PEOPLES OF THE ROMAN WORLD

In this generously illustrated book, Mary T. Boatwright examines five of the peoples absorbed into the Roman world from the Republican through the Imperial periods: northerners, Greeks, Egyptians, Jews, and Christians. She explores the tension that developed between assimilation and distinctiveness in the Roman world over time, as well as the changes effected in Rome by its multicultural nature. Underlining the fundamental importance of diversity to Rome's self-identity, the book explores Romans' tolerance of difference and community as they expanded and consolidated their power and incorporated other peoples into their empire. *Peoples of the Roman World* provides an accessible account of the empire's social, cultural, religious, and political history as it explores the rich literary, documentary, and visual evidence of these peoples and Rome's reactions to them.

Mary T. Boatwright is Professor of Ancient History in the Department of Classical Studies at Duke University. She is the author of several books, including *Hadrian and the City of Rome*, *Hadrian and the Cities of the Roman Empire*, *The Romans: From Village to Empire*, *A History of Ancient Rome from Earliest Times to Constantine* (with Daniel J. Gargola and Richard J. A. Talbert), and *A Brief History of the Romans* (with Daniel J. Gargola and Richard J. A. Talbert).

CAMBRIDGE INTRODUCTION TO ROMAN CIVILIZATION

The Cambridge Introduction to Roman Civilization is a program of books designed for use by students who have no prior knowledge of or familiarity with Roman antiquity. Books in this series focus on key topics, such as slavery, warfare, and women. They are intended to serve as a first point of reference for students who will then be equipped to pursue more specialized scholarly and critical studies. The texts of these volumes are written in clear, jargon-free language and integrate primary texts into syntheses that reflect the most up-to-date research. All volumes in the series will be closely linked to readings and topics presented in the Cambridge Latin Course.

Also in the Series
Roman Religion by Valerie M. Warrior
Roman Women by Eve D'Ambra
Roman Warfare by Jonathan P. Roth
Slavery in the Roman World by Sandra R. Joshel

PEOPLES OF THE ROMAN WORLD

MARY T. BOATWRIGHT

Duke University

CAMBRIDGE
UNIVERSITY PRESS

CAMBRIDGE UNIVERSITY PRESS
Cambridge, New York, Melbourne, Madrid, Cape Town,
Singapore, São Paulo, Delhi, Tokyo, Mexico City

Cambridge University Press
32 Avenue of the Americas, New York, NY 10013-2473, USA

www.cambridge.org
Information on this title: www.cambridge.org/9780521549943

First published 2012

Printed in the United States of America

A catalog record for this publication is available from the British Library.

Library of Congress Cataloging in Publication data
Boatwright, Mary Taliaferro.
Peoples of the Roman world / Mary T. Boatwright.
p.   cm. – (Cambridge introduction to Roman civilization)
Includes bibliographical references and index.
ISBN 978-0-521-84062-0 (hbk.) – ISBN 978-0-521-54994-3 (pbk.)
1. Rome – Ethnic relations.   2. Ethnology – Rome – History.
3. Minorities – Rome – History.   4. Ethnicity – Rome – History.
5. Assimilation (Sociology) – Rome – History.   6. Acculturation – Rome – History.
7. Cultural pluralism – Rome – History.   8. Rome – Social conditions.
9. Imperialism – Social aspects – Rome – History.
10. Rome – Territorial expansion.   I. Title.   II. Series.
DG190.B63   2011
937–dc22   2011016120

ISBN 978-0-521-84062-0 Hardback
ISBN 978-0-521-54994-3 Paperback

CONTENTS

ILLUSTRATIONS AND MAPS

COLOR PLATES

NOTES TO THE READER

Because this book covers many regions and periods, some perhaps unfamiliar to readers, I have explained and located places, people, and events throughout. In-text references to ancient cities, all identified by their Roman names with the exception of Rome, Athens, and Milan, are followed by their modern equivalents (e.g., Arelate, modern Arles, France), and I also approximately locate Rome's provinces in relation to modern countries. "Macedon" refers to the autonomous Kingdom of Macedon, whereas "Macedonia" refers to the Roman province that later included Macedon's territory in the northern Balkans. "Achaia" is used to refer to the province established by the Romans in the lower Balkans; and "Judaea" designates the area considered by Jews as their homeland, which includes smaller regions such as Judaea, Galilee, and Idumaea. (I do not use "Palestine," as it derives from the official Roman name of the province, Syria Palaestina, imposed on the area after the Third Jewish Revolt of 132–135 CE.) I provide full Roman proper names the first time I mention individuals other than the emperors, normalizing the Roman *praenomina* or personal names Caius and Cnaeus to Gaius and Gnaeus, and using "J" for consonantal "I" (as in Julius for Iulius).

Other conventions are helpful to note here. I use BCE (Before the Common Era) in preference to BC (Before Christ) and CE (Common Era) instead of AD (Anno Domini, Latin for "Year of Our Lord"). The uncapitalized word "empire" refers to Rome's geographical holdings. In contrast, "Empire" (often preceded by "Roman") refers to the chronological period of Rome's empire. This is traditionally dated from 27 BCE, when Octavian, who rose to power in the civil wars following Julius Caesar's assassination in 44 BCE, was given the name Augustus and had his authority ratified by the Senate and the People of Rome, until the end of the third century CE. In deriving from political concepts, "Roman Empire" complements the "Roman Republic." I use Roman Republic to designate the chronological period traditionally dated from 510/509 BCE, when Rome's system of annually elected power-sharing magistrates was established, until Octavian's overthrow of that system and consolidation of his own authority in 27 BCE.

My main sources are literary, documentary, and visual, and their varying quantity and quality as related to the subject of each chapter precluded my adopting a standardized format for my chapters. With important exceptions for the Jews and the Christians, the primary literary evidence usually reflects attitudes of Rome's elite that were based on age-old traditions and prejudices, and most of it comes from Rome itself, a densely crowded city housing up to a million inhabitants from the empire and beyond. I identify all authors and works by date and other useful information the first time they figure in the narrative. All authors cited more than once are also identified in the Glossary, and the dates of their relevant works are found in the Timeline.

Except where noted, I am responsible for the English translations of the passages provided. Almost all authors and works can easily be found in the Loeb Classical Library, a series of books presenting the original Greek or Latin text on each left-hand page and a somewhat literal but accessible translation facing it. (The series is now published by Harvard University Press.) I have noted when I have used a Loeb or some other translation and have included the full reference in the Suggested Further Reading section after each chapter.

Documentary sources can provide great insight into less highly placed individuals, commemorating individual shopkeepers or soldiers at their death, for example, or preserving the texts of laws affecting Roman citizens and peoples. Individual documents discussed in my text also have citations referring to where they can be found in full and in translation. Visual resources include maps as well as photographs of sculpture, paintings, coins, and other material culture for official and private representations of Rome's peoples. Illustrations are chosen to complement and expand the narrative they accompany, and I provide specific information in each of the captions.

Each chapter is followed by a short list of suggested readings, a few of which are referred to in the text. At the book's end is a Timeline that displays all the discussed events, individuals, and ancient sources, followed by a Glossary of authors and works, abbreviations, and unusual words that appear more than once in the narrative.

ACKNOWLEDGMENTS

While finishing *Hadrian and the Cities of the Roman Empire* more than a decade ago I increasingly felt the need to explore the Roman world from "below" – that is, to look at it not as Hadrian or the Roman governing elite might have, but from the perspectives of those incorporated into, and governed by, the Roman state. My desire to acquaint myself with Rome's "exiles on Main Street" – individuals I (and most) can identify with on many grounds – became all the stronger once I could turn to this *Peoples* project. It caused me to read Roman texts and material culture in changed ways, undertake different types of research, teach new courses, and be more open to Roman social and cultural history. In all these endeavors I found great support and learned a tremendous amount.

Although any errors that may be detected are due to me alone, whatever strengths there are in *Peoples of the Roman World* come from the friends, colleagues, and students I worked with as this book took its time to completion. Many individuals directly or indirectly aided me, from Ljubljana and Budapest, to London and Durham, often by introducing me to new material culture on site or in museums. I benefited greatly from the interests and expertise of my Duke University colleagues Carla Antonaccio and Josh Sosin; colleagues elsewhere – such as Susan Walker – also offered invaluable discussion. The intellectual setting at Duke has been invigorating; in particular, Duke's Center for Late Ancient Studies and its energetic participants have deeply influenced my thinking about Rome's Jews and Christians. Graduate students from Duke University and the University of North Carolina–Chapel Hill explored with me many of the texts that undergird my book, and some of their dissertation work – particularly that of Charlie Muntz, Alex Meyer, and Jessica Vahl – furthered my awareness of specific authors, events, and trends. Duke undergraduates "kept me honest" by pressing me to explain clearly and illustrate memorably what I try to convey. Tolerant, occasionally baffled questions from friends and family, usually in non-academic circumstances such as alongside a youth soccer field, similarly helped hone my thinking.

Additional thanks are due to my undergraduate and graduate research assistants over the years, a talented group that includes Elizabeth Rudisill, Laura Puleo, Adrienne Cohen, Alex Jorn, Jessica Vahl, and Mack Zalin. Brian Turner, Director of the Ancient World Mapping Center in 2010–11, was vital for my maps. Cambridge University Press was unfailingly supportive: Beatrice Rehl graciously and patiently provided excellent guidance and friendship through the expiration of deadlines; James Dunn quickly and accurately made my three city plans; and Holly Johnson was a serene and sensitive editor. Individuals at the many organizations credited in my captions responded generously to my requests for images. Duke University provided research assistance. With such support I hope to have translated my ambition into this book so that others, too, can appreciate at least some of the fascinating diversity of the Roman world.

I dedicate this to Paul, Joseph, and Sammy, my beloved fellow travelers in antiquity and the present alike.

CHAPTER 1

ROME AND ITS

PEOPLES

Introduction

Although now many may consider Rome and the Romans as a distinct, single-minded culture, Rome always encompassed many peoples and lands. Cicero called Rome the *populus Romanus omnium gentium victor*, a phrase that well expresses Rome's growth and inherent tensions: the Latin can mean both "the Roman people triumphant over all the races" and "the victorious Roman people of all races" (Cicero, *On the Orator* 2.76; 55 BCE). One of the Romans' most characteristic traits was their drive to conquer and incorporate others. Julius Caesar, for example, is supposed to have proclaimed to his lieutenants in 58 BCE:

> [O]ur ancestors made Rome so great ... by bringing their minds to venture readily all that they ought to do, and their bodies to work out eagerly all the plans they had determined upon; by risking their own possessions as if they belonged to others, but acquiring readily the possessions of their neighbors as their own.... They thought that happiness was nothing else than doing their duty, and they held that misfortune was nothing else than resting inactive. It was in consequence of these principles, therefore, that those men, who were in the beginning very few and dwelt in a city at first as small as any, conquered the Latins, subdued the Sabines, mastered the Etruscans ... [and] subjugated the whole land south of the Alps.... The later Romans, likewise, and our own fathers imitated them, not satisfied with what they had inherited but regarding sloth as their sure destruction and hardship as their certain safety. They feared that if their treasures were not increased the goods would waste away of themselves and wear out with age, and they themselves were ashamed after receiving so rich a heritage to add nothing to

it; accordingly they effected much greater and more numerous conquests. (Cassius Dio, *Roman History* 38.37–38, written 220s CE; adapted from Loeb translation)

Caesar and other Romans were exceptionally successful conquerors, and at its peak in the second century CE, "Rome" extended from northern Britain to Mesopotamia, and from the Rhine and Danube rivers to the upper reaches of the Nile. Those inhabiting this expansive territory numbered some 60 million at Rome's acme in the second century CE, and they included many different peoples and cultures (Fig. 1).

This book examines five of these groups, exploring the tension between assimilation and distinctiveness in Rome's expanding populace, as well as the transformations brought to Rome by its multicultural nature. The five groups I have chosen – "northerners," Greeks, Egyptians, Jews, and Christians – were distinct within the Roman world. Yet all were, or became, Romans, and all contributed inestimably to Roman history. As we shall see in this book, the criteria for their distinctiveness included culture, language, religion, physical features, customs, and ethnicity; also, the groups were not unitary within themselves. I do not explore Rome's interactions with Sabines, Samnites, Etruscans, and other Italic peoples, although claims based on these ethnic groups figured in Republican history. Other groups important during the Empire could also be investigated fruitfully: for instance, Africans and blacks within the Roman world have been the subject of important studies. But the groups I examine here offer relatively full and accessible evidence that overlaps and differs in interesting ways. The following chapters thus illuminate aspects of Rome's social, cultural, religious, and political history even while exploring the value, and the limitations, of diverse types of Roman evidence. My primary purpose is not to discern what constituted "Romanness" (or *Romanitas*, to use a word now sometimes found in scholarship), or how non-Romans "became Roman," a phenomenon often termed "Romanization." Rather, I examine Roman concepts and tolerance of community and difference in regard to five groups, the changing relationships these groups had with Rome (and other groups)

1. Map of the Roman world at its height in the second century CE, noting lands, rivers, and most provinces of the time, as well as cities and sites mentioned in the text. Map © 2011, Ancient World Mapping Center (www.unc.edu/awmc). Used by permission.

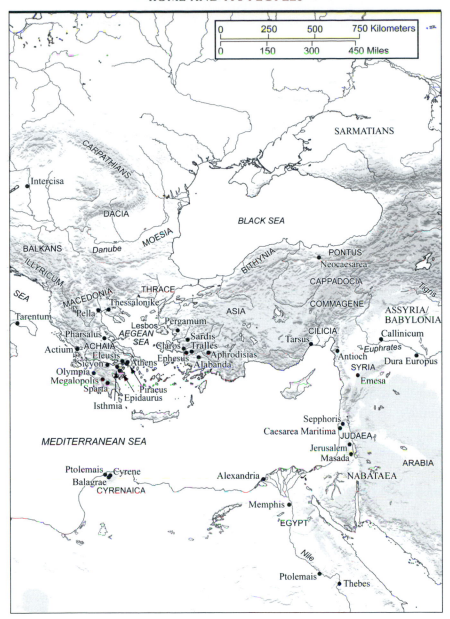

| 0 | 250 | 500 | 750 Kilometers |
| 0 | 150 | 300 | 450 Miles |

SARMATIANS

CARPATHIANS

Intercisa

DACIA

BLACK SEA

BALKANS   Danube   MOESIA

ILLYRICUM

BITHYNIA   PONTUS
Neocaesarea

SEA   MACEDONIA   THRACE   CAPPADOCIA

Tigris

Tarentum   Pella   Thessalonike   COMMAGENE   ASSYRIA/
BABYLONIA

Lesbos   Pergamum   ASIA   Callinicum

Pharsalus   AEGEAN   Sardis   CILICIA   Euphrates

Actium   SEA   Claros   Tralles   Tarsus   Antioch   Dura Europus

ACHAIA   Eleusis   Ephesus   Aphrodisias   SYRIA

Sicyon   Athens   Alabanda   Emesa

Olympia

Megalopolis   Piraeus

Sparta   Epidaurus

Isthmia

Sepphoris

MEDITERRANEAN SEA   Caesarea Maritima   JUDAEA

Jerusalem

Masada   ARABIA

Ptolemais   Cyrene   Alexandria   NABATAEA

Balagrae

CYRENAICA

Memphis

EGYPT

Nile

Ptolemais

Thebes

5

over time, and some reciprocal effects of the incorporation of these groups into Rome's world.

Diversity from Rome's Beginnings, One of Rome's Characteristics

Romans emphasized their varied origins even though often speaking about "the Romans" or "the Roman populace" as though it were homogeneous, as does Cicero in our opening quotation. Their founding legends, dynamic throughout Rome's history, were memorably elaborated in literature and the visual arts during the Augustan period. Vergil, Livy, and others are clear that Aeneas, the ancestor of all Romans and one of the few Trojans to survive the epic Trojan War, emigrated to Italy, where he overcame Latin peoples to establish himself in Latium. Aeneas' descendant Romulus, founder of the city of Rome and its first king in the eighth century BCE, created an "asylum" on the Capitoline Hill to enroll Italian and other immigrants in his new state. In need of citizen children for the new Rome, Romulus also masterminded the violent seizure of women from the neighboring Sabine tribe, joining Sabines to Romans to further enlarge the citizen base.

Roman authors show both negative and positive reactions to the diversity of the Romans. In *On Behalf of Balbus* (chap. 31; 56 BCE), Cicero claims that what was paramount in founding Rome's empire and increasing the reputation of the Roman people was Romulus' example of enlarging the state by taking in former enemies. In the Augustan era, on the other hand, Dionysius of Halicarnassus criticized the Romans for their "mongrel" nature, emphasizing that criminals, hoodlums, and other undesirables were among Romulus' new citizens (Dionysius of Halicarnassus, *Roman Antiquities* 2.15.4). In the second century CE, the orator Aelius Aristides positively valued Rome's heterogeneity as a reflection of meritocracy. (The contrasting opinions of these last two authors, both from Rome's eastern provinces and writing in Greek for an educated, Greek-speaking audience in the Roman world, warn us against typecasting any of our groups.) Still other authors, like Pliny the Elder from northern Italy, downplayed Rome's multiculturalism in relation to a sweeping glorification of Roman assimilation. Pliny praises Italy as:

> At one and the same time the foster child and parent of all the lands, chosen by the power of the gods ... to gather together scattered realms and soften their customs, to unite the discordant wild tongues of so many peoples (*populi*) into a common speech for communication, and to give civilization (*humanitas*) to mankind, and, in short, to become the one homeland of all the peoples (*gentes*) in the entire world. (*Natural History* 3.39; published ca. 77–79 CE)

Rome's assimilation of various peoples was never uncontested or uncomplicated. Some groups, such as various tribes of the Britons, rose up against their Roman conquerors, and the Jews were particularly rebellious, breaking out in three dangerous revolts from 66 to 135 CE. Languages other than Latin were in use throughout Roman territories, and even in Rome itself. Greek was a special case, for Romans considered Greek the main language of civilization and literature. From the third century BCE through the third century CE those in Rome's elite ranks knew it, and in the Roman world it was employed equally with Latin as an administrative language. Jews and Egyptians retained or even developed distinct customs and rites despite their incorporation into the Roman empire, and the elite of both groups used Greek for their writings.

Many of the groups we discuss in this book – with the notable exception of the Christians – apparently retained their original cults and religious beliefs even while participating in Roman public religion, and the monotheistic Jews frequently worked out compromises with their imperial Roman rulers. Individuals and groups, it seems, could take on Roman "civilization" (Pliny's *humanitas*) without losing a primary identity. A non-Christian speaker in Minucius Felix's *Octavius*, a Christian dialogue written in the late second or early third century, emphasizes Rome's acceptance of other religions:

Hence it is that throughout the wide [Roman] empire, provinces, and towns, we see each people having its own individual rites and worshipping its local gods, the Eleusinians Ceres, the Phrygians the Great Mother, the Epidaurians Aesculapius, the Chaldaeans Bel, the Syrians Astarte, the Taurians Diana, the Gauls Mercury, the Romans all of these.... Thus [the Romans'] power and authority has occupied the scope of the whole earth, thus their empire has expanded beyond the routes of the sun and the limits of the Ocean itself, while they exercise religious virtue even in arms ... while everywhere they seek out the gods of others and make them their own, while they build altars even to unknown divinities.... Thus, in that they take on for themselves the sacred institutions of all peoples (*gentes*), they also deserve their dominion. (Minucius Felix, *Octavius* 6.1–3)

In the preceding quotations, as in others in this book, diversity is considered fundamental to Rome and the Romans. This contrasts an important definition of "Greekness" that was articulated in the 430s BCE by the influential Greek historian Herodotus. In Herodotus' *Histories*, which investigated the Persian Wars and underlying Greek and Persian antagonism, the Athenians, Spartans, and other Greeks are said to share a certain "Greekness" because of their shared blood (i.e., a common descent), shared language, shared way of life, and shared religious practices (*Histories* 8.144.2). Such commonalities did not hold for the Romans, whose phenomenal geopolitical growth instead forced them to continually reassess who and what they were.

The Growth of Rome, Roman Provinces, and Roman Citizenship

Throughout Rome's history many, if not most, of those identified with Rome were of non-Roman origin even if they held Roman citizenship; furthermore, from the establishment of Rome's Republic at the end of the sixth century BCE until the early third century CE, those who enjoyed full Roman citizenship comprised at most perhaps only half of those associated with Rome, and usually much less. These facts about Rome's population are due to many phenomena, most obviously its prodigious growth. Rome's expansion, especially remarkable during the Republic when it grew from a small city-state on the seven hills of Rome to encompass almost all of the lands around the Mediterranean, depended on its ability to field armies continuously. Engaging yearly in hostilities ever farther from the city, the Romans developed a system of alliances that ensured copious manpower under the command of Roman generals. The conquered were often incorporated into Rome's army – by the end of the Republic as auxiliary or allied troops – and then eventually into the Roman state. Elaborate public rituals and justification of wars as defensive ones undertaken for their mutual protection encouraged the rapport of Romans and their comrades-in-arms, the Italian allies. The Social War of 91–88/87 BCE resulted in the enrollment of the Italian allies as Roman citizens. Also, during the late Republic (ending at 27 BCE), and continuing throughout the Empire, generals and emperors granted Roman citizenship to individuals and groups in return for anticipated and rendered services, particularly military and political ones. By the second century CE, Rome had devised ways to grant citizenship automatically to those who had served as auxiliary soldiers or as local magistrates, that is to say, had assumed roles considered useful to the growth and perpetuation of the state.

But such grants of Roman citizenship were relatively rare and often begrudged until the third century CE. Augustus is reported to have refused his wife Livia when she asked him to grant a certain Gallic man Roman citizenship. He gave the man tax-exempt status instead, stating that he would more readily allow money to be taken from the treasury than the honor of Roman citizenship to be made common (Suetonius, *Life of Augustus* 40.3). Until 212 CE, most people in Rome's provinces were not Roman citizens.

And Rome's provinces were many and widespread. The provincial system enlarged Rome's territory and control of peoples both outside

and within the northern Italian peninsula, starting with the two provinces of Sicily and Sardinia/Corsica (227 BCE), continuing with the
provinces of Closer and Farther Spain, Macedonia, and other provinces
in the eastern Mediterranean in the second century BCE, and intensify-
ing after about 100 BCE. Successful wars enabled Rome to seize land
outside of Italy that it then retained as provinces; other overseas lands (and
their associated peoples), such as Asia (in 133/129 BCE) and Bithynia
(in 75/74 BCE; both in modern Turkey), were actually bequeathed by
their kings to the ever-growing Rome. Such overseas territory was con-
ceived of as the peoples inhabiting it. Velleius Paterculus, for example,
writes in his *Roman History*, "It seems not at all useless to digress here
to say which race and tribe (*gens et natio*), reduced to provincial status,
was made tax-paying, and under whose military command ..." (2.38.1;
composed before 31 CE). Over a century later, the historian Appian
arranged his *Roman History* according to the peoples and lands Rome
had conquered, devoting separate books to, for example, the wars by
which Rome conquered the inhabitants of Spain, and those by which
the Egyptians fell into Roman control (the latter, known only from its
title, has now perished). In other words, Rome's lands were those who
inhabited them; Rome's power was Rome's peoples. In 60 BCE, before
Caesar conquered Gaul, Rome controlled over ten sprawling provinces;
after Augustus' death in 14 CE, the provinces numbered around twenty-
five; and at the time of Rome's greatest expansion, in the first half of the
second century CE, the empire administered some forty provinces.

Until 212 CE, when an imperial law was passed granting Roman
citizenship to virtually all the free inhabitants of the Roman state, the
provinces were populated primarily by free individuals who were not
considered or treated as Roman citizens. Romans generally referred
to these persons as *peregrini* or *alieni*: both terms are often translated as
"foreigners," although *peregrini* properly indicates free (non-slave) provincials, and *alieni* free persons from outside Roman territory. When in
the late Republican and early Imperial periods Rome sent out colonists
to the provinces, Roman military veterans and other new settlers in a
city either expelled the indigenous population or reduced them to a

status whereby they were liable to various duties but had fewer rights and privileges than the Romans. Originally, provincials lacked most Roman rights such as voting and access to Roman law, and they were liable to many burdens, especially those of taxes and tribute. But even by the end of the Republic some few were being granted Roman citizenship. Like Aulus Licinius Archias, whom I discuss in Chapter 3, such new citizens were deemed acceptable because of the benefits they brought to Rome. Later, individual and small-group grants of citizenship figured among imperial benefactions. Finally, by a decree of 212 CE now called the *Constitutio Antoniniana*, the emperor Caracalla made Rome's *peregrini* – the free inhabitants of Rome's provinces – Roman citizens, whose civic status would pass to their descendants. Caracalla himself was descended from a *peregrinus* who had gained Roman citizenship by holding local office in the provincial African city of Leptis Magna (near modern Al Khums, Libya), but there is no clear and single explanation for his decisive act.

Ethnicity and Other Types of Identity in Rome

My use of the term "peoples," like some of the discussion in the following chapters, raises the subject of ethnicity. Ethnicity has been a major concern since the late eighteenth-century formation of nation-states in western Europe posited ethnic ties as one basis of nationalism. It has great relevance today. Modern societies and nations are grappling with a globalized economy and escalating movements of refugees and immigrants; increasing numbers of people identify themselves as multiracial, or refuse such categorizations. "Identity politics" is at the forefront of much political, religious, and social activity, and ethnicity was key as identity politics developed in the twentieth century. One formulation of ethnicity that many classicists now use emphasizes it as a "social phenomenon" that "can only be constructed by opposition to other ethnic identities" (Hall 1997, 32). In ancient Rome as in other cultures, concepts of ethnicity commonly figured in the description of genetic, cultural, and social variations that shaped identity and "alterity," or otherness. But features, traits, and practices often claimed as marks of ethnic distinction – a common homeland, descent, language, religion, and culture – are beliefs and symbols, not inalterable characteristics. One can always learn a new language, for example; homeland, even alleged descent, can be changed and contested. The Latin and Greek words that we translate as "people," "tribe," "race," and the like – *gens, natio, populus, ethnos* (pl. *gentes, nationes, populi, ethne*), and other terms I use in translated texts – are themselves imprecise.

At first sight the understanding of ethnicity as relative – that is, ethnic identity determined by distinction from "other" rather than by some immutable element – seems contradicted by other ancient concepts that look universal and not contextual. In the later fifth century BCE, Herodotus postulated essential Greekness, as we have seen, in a passage that still influences conceptions of ethnicity. Around the same time the Hippocratic treatise *Airs, Waters, Places* (16.22–23) proposed an oft-repeated dictum – namely, that climate and environment/geography conclusively affect people's characters, body types, and behavior. Numerous ancient authors associated eastern peoples and locales with luxury and effeminacy. The influential fourth-century Greek philosopher Plato adds, "the peoples of Asia are characteristically servile, although otherwise intelligent and artistically endowed." The Roman Vitruvius wrote in the Augustan period: "Because of the thinness of their sky the southern tribes (*nationes*), with their intense fervor, are stimulated rather quickly to form plans. The northern races (*gentes*), saturated by their thick sky, have dull minds because of the pressure of the wet and chill air ... but they have military boldness" (Vitruvius, *On Architecture* 6.1.9–10). The relativity of such concepts is clear, however, in Vitruvius' idea that the Roman people (*populus Romanus*) were situated in the middle of the world, and thus enjoyed the best of every environment while escaping the worst. He further held that the Romans optimized their situation through their political and military discipline: "By its policies and planning Rome checks the military virtues of the [northern] barbarians, and by its firm hand the schemes of the southerners.

The divine mind so located the state of the Roman people (*civitas populi Romani*) and its excellent and tempered region so that it might gain the rule of the entire world" (6.1.11).

As we shall see in the following chapters, totalizing judgments were frequently expressed by Romans, especially when characterizing enemies, rebellious provincials, or new slave or free immigrants to Rome. But climatic and geographic determinism, powerful though the concept was, was undermined by its connection to place. What kind of character was "fated" for children born to Romans living in Asia and the "servile" East? What about a child born in Rome to a couple originally from the north? How long did it take someone to become Roman by moving to the city? And how long did it take for the "corrupting" influence of climate and locale to influence a Roman traveler or settler in the provinces? Climatic determinism for ethnic identification was particularly ill-suited to the Romans, who moved frequently for the purposes of war, politics, trade, and other causes.

Sources for Understanding Rome's Peoples

Discussion of the peoples of the Roman world is further complicated by differences between the city of Rome and elsewhere. The literary evidence usually reflects attitudes of Rome's elite that were based on age-old traditions and prejudices particularly deep-seated in the capital city. To these must have been added the stresses of living in a dense and overcrowded city housing about 700,000 (in the Augustan era) to a million (second century CE) inhabitants from the entire empire and beyond. Most of our evidence comes from Rome, and denunciation of various groups – northerners, Christians, or others – is often couched as fear of overwhelming numbers, reflecting anxiety at the pace of cultural change. In the late Republic and early Empire, the city sporadically expelled ethnic groups, such as Germans (9 CE) and Egyptians and Jews (19 CE), but our information is very deficient for numbers, motivations, and results. Although periodic censuses were taken in the

Roman provinces and Italy itself, we almost never have those figures (other than from Egypt, and these are not complete), and the categories used were not race or ethnicity, but rather Roman, non-Roman, and other civic statuses. Furthermore, in the capital city various social and political distinctions seem to have been more strictly observed than elsewhere. Augustus, for instance, stipulated that when at Rome's Forum or the Circus Maximus, presumably whether they were engaged in business or at leisure, all Roman citizens wear the toga. This ceremonial garment, woven of white wool and wrapped over a man's tunic in intricate set patterns, was forbidden to non-Romans (Fig. 2). But this distinct mark of Roman citizenship, insisted upon by the man whose struggles to attain power as the first *princeps* or emperor had overturned the Roman world, appears to have been ignored in the provinces and even in the smaller towns of Italy. Visual, epigraphic, and literary evidence indicates a higher tolerance of diversity in the countryside and provinces.

It is also not so clear who or how many in the Roman world recognized difference and diversity. Our distance from that world leaves us with many unanswerable questions. Ethnic identification, like other identities, depends both on an individual's self-identification as part of a group, and on others' acceptance of that person's inclusion in the group. Even in the modern world the interplay of objective and subjective identity is often impossible to untangle; for the Roman world the task is aggravated by the infinitely more scarce and fragmentary nature of the evidence. Theoretical archaeologists hold that identity is constructed and negotiated through the use and experiencing of objects. But specific pieces of art, decoration, or furnishings only very rarely can be identified with one person, family, or group, and objects of Roman material culture, such as terracotta lamps decorated with circus or gladiatorial scenes, are found throughout the Roman world. The find-spots and use of many objects are now long lost to us.

We are often forced back upon the words of the Romans, either in literature or in documents. When our sources identify a person or group

2. Statue of Augustus draped in a toga (marble, 2.17 m H). One fold is pulled over his head, since he is shown while sacrificing as Rome's chief priest (*pontifex maximus*). His depiction in a toga, a garment he required Roman citizens to wear on public occasions in Rome and that was forbidden to non-Romans, emphasizes the civil authority of this first *princeps*. The arrangement of his long, voluminous outer wrap is particularly elaborate in its special folds over the chest region. From Rome, now in the Museo Nazionale Romano, Terme di Diocleziano, inv. 56230. Published by permission of the Ministero per i Beni e le Attività Culturali – Soprintendenza Speciale per i Beni Archeologici di Roma.

as ethnically different – "born in Dacia" for example – who demarcated that difference? The individual, the group, or someone else? Further, most sources are of a public nature, and we have very few personal accounts that were not aimed at a public audience. To say this, however, is to ask again, "What public?": was it the smaller self-identified group or society at large? When an epitaph from Rome identifies the deceased as Jewish, was that identification chosen by the deceased or by the commemorator? Was it intended primarily for the Jewish community or for others who might see the tombstone? Can we discern specific political or social goals for publicizing an ethnic identity? Such conundrums, none of which can be answered with certainty, should be borne in mind throughout the following chapters.

Ideas of Peoples in the Roman World

Yet Romans definitely had notions about various peoples, races, and groups. Some taggings – often sheerly prejudicial – were expressed incidentally in literature and documentary material, as we shall see repeatedly in the following chapters. Others took ethnic matters more seriously: in 43 BCE, for example, the polymath Varro's book *On the Race of the Roman People* included a section discussing what, and from what people, the Romans copied. Romans also wrote and read ethnographies. There are a few focused ones like Tacitus' *Germania* (late first century CE), but most extant ethnographies are part of larger historical works. Caesar has a long ethnographic digression on the Gauls in Book 6 of *War against Gaul* – our earliest surviving Roman ethnography – and Tacitus provides a long ethnography of the Jews in *Histories* 5. The geographer Strabo, who wrote during the Augustan and early Tiberian periods, explicitly stressed how useful geography – closely tied to ethnography – was in his own day, for the greatest generals were those who could unite peoples and cities under one government and political management (*Geography* 1.1.16). Strabo devotes Book 4 of his *Geography* to Gaul, Book 17 to Egypt, and other books to other areas. Pliny the Elder wrote (ca. 60 CE) a history of all the wars between the Romans and Germans; although it is now lost, his research occasionally surfaces in his *Natural History* (e.g., 30.4, on Celtic words) and was used by subsequent writers including Tacitus (Tacitus, *Annals* 1.69). The scarcity and formulaic aspects of surviving ethnographies make it hard to distinguish what purports to be new and factual from what may be simply uninformed clichés, but at the least such writings reveal Roman interest in ethnic differences. On the other hand, these ethnographic works were accessible mainly to Rome's elite, and we cannot gauge their influence on the many in Rome's world who could not read, estimated as 80–90 percent of the total population.

Roman notions of ethnicity and difference were also expressed in art and public monuments, where they glorified Roman conquests. Cicero, for example, boasts: "Tribes of Gaul have been made noteworthy because of our triumphs and monuments" (Cicero, *On Behalf of Fonteius* 12; 69 BCE). Rome's triumphal processions, of which some three hundred are known, celebrated victorious expansion and conquest: beginning at the latest in the second century BCE, soldiers of a triumphing general in Rome paraded depictions of battles, city sieges, and other victorious military moments on paintings, tapestries, and perhaps three-dimensional models that were subsequently exhibited in temples. Triumphal arches depicted not only the conquering Roman commander but also the peoples he had overcome. Trophies, ritualized heaps of non-Roman armor rendered in bronze or stone, were erected in Rome and elsewhere; their images decorated the breastplates of imperial statues and, on a larger scale, temples like the rebuilt Apollo Sosianus of the early Augustan period (Fig. 3). Yet, as with the trophy and triumph depicted on the frieze of the Temple of Apollo Sosianus, at times it is difficult to detect exactly which defeated enemy is being referred to. Attitudes of subjugation and non-Roman dress, perhaps also unusual hairstyles and wild grimacing, are enough to earmark the enemy, a not (yet) Roman person.

Long after provincials and freed persons became Roman citizens, such visual characteristics memorialized the brutal subjugation of non-Romans by Romans. These two crudely opposed groups were distinguished in the sculpted battle scenes and other historical narratives decorating monuments of the Empire (Fig. 4). More nuanced personifications of non-Roman countries or peoples also enlivened coins, where they were usually portrayed as violent and unkempt in the last century BCE and the first CE but as docile thereafter; and sculptural personifications of groups, peoples, and places exhibited in Rome and elsewhere exalted the Roman general or family credited with defeating them (Fig. 5). Part of the Theater of Pompey exhibited personifications of the fourteen "nations" (*gentes*) over which Pompey had triumphed in the East in 66–63 BCE. Although such images also appeared on official state monuments in other cities and locales from the time of Augustus' rule (27 BCE–14 CE) and after, they were particularly numerous in the capital city (Fig. 6).

3. A Roman triumphal procession on a frieze from the Augustan Temple of Apollo Sosianus in Rome, as rebuilt and rededicated probably by Gaius Sosius after his triumph over the Jews in 34 BCE. An older and a younger "barbarian," both males with their hands tied behind their backs and flanking a trophy, are paraded through Rome, followed by attendants and victims for the culminating sacrifice. Rome's humiliated enemy has no clearly discernible ethnic characteristics. The frieze is now in the Musei Capitolini and exhibited in the Centrale Montemartini, Rome. Photo by permission of the Sovraintendenza ai Beni Culturali di Roma Capitale.

Together with Rome's history and literature, Roman material culture helps to explain Rome's self-definition as *populus victor omnium gentium*, their ambiguous identity as both "the people triumphant over all the races" and "the victorious people of all races."

Given the diverse makeup of Rome and the Romans, ethnicity could not be immutable and is thus but one marker of difference and identity in the Roman world. In *On the Republic*, for example, Cicero has his discussants debate whether Romulus was a king over barbarians. They conclude that, although the Greeks defined barbarism in terms of language (*linguae*), Romans saw it in terms of customs or behavior (*mores*), and it was more important to look into character (*ingenia*) than race (*gens*) (Cicero, *On the Republic* 1.58; written 51 BCE). It will frequently emerge in this book that no one clear criterion existed for defining "barbarians" or other non-Romans. Identity in Rome seems to have been constantly renegotiated as the Roman citizen base expanded and citizens and others changed their locations and circumstances.

4. Northerners and Romans on a relief from a mid-second century CE arch on the Via Lata, Rome's main road leading in from the north. The relief is heavily restored in its background section, and also for the head and right hand of the emperor. Barbarians, including a young boy, supplicate a Roman emperor, whose toga shows that the scene is set in Rome. The greater size and togas of the Romans contrast with the massed and humbled non-Romans entreating them. The relief is now in the Torlonia Collection in Rome; photo is from the plaster cast in the Museo della Civiltà Romana, used by permission of Roma, Museo della Civiltà Romana.

Movement in the City of Rome and Rome's Empire

There was always a certain amount of free movement within the empire to Rome, and from beyond Rome's borders into the empire, particularly in times of peace and prosperity. The capital city, whose population is estimated as peaking around a million ca. 100 to 167 CE, always attracted many who came to visit or stay temporarily. In the middle of the first century CE, Seneca described the variety of individuals encountered in Rome:

Look at this crush of people for whom the housing of this immense city scarcely suffices: most of them are far from their

5. Coins with personifications of subjugated non-Roman peoples, lands, and places. (*Upper left*) Silver denarius of Julius Caesar, 48–47 BCE. On the obverse is a head of Venus, Caesar's reputed ancestor, wearing an oak-wreath, a diadem, and showy jewelry; a small inscription is behind her neck. On the reverse, flanked by Caesar's name, is a trophy with a Gallic shield and Gallic military trumpet. Below it sits a captive with his arms bound behind his back. His long, straggly hair and unkempt beard mark him as distinctively Gallic. Now in the British Museum. Object no.: 1867,0101.1267, CM RR1p506.3959. © The Trustees of the British Academy.

(*Lower right*) Gold aureus struck under Hadrian in Rome, 128–138 CE. On the obverse is Hadrian, wearing a laurel diadem and titled "Augustus, consul three times, Father of the Fatherland." On the reverse sits the male personification of the Nile River, identified as NILVS. In his right hand he holds a cornucopia, symbolic of the fertility the annual Nile floods brought to Egypt and the Roman world. His left arm, cradling a reed, rests on a sphinx. Below him is a crocodile, and a hippopotamus faces him. Object no.: R.12312, CM 1864, 1128.63. © The Trustees of the British Academy.

place of birth. They have come together from their towns and cities, in fact from the whole world. Some ambition drew; others, the necessity of a public job or a diplomatic task; still others, the pull of extravagance, as they search out a place ready and ripe for depravity. Some the desire of higher education brings, others the public spectacles; some men a friendship has drawn, and

6. Personification of a province, tentatively identified as Thrace, from the Temple of the deified Hadrian in Rome (139–145 CE). The fringed outer cloak helps to identify the female personification as non-Roman. She has one breast bared, as would the Amazons, who were thought to be from near Thrace. She carries a scythe and grain (although her lower arms and hands are restored), perhaps indicating the grain tribute paid by Thrace to Rome. Proconnesian marble. 164 cm H; 144 cm W. Now in the Museo Nazionale Romano, Palazzo Massimo, inv. 428496. Published by permission of the Ministero per i Beni e le Attività Culturali – Soprintendenza Speciale per i Beni Archeologici di Roma.

some, the work [in Rome] that offers plenty of opportunities to show their worth. Some arrivals have brought their body to sell, some their eloquence. All types of men have rushed to this city that values highly virtues and vices alike.... Then go from this megalopolis, which can be called shared, so to speak, to the cities all around: most [of these also] have some foreign population. (Seneca, *To Helvia, on Consolation* 6.2–3)

Slightly later, when in 80 CE the poet Martial celebrated the opening of the Flavian amphitheater (later called the Colosseum), he held that its amazing wonder brought to Rome even far-off barbarous peoples such as "Thracians, Sarmatians, Egyptians, Arabs, Germans, and Ethiopians." He concludes by stressing that these discordant peoples were united by the paternalistic benevolence of the ruling emperor, Titus (*On the Spectacles* 3).

Inscriptions furnish slightly less impressionistic information than such literary remarks about non-Romans in Rome, identifying them individually as *peregrinus, hospis* (foreigner, guest), with an ethnic designation, by specification of birth in a town or city not in Italy and/or a province, or the like. Such documentary material confirms that there were a large number of non-Romans in the city. According to a recent study, some two thousand inscriptions from Rome record about 3,500 "foreign" persons. Few of these inscriptions can be dated more than roughly, and very few indicate how the commemorated individuals came to the capital city. Overall, however, the epigraphic evidence seems to indicate that of second-century CE Rome's million inhabitants about 35 percent were free male citizens, about 30 percent free women, and 25 percent slaves and non-Romans in an unknowable proportion. A high mortality rate caused by poor hygienic conditions, crowding, natural disasters like fires, floods, or plagues, and the general lack of medical understanding, among other demographic factors, demanded continual replenishment of the population in the closely packed capital city. Perhaps some ten thousand new immigrants came yearly, enabling Rome's population to remain at its high levels, and during the Empire most of these would have been free provincials.

As Seneca suggests, Rome's immigrants and sojourners were of all sorts. Provincials who came to Rome to fulfill military duties stood out more than others (see, e.g., Tacitus, *Histories* 2.88). Epitaphs and other evidence allow us to estimate this group as between 11,000 and 27–30,000 in the first to the third centuries CE. Almost no soldiers were actually recruited in Rome, although in the first and second centuries Italy furnished the majority of the men serving the ca. 9,000-strong Praetorian Guard. In the third century, however, about three-fifths of the Praetorian Guard came from Pannonia and neighboring provinces, and the remainder from the East. In standard denigration of northern-ers (see Chapter 2), the third-century historian Cassius Dio remarks that the shift in recruitment practices "fill[ed] the city with a swarm of ill-assorted soldiers most savage in their looks, most frightening in their shouting, and most uncouth in their exchanges" (*Roman History* 75.2.6). But much earlier the Julio-Claudians had employed German private bodyguards, probably because of their reputation for "military boldness" and lack of deviousness (see Vitruvius, previously quoted). At the begin-ning of the second century CE the German bodyguard was replaced by the *equites singulares* (select cavalrymen), a group of some thousand men similarly from the north (now the northwest and northeast). Some sail-ors in Rome, drawn from the fleets in Italy to work at the Colosseum and perform other duties, may have been Egyptian or Alexandrian (see Chapter 4). Including family members, perhaps 2 percent of the popu-lation of third-century Rome is estimated to have come from outside Italy for military service in the city. The power these "foreign" soldiers and marines wielded must have made them more conspicuous than their relatively small numbers suggest.

Although troops would not have been common in cities other than Rome, immigration and rapid population turnover were undoubtedly present, especially in the Empire's other three great cities – Alexandria (Egypt), Antioch (Syria, modern Antakya, Turkey), and Carthage (near Tunis, Tunisia) – whose populations seem to have numbered in the hundreds of thousands, and in smaller cities as well. Many newcom-ers, whose motives for moving ranged from employment, business, and politics to entertainment as performers, may have come from nearby regions, but some must also have come from farther afield; studies of names on inscriptions suggest that Syria, Asia, and other provinces in the Greek East supplied a steady stream of persons to Africa and other provinces in the west. Despite the great difficulties and costs involved in travel and communication, intentional movement of individuals and families certainly contributed to the diversity of the Roman people. We also see later the great admixture of peoples that slavery caused in Rome.

"Peoples" in Rome's Social and Political Ranks

Grants of Roman citizenship and movement of individuals during the Empire ultimately contributed to the renewal of Rome's ruling elite as well as to that of other echelons in Rome. Inscriptions and other evidence show that during the Empire senators with known origins in Rome's western and eastern provinces rather than in Italy rose from 17 percent of the senate ca. 69–79 CE, to 23 percent ca. 81–96, to 34 percent when Trajan was emperor (98–117), to 44 percent under the emperor Hadrian (117–138), finally reaching 57 percent of the senate under the emperors Septimius Severus and Caracalla (193–217). Trajan himself, from Italica (near Sevilla, Spain), was the first of many emperors with origins in the provinces. But Roman literary and visual evidence, much of which comes from individuals of senatorial and equestrian standing, make it dubious that non-Italian senators and emperors saw themselves as representatives of their provinces. Rather, once they and their families had "made it" in the Roman world, they seem to have identified with the traditional Roman elite in the kind of self-congratulatory assimilationist vision of Rome voiced by Pliny the Elder (quoted earlier; see also the discussion of the Lyon Tablet in Chapter 2).

On a vastly lower social and political level were foreign- or provincial-born slaves and freedmen in Rome, Italy, and the provinces, most of whom had come from outside Italy. Slaves have been estimated as constituting 10 percent of the overall population of the Roman Empire, that is six million of sixty million at Rome's peak. Although this proportion was not the same in all regions and eras, slaves and their descendants are critical to the investigation of the peoples of the Roman world. Some individuals remained slaves throughout their lives. Others, predominantly domestic slaves, were eventually freed by their masters and became Roman citizens; they were then known as freedmen (*liberti*) or freedwomen (*libertae*), and had almost full citizenship rights. In comparison to other slave-owning societies, Romans freed slaves relatively frequently, although this seems to have pertained mostly to skilled domestic slaves.

In any case, enormous and perhaps insoluble questions adhere to Rome's slaves and freed persons. Most slaves have left no trace. Slaves were generally considered "talking tools" (see Varro, *On Agriculture* 1.17.1; written at the end of the Republic): upon enslavement they lost their names, families, land, belongings, and other marks of identity, and thereafter were simply possessions of their Roman masters. Untold numbers lived and died with no record that survives. Similarly, the great mass of landless and/or impoverished Roman citizens left little or no trace in the material and literary record. In the capital city, freed persons and slaves with origins outside of Italy together may have constituted 35 to 40 percent of the population at any one time. Our greatest source of information for such individuals is epigraphic, but inscriptions tend to memorialize only those who had some wealth or power, and they are usually formulaic. Epitaphs, which constitute most of our data, usually provide little other than the names of the deceased and commemorator (at times not even the latter), along with an epithet, occupation, or quality of the deceased. Most names attested in Rome are either Latin or Greek, and very few come from another language. "Greek" names predominate among slaves, freed persons, and Christians. We cannot, for example, determine whether a humble Christian woman named Irene (Greek for "peace") was from Asia, Achaia, Bithynia, or elsewhere, was called "Peace" because of the Christian associations of the name, or had acquired her Greek name from a Greek slave trader. At the end of the Republic Varro said that slaves might be named for their sellers or the region or city in which they were purchased (*On the Latin Language* 8.9.21); this would render a name useless for determining origins. Seemingly ethnic designations or names such as "Gallus" might have been used as a *cognomen* rather than to designate someone as "Gallic" or Celtic; in any case, the "Gallic" designation itself was very imprecise (see Chapter 2). An epithet or name evocative of a physical characteristic sometimes linked with ethnicity might not have been an ethnic designation at all (like *maurus*, brown; cf. the modern surname Brown).

Difficulties in Determining Non-Roman Identities
in Rome and the Empire

Despite modern estimates of high numbers in Rome of freed and enslaved individuals of non-Roman origins, we do not know whether slaves retained an ethnic identity within their *familia* (group of persons under the legal guardianship of a citizen), passed that ethnicity on to their slave-born offspring, and/or regained their original ethnic identity upon manumission. Masters may have actively discouraged the perpetuation of ethnic identity among their slaves. The famous Revolt of Spartacus (73–71 BCE), led and fueled by slaves identified as Thracians and Gauls, emphasized the dangers of alienation and separatism. Over a century later, a slave's murder of his master occasioned a senatorial meeting in 62 CE at which was denounced the Roman practice of owning veritable slave "nations" with divergent and non-Roman religions and customs. Epigraphic and other evidence suggests that the numerous slaves and freedmen of an elite household participated in the religion of the house, often centered around the *genius* (or life force) of the head of the family, and that they normally used Latin for their daily transactions. Slaves' allegiance to, and identification with, their original homelands must have been difficult to maintain. Even if a slave's ethnicity could endure while he or she was under a master's control, it may have coexisted with other types of distinctiveness, such as an occupational identity tied to the job or position the slave assumed within the *familia*.

Former slaves, that is to say freed persons, seem disproportionately well represented in epitaphs and on funerary monuments, especially in and around Rome, the Bay of Naples, North Italy, and some cities in the provinces. In these contexts they often tend to assume a "Roman" identity marked by the use of the Roman *tria nomina* – a Roman *praenomen* like Gaius, a family name like Julius, and a specialized family name like Caesar. Other Roman signifiers are the special male costume of the long, draped toga, the *dextrarum iunctio* (clasping of right hands between man and wife, a symbol of legal marriage), the papyrus scroll (a symbol of manumission or honorable discharge papers), and/or (especially in the

7. Funerary relief of the family of the freedman Sextus Maelius Stabilio, from the Augustan period. In a convention of this era's tombstones from around Rome, the commemorated individuals are arranged as though they were looking through a window and are identified underneath their portraits. We see (*left to right*) Sextus Maelius Stabilio, the freedman of Sextus; Vesinia Jucunda, the freedwoman of a woman (denoted by the backwards C, and probably also named Vesinia); and Sextus Maelius Faustus, freedman of Sextus. The clasped right hands of the older couple indicate that they are married, as does Vesinia's modest gesture of pulling her veil forward over her hair and face. The inclusion of the younger man indicates that he is their son. Both father and son wear the Roman toga, the mark of Roman citizenship that they acquired upon manumission by their owner Sextus Maelius (whose *nomen* they now carry). Their names and identification confirm that they all were former slaves, but their gestures and clothing declare that they are now Roman. Monument now in the North Carolina Museum of Art; image from Corbis Museum collection (and copyrighted North Carolina Museum of Art / Corbis), Standard Rights Managed (RM) NC001978.

case of women) hairstyles and even physiognomies modeled on those of the imperial family (Fig. 7). Such visual symbols of Roman citizenship, or at least of the desire to seem Roman, indicate the power of Rome's assimilating myths and the tendency of Roman identity to eclipse ethnic and other types of distinctions. On the other hand, the persistence of non-Latin languages and names, and of non-Roman customs and religions, reveals that many peoples retained a distinct identity despite their incorporation into Rome. This book explores that tension, as well as the contributions of some of Rome's peoples.

Further Guide to This Book

Although most of the following chapters begin with the Republican period, I do not detail the wars by which various peoples became subjected to Roman power. Concentration on Rome's military activity and conquests can too broadly objectify Rome's many opponents simply as the "enemy," obscuring the individuality of peoples and cultures in the Roman world. More nuanced depictions, including self-portrayals, come from after each group and its constituents were taken over by Rome. Such visual and documentary sources, as well as better-known literary passages, date mainly to the Empire. Rome's foundations and earliest growth are famous because of much later literary material: as we saw in the opening pages of this chapter, Livy and Dionysius Halicarnassus described Romulus' actions some 750 years after the events were reckoned to have occurred. Such descriptions can elucidate the period when they were written more sensibly than the times they depict. I turn more directly to the later Republican and Imperial eras, and my treatments generally stop in the fourth century CE.

We shall see in Chapter 2 that those the Romans loosely categorized as (northern) Celts, Gauls, and Germans left no literature and little documentary material of their own, forcing us to decipher and interpret Roman descriptions. These illuminate the stereotype of the "northern barbarian" and its shifting application over time as Romans contrasted it with themselves, more or less explicitly, as a means of self-identification. Rather than investigating each northern group the Romans identified in this way, I focus on the stereotype itself and Rome's ambivalence toward northerners. The Greeks, the subject of Chapter 3, also constituted for the Romans a culture against which they defined themselves both positively and negatively. They eagerly emulated Greek literature, art and architecture, and philosophical thought even as they prided themselves on their military and political superiority to the Greeks. Rome's assimilation of Greek culture was fundamental to its own culture and development; in turn, many Greeks apparently flourished in the Roman world. Egyptians and Egypt, the subject of Chapter 4, were much more marginalized in Roman thought and history, although a source of great wealth and never-ending fascination. Yet papyri documents and portraits from Roman Egypt reveal aspects of daily life and representation that belie essential distinctions between Romans and Roman-Egyptians. While investigating Jews and Christians in Chapters 5 and 6, we see a minority perspective articulated eloquently by members of these groups; in turn, we frequently encounter overt prejudice against them. Added complications for the investigation are the sometimes contentious relations between Jews and Christians, and the relative lack of figural representations for both. Rome's official relations with the two groups indicate both attempts at cautious assimilation or accommodation and outbreaks of exasperation and violent intolerance.

In sum, the individual and collective histories of these five groups should reveal the ongoing cultural transformation of Rome and the many contributions Rome's peoples made to the empire, even as we see the impossibility of identifying any group in Rome, or indeed the Romans themselves, definitively. Identities were contested at any one moment and shifted over time and space. One great source of Rome's power and longevity was its ability to adapt to such changes and continually reconfigure the notion of what being Roman was.

SUGGESTED FURTHER READING

Adams, C., and Laurence, R. (eds.). 2001. *Travel and Geography in the Roman Empire*. London: Routledge.

Beard, M. 2007. *The Roman Triumph*. Cambridge, MA: Harvard University Press.

Beard, M., North, J., and Price, S. 1998. *Religions of Rome*. Vol. I, *A History*; Vol. II, *A Sourcebook*. Cambridge: Cambridge University Press.

Brunt, P. A. 1971. *Social Conflicts in the Roman Republic*. London: Chatto and Windus.

D'Ambra, E. 1998. *Roman Art*. Cambridge: Cambridge University Press.

Dench, E. 2005. *Romulus' Asylum: Roman Identities from the Age of Alexander to the Age of Hadrian*. Oxford: Oxford University Press.

Edwards, C., and Woolf, G. (eds.). 2003. *Rome the Cosmopolis*. Cambridge: Cambridge University Press.

Farney, G. D. 2007. *Ethnic Identity and Aristocratic Competition in Republican Rome*. Cambridge: Cambridge University Press.

Frier, B. 2000. "Demography." In *The Cambridge Ancient History*, vol. 11 (2nd ed.): 787–816.

Gardner, J. F. 1993. *Being a Roman Citizen*. London: Routledge.

Gordon, M. L. 1924. "The Nationality of Slaves under the Early Roman Empire." *The Journal of Roman Studies* 14: 93–111.

Hall, J. M. 1997. *Ethnic Identity in Greek Antiquity*. Cambridge: Cambridge University Press.

Holliday, P. J. 2002. *The Origins of Roman Historical Commemoration in the Visual Arts*. Cambridge: Cambridge University Press.

Huskinson, J. (ed.). 2000. *Experiencing Rome: Culture, Identity and Power in the Roman Empire*. London: Routledge.

Isaac, B. H. 2004. *The Invention of Racism in Classical Antiquity*. Princeton, NJ: Princeton University Press.

Joshel, S. R. 1992. *Work, Identity, and Legal Status at Rome: A Study of the Occupational Inscriptions*. Norman: University of Oklahoma Press.

La Piana, G. 1927. "Foreign Groups in Rome." *Harvard Theological Review* 20: 183–403.

Lawrence, R., and Berry, J. (eds.). 1998. *Cultural Identity in the Roman Empire*. London: Routledge.

Millar, F., et al. 1967. *The Roman Empire and Its Neighbours*. London: Weidenfeld and Nicolson.

Noy, D. 2000. *Foreigners at Rome: Citizens and Strangers*. London: Duckworth.

Scheidel, W. 1997. "Quantifying the Sources of Slaves in the Early Roman Empire." *The Journal of Roman Studies* 87: 156–69.

Scott, S., and Webster, J. (eds.). 2003. *Roman Imperialism and Provincial Art*. Cambridge: Cambridge University Press.

Snowden, F. M., Jr. 1970. *Blacks in Antiquity: Ethiopians in the Greco-Roman Experience*. Cambridge, MA: Harvard University Press.

Thompson, L. A. 1989. *Romans and Blacks*. Norman: University of Oklahoma Press.

Wells, P. S. 1999. *The Barbarians Speak: How the Conquered Peoples Shaped Roman Europe*. Princeton, NJ: Princeton University Press.

Woolf, G. 1998. *Becoming Roman: The Origins of Provincial Civilization in Gaul*. Cambridge: Cambridge University Press.

CHAPTER 2

GAULS, CELTS, GERMANS, AND OTHER "NORTHERNERS"

D | M
LICINIAE L·F | SEX·ADGENN·II
FLAVILLAE | MACRN·TRIB·LEG·V
| VICH·IIVIR·IVR·DIC
FLAMINICAVG | PONT·EPRAEF·FABR

Introduction

Italy, a long and mountainous peninsula with few good harbors, may seem forbidding and inaccessible, but its permeable northern boundary of the Alps allowed recurrent interaction with northerners. These dealings led to Romans forming stereotypes about their northern neighbors. In the sixth century BCE and again around 400 BCE, groups north of the Alps migrated in significant numbers throughout and below central Europe, moving west into the Iberian Peninsula, east into the Balkans and Asia Minor, and south into Italy (Fig. 8). Throughout the Republic, again in the second century CE, and more intensively thereafter, migrations and invasions from the north entered or threatened Italy and Roman territory. The infamous Gallic Sack of Rome, traditionally dated to 390 or 387/386 BCE, was particularly scarring for the Romans. Thereafter Gauls and other northerners symbolized for Rome an aggressive external foe with warlike capabilities matching Rome's own, in contrast to Greeks, Egyptians, Jews, and others whom the Romans conquered in their own lands. This may account for the Romans' imprecise but deep-seated stereotyping of "northern barbarians" that endured even as successive groups of trans-Alpine Europeans were assimilated, first as provincials and later as Roman citizens. Further, although some individual "Gauls" and other northerners reached Rome's highest levels – the family of Antoninus Pius, who served as Rome's emperor from 138 to 161, had origins in Nemausus (modern Nîmes, France) – Romans seem never to have relinquished their association of barbarism with the north.

Northern Europeans encountered by Greeks and Romans were regularly identified by various imprecise terms throughout the Roman period. Names translated as Celts, Gauls, and Galatians (*Celtae, Galli, Keltoi, Galatae*, and others) designated peoples sharing a common background of language and artistic traditions now identified as the la Tène culture. Germans (*Germani*) were thought of as originating farther north and east of the Rhine: geographically more remote from Greeks and Romans, they were considered more barbaric. Generalized group names and stereotypes long persisted for Greeks and Romans despite more contacts with northern Europeans. After 600 BCE, when Greeks from Phocaea (modern Foça, Turkey) colonized Massalia (the Latin Massilia, modern Marseilles, France) at the mouth of the Rhône River, commerce and other personal exchanges occurred regularly between northerners in temperate Europe and inhabitants along the Mediterranean. Greek ethnographic and geographic works on Gauls, Celts, and others in northern regions appeared by the second century BCE and increased in the first; one on the Celts, considered highly influential for Caesar and Tacitus but now lost, was written by the great polymath Posidonius of Apamea (d. ca. 51 BCE; Apamea is modern Afamia or Kalat el-Mudik in northwestern Syria).

By the last century of the Republic Romans had repeatedly fought various Gauls and Germans. Although now the best-known hostilities are the conquest of Gaul undertaken by Julius Caesar from 58 to 51 BCE (which included skirmishes in Britain and Germany), many others were defensive and unsuccessful for Rome. When the Romans encountered northern tribes or groups in Pannonia, Dacia, and elsewhere, they often classified them conventionally as barbarian, Celt or Gallic, and/or German. We can see this, for example, in the honorific epithet "Germanicus" that was commonly used for emperors in the first through third centuries, even for Marcus Aurelius and others whose victories against northern "barbarians" were not in Germany or along the Rhine River.

Roman Ideas of Northerners

Literary descriptions and images cast these loosely defined northerners as uncultured and unsophisticated, but often imposing (Fig. 9). As no literature and few inscriptions written by these peoples remain, we hear only Roman and Greek views. Among the stereotypes figure

8. Map showing spread of Celtic-language speakers at maximum extent, ca. 200 BCE, and designating approximate areas of tribes mentioned in the text (some of which, like the Iceni, are securely documented only in later periods). Some Gallic settlements (e.g., Narbo) are identified by their later Roman names. Map © 2011, Ancient World Mapping Center (www.unc.edu/awmc). Used by permission.

honesty in warfare and a lack of wiliness (*The African War* 73.2; written 40s BCE); preference for fighting and arms over farming and crafts (e.g., Strabo, *Geography* 4.1.2; Augustan period); great courage (e.g., Caesar, *War against Gaul* 2.27); reluctance to live in cities or even to have fixed homes; inconsistency and quickness to anger; uncontrollable greed for gold, wine, and other sensual pleasures (see Livy on the fourth-century Gallic Sack of Rome); and women's visibility and participation in men's affairs, including warfare and religion (e.g., Tacitus, *Annals* 14.35). Strabo

holds that the Gauls were war-mad, high-spirited, and quick for battle, although somewhat simple (*Geography* 4.4.2). Over two centuries later the historian Herodian remarked, "The inhabitants of Pannonia [modern Hungary] are tall men of fine physique, natural and fierce fighters, but intellectually dull and slow-witted when it comes to crafty words or subtle actions" (*Roman History* 2.9.11; Loeb trans.). Roman art distinguished northern barbarians from Romans more strikingly, for the northerners are often depicted semi-naked, frighteningly large, and uncontrolled. Men characteristically wear "breeches," or trousers with tight leggings, in contrast to the Roman toga and the Greco-Roman tunic. Men and women have long, disheveled hair – the farther north the blonder – that

9. Statue group of the murder-suicide of a Gallic couple. This freestanding statuary group, often called the "Ludovisi Gaul" because of its former inclusion in the collection of the Ludovisi family at Rome, depicts the suicide murder of a Gaul and his wife. She wears a fringed outer cloak (see Fig. 6); he is heroically naked except for his short fighting cloak. Gallic women were thought to participate in warfare, at least as spectators who would encourage and shame their men into greater acts of courage. This is a Roman copy (2.11 m H = 6 ft. 11 in.; marble) of a group from a monument built by Attalus I of Pergamon after his victory over Galatians in central Asia Minor, ca. 220 BCE. Now in the Museo Nazionale Romano, Palazzo Altemps, inv. 8608. Published by permission of the Ministero per i Beni e le Attività Culturali – Soprintendenza Speciale per i Beni Archeologici di Roma.

is matched by unkempt beards and mustaches on men. This image was perpetuated later by the Roman term "Gallia Comata," or "long-haired Gaul," to describe the more northern and supposedly more uncivilized part of Gaul in contrast to "Gallia Togata," or "Gaul in the Roman toga," for Gallic lands on the Mediterranean and closer to Rome.

As is clear in Tacitus' *Germania*, written 98 CE, some of these qualities were ones Romans saw in themselves, with pride as traditional virtues (courage and militarism) or with shame as signs of their own degeneration (sensuality and greed). Tacitus seems to have thought that the Germans' militarism posed an elemental threat to Rome deterred only by the gods' favor and the Germans' inherent dissension (*Germania* 33): this last quality is implicitly compared to the Romans' own political organization and discipline, which they considered superior to those of other groups. Other qualities attributed to northerners, such as intellectual dullness and inconsistency, derived from the essentialist concepts of the influence of climate and geography on humans that we discussed in Chapter 1. But in general the northerners' wild and unruly behavior, temperament, and appearance were presented in opposition to the Roman virtues of order, self-restraint, and respect for authority. For the Romans, northerners manifested a barbarian nature by their unruliness and unpredictability as well as by their chronic aggression and resistance to Rome.

The Gallic Sack of Rome in 390 (or 387/386) BCE

Such stereotypes feature particularly in Livy's elaborate description of the Gallic Sack of Rome. His description of this event (5.33–49, written in the Augustan period), like others now extant, was written long after the event occurred in 390 BCE (387/6 by Polybius' reckoning in the mid-second century BCE, *Histories* 1.6.1). The background Livy and others give for the sack is the movement south of Gauls, who had earlier settled along the upper Adriatic Sea area and in the Po River valley (see Fig. 8). After failed negotiations, the northerners crushed the Romans at the

Allia River (some 9 km north of Rome) and continued south to capture the city of Rome itself. Only the Capitoline, Rome's citadel, remained in Roman hands. Livy's dramatic description of the Gauls' first night in the city emphasizes Rome's vulnerability to the countless invaders:

> As the Romans beheld from the Citadel the City filled with the enemy, who were running about in all the streets, as some new disaster was constantly occurring first in one quarter then in another, they could no longer control their eyes and ears, let alone their thoughts and feelings. Wherever their attention was drawn by the shouts of the enemy, the shrieks of women and boys, the roar of flames, and the crash of houses falling in, there they turned their eyes and minds as though they had been set by Fortune to be spectators of their country's fall, powerless to protect anything they possessed beyond their lives. Above all others who have ever stood a siege were they to be pitied, cut off as they were from the land of their birth and seeing all that had been theirs in the possession of the enemy. (Livy 5.42)

Most Romans forsook the city as the Gauls besieged the few defenders on the Capitoline for seven months. The besiegers finally left only for a price, with their leader Brennus famously exclaiming, "Woe to the conquered!" and flinging his sword on the balance to increase the amount of gold the Romans had to pay (Livy 5.48.9).

This early defeat and humiliation at Gallic hands undoubtedly influenced the Romans' views of northern peoples. The Gauls were the only external foe acknowledged to have conquered the city in the thousand-plus years from the establishment of the Republic in the late sixth century BCE, up until the fifth century CE. As we shall see later, northerners would again invade Roman territory (though not Rome itself) many times, even though Romans would repeatedly best them. We may perhaps see Roman vanity at work in the speech Livy attributes to the great Roman leader Marcus Furius Camillus during the seven-month Gallic siege of Rome. Camillus scorns the Gauls as disorderly and gluttonous:

Already the irksomeness of a siege has proved too much for them; they are giving it up and wandering through the fields in straggling parties. When they are gorged with food and the wine they drink so greedily, they throw themselves down like wild beasts on the approach of night in all directions by the streams, without entrenching themselves or setting any outposts or pickets on guard. (Livy 5.44)

His words implicitly contrast the Gauls' behavior to Roman military discipline. Romans attributed their military success to this characteristic, and it was one way in which they distinguished themselves from their belligerent but careless northern foes.

Other Roman Hostilities with Northerners in Italy during the Republic

The Gallic Sack was only the first of many hostile encounters between Romans and Gauls in Italy during the Republic. As we have seen, by the fourth century BCE, Gauls were inhabiting Italy in the Po valley and along the Adriatic north of the Apennines. Some of the wars of the fourth and third centuries took place in this region as Rome invaded Gallic territory, while others occurred farther south in land under Roman or allied control (Fig. 10). Victorious Romans claimed for themselves the area from modern Rimini to below the Metaurus River as *ager Gallicus* ("Gallic land"), brought back slaves, and colonized the land. Disregarding their own aggression, Romans saw Gauls as rootless plunderers, broadly objectifying them in ways that now seem absurd. For example, Claudius Quadrigarius, a historian of the early first century BCE, wrote:

Then came forward [at a standoff in 361 BCE] a certain Gaul, decorated by a torque necklace and armbands but otherwise naked except for his shield and two swords, who stood out from the others for his strength, size, and manly youth, and likewise

10. Map of northern Italy in the mid- to late Roman Republic, showing geographical features, regions, tribes, and cities. From the fourth century BCE the area of the Padus (Po) River valley between the Alps and the Apennines was known to the Romans as Cisalpine Gaul, "Gaul this side of the Alps." The Metaurus River south of Ariminum (modern Rimini) roughly marks Cisalpine Gaul's southeastern limits. Map © 2011, Ancient World Mapping Center (www.unc.edu/awmc). Used by permission.

11. Civitalba relief. This terracotta relief (ca. 45 cm H), found in Civitalba, Italy (southwest of Ariminum and just south of Cisalpine Gaul) apparently once decorated a temple of the early second century BCE. We see a local version of a motif that became common in Greece and Asia after Gauls attempted to sack Delphi in 279/278 BCE but were allegedly deterred by Delphi's tutelary god, Apollo. The relief depicts two Gauls fleeing in terror and dropping their booty of precious temple dedications that includes an (upside-down) urn and a round shield. They are shown mostly naked, with exaggerated sexual organs and long disheveled hair; one wears a torque around his neck. The frieze, now in Ancona, Museo Archeologico Nazionale delle Marche (Soprintendenza per i Beni Archeologici delle Marche di Ancona, inv. nn. 66268 and 66269; slide n. 179520, Archivio Fotografico), is published by permission of the Ministero per i Beni e le Attività Culturali – Direzione Regionale per i Beni Culturali e Paesaggistici delle Marche – Soprintendenza per i Beni Archeologici delle Marche.

> for his courage. [He called for single battle, and] no one dared to
> meet him because of his immense size and ferocious appearance.
> Then the Gaul began mocking [the Romans] and sticking out
> his tongue....

This provoked the Roman Titus Manlius to take him on, subsequently besting him in a terrific battle (quoted in Aulus Gellius, *Attic Nights* 9.13.7–19) (Fig. 11). Underscoring the Romans' ambivalence toward the belligerent northerners, in another version of the story Livy has the

Gaul explicitly challenge the Romans to determine "which race is better in war" (7.9.8). In 225 BCE the Romans and their allies turned back a Gallic invasion at Telamon in Etruria, only some 90 miles northwest of Rome.

After the late third century BCE a great deal of Roman energy seems to have been aimed at acquiring "Cisalpine Gaul," the area of modern Italy "this side" (*cis*, according to perspectives from Rome) of the Alps that had been settled by Gallic peoples. Gallic tribes in this region had supported Hannibal as he crossed the Alps and invaded Italy in 218 BCE, and Rome's final victory in the Hannibalic or Second Punic War (218–201) ultimately doomed the northerners. But the conquest was a lengthy and difficult process. (See Fig. 10.) By 191 BCE the Romans had defeated the Boii around Bononia (Bologna, Italy). During the next eight years they settled numerous colonies at important crossroads and locales, mostly south of the Po. In 187 they built the Via Aemilia from Ariminum to Placentia to solidify their gains. As they secured for themselves the territory south of the Po during the next century, its former Celtic/Gallic inhabitants moved north of the river, thereby gaining the name "Transpadani" ("those across the Padanus [Po] River").

Cisalpine Gaul can serve as an example of Rome's ambivalence toward the incorporation of other peoples. When the region was made a province after the Social War (91–88/87 BCE), the inhabitants of Rome's earlier colonies there were granted Roman citizenship; one such family was that of the poet Catullus. But the rest of the free population, the Celtic/Gallic Transpadani, did not receive full Roman citizenship until forty years later, in a grant due to Julius Caesar in 49 BCE. Furthermore, the territory of "Cisalpine Gaul" between the Italian Alps and the Apennines lost its provincial status to become fully integrated into Roman Italy only in 42 BCE. Despite Rome's apparent reluctance to accept Cisalpine Gaul officially as part of its homeland, the area was celebrated in the late Republic as "the flower of Italy, the pride and bulwark of the Roman people" (Cicero, *Philippics* 3.13; 44 BCE). A century or more later the elite of Rome – respected senators, officials, and Latin authors – included Pliny the Elder, Pliny the Younger, and others from this region (perhaps also Tacitus, although Tacitus has also been said to have been from Narbonese Gaul). Many now consider as quintessentially Italian the Po River region and other areas the Romans originally thought of as "Cisalpine Gaul" and Gallic.

Romans and Northerners across the Alps

The Second Punic War (218–201 BCE) had also brought the Romans into conflict with Gallic/Celtic groups across the Alps, because Rome's alliance with the Greek colony of Massalia (Latin: Massilia) led to problems with Massalia's Gallic neighbors, the Salluvii, Arverni, Allobroges, and other tribes, despite benefiting Rome during the war. During the Second Punic War Rome also invaded the area of modern eastern Spain, where the Carthaginians had established strongholds and good relations with Celtiberians, the culture fused from indigenous Iberians and Celtic immigrants of the sixth century BCE and again around 400 BCE. Rome's victories in the Iberian Peninsula during the Second Punic War against the Carthaginians and their allies led to the establishment of Rome's provinces of Closer and Farther Spain in a brutal process that took from 197 to 133 BCE. This pitted Rome against Celtiberians in Spain as well as against the Gallic tribes controlling land routes from Italy to the Iberian Peninsula (Fig. 12). The interaction was legendarily bloody and extended: for example, when Gnaeus Domitius Ahenobarbus fought the Allobroges in 122 BCE, Roman forces are said to have killed twenty thousand Gauls and captured three thousand others. By 117 BCE Rome had established in this region another Gallic province, that of Narbonese Gaul, which had its administrative center at Narbo, one of Rome's first overseas colonies (settled probably 118 BCE; modern Narbonne, France).

Narbonese Gaul provides another example of Roman ambivalence toward Gauls and other provincial peoples, and of the shifting location of northern barbarism. At first Roman command of southwestern Gaul was tied to exploitation so flagrant that it incited intermittent revolts and

Ancient World Mapping Center 2011

12. Map of Transalpine Gaul in the later Roman Republic. Transalpine Gaul, or "Gaul across the Alps," was the site of much contact between northerners and Romans beginning in the late third century BCE. Rome was drawn into the power relationships of Gaul by the military problems her ally Massilia encountered with local Celtic and other peoples, and by her own need for communications with Spain. Narbo became a Roman colony around 117 BCE. Map © 2011, Ancient World Mapping Center (www.unc.edu/awmc). Used by permission.

was decried even at Rome in 107 and the 70s BCE. In the later scandal Cicero defended Marcus Fonteius, who was charged with corruption while governor there in the 70s. In the extant speech the orator repeatedly disparages the "barbarian" Gauls in contrast to "our fellow citizens" (e.g., *On Behalf of Fonteius* 4 and 15). But even within a decade Cicero, and presumably his audience, could shift the location of hostile Gauls to temperate France north and northeast of Narbonese Gaul (Cicero, *Catilinarians*

3.22; from 63 BCE). The alleged savagery of this more northern region, Gallia Comata, helped to justify the attacks of Julius Caesar that began in 58 BCE. Narbonese Gaul itself continued to be integrated with Rome in a process that underlines the relativity of "barbarian" rhetoric. In the 70s CE Pliny the Elder wrote, with some satisfaction, "in the cultivation of its fields, the dignified honor of its men and morals, the extent of its wealth, [Narbonese Gaul] must be put behind no other province, and in short is more like Italy than like a province" (*Natural History* 3.31).

One means of integration (which we shall see also with "the Greeks" in Chapter 3) was the imperial cult, which provided provincials with a chance for social and political advancement into positions of prominence in the imperial Roman world. Two detailed inscriptions survive from different faces of an altar erected and dedicated in 11/13 CE for use of the imperial cult in Narbo (English translation in Lewis and Reinhold 1990: I, 622–3). The inscription details vows for Augustus' worship that the people of Narbo have taken in perpetuity, as well as protocols for three annual sacrifices of animals (accompanied by incense and wine), and two annual offerings of just incense and wine, to be overseen by three Roman equestrians and three freedmen from Narbonese Gaul. The safety of Augustus, of his wife, children and clan, and of the Senate and the People of Rome is tied to that of Narbo. Other inscriptions and tombstones show us some of the individuals who served as priests and priestesses of the imperial cult (Fig. 13). Individuals from southern Gaul played essential roles in the Roman world as religious personnel, local town councilors, magistrates, and priests, landowners, and merchants. By the mid-second century CE the area had reached the pinnacle of Roman power in the person of the emperor Antoninus Pius (r. 138–161 CE), whose family was from Nemausus.

Germans and Gauls from Temperate Europe

In the late Republic, however, the assimilation of Mediterranean Gauls may have been due as much to the emergence of more distant "barbarian"

13. "Romano-Gallic" couple from Nemausus. Funerary relief from Nemausus (modern Nîmes, France), showing a respectable Roman couple of the beginning of the second century CE. The epitaph translates as: "To the spirits of the dead of Licinia Flavilla, daughter of Lucius, flaminica Augustalis, and of Sextus Adgennius Macrinus, tribune of the 6th Legion Victrix, quattuorvir to decide the law, pontifex, and chief of the engineers." The man's *nomen* Adgennius indicates a Gallic background. Although he was a local town councilor (as one of four men appointed to a judicial board) and priest (or *pontifex*), his military uniform and the order in which his positions are placed in his epitaph give pride of place to his military service as tribune of the 6th ("Victorious") Legion and head of the army engineers. His hair is arranged like that of Trajan (r. 98–117). The woman, presumably his wife, has elaborately curled hair crowning her head in a hairstyle popular among imperial women and others during the late first and early second century CE. Her title, flaminica Augustalis, identifies her as a priestess of the imperial cult. Published by permission of le Musée archéologique de Nîmes. © Ville de Nîmes. Photo: Dejan Stokic.

threats as to familiarity, cultural interchange, and shared economic concerns. Beginning in 113 BCE Cimbri, Teutoni, Ambrones, and other Germanic tribes originating in the North Sea region repeatedly clashed with Romans in southern Gaul and in Illyricum (north and east of the Adriatic Sea), crushing Roman armies and inflicting other disasters. The Helvetii and a few other southern Gallic tribes joined the invaders against Rome. The origins and ethnicity of these "barbarians" are unclear, and Sallust, writing in the mid-first century BCE, even loosely calls them Gauls as he emphasizes their military valor:

> Just about the same time [108 BCE], war was feebly waged against the Gauls under our leaders Quintus Caepio and Gnaeus Manlius, and all Italy shuddered with fear. Thus even up to our own day Romans judge that although all other things and peoples yield to our virtue, with the Gauls we strive for our safety, not for our glory. (Sallust, *War against Jugurtha* 114)

Plutarch, in a fuller description from the early second century CE, states:

> [The invaders'] numbers, however, are given by many writers as not less, but more, than [Plutarch's own number of 300,000 fighting men accompanied by women and children]. Moreover, their courage and daring made them irresistible, and when they engaged in battle they came on with the swiftness and force of fire, so that no one could withstand their onset, but all who came in their way became their prey and booty, and even many large Roman armies, with their commanders, who had been stationed to protect Transalpine Gaul, were destroyed ingloriously. Indeed, by their feeble resistance [these Roman armies] were mainly instrumental in drawing the on-rushing barbarians down upon Rome. (*Life of Marius* 11.8; Loeb trans. by B. Perrin)

Emphasizing the stereotypical wildness of northerners, Plutarch presents the Ambrones and others as barely human. After a clash at Aquae Sextiae (modern Aix-en-Provence, France), their "lamentation all night long [was] not like the wails and groans of men, but like howls and bellows with a strain of the wild beast in them, mingled with threats and cries of grief.... The whole plain was filled with a terrible din" (*Life of Marius* 20; based on Loeb trans.). After repeated setbacks the Romans repulsed the invaders, and at the final clash, at Cisalpine Gaul's Vercellae (modern Vercelli in northwestern Italy), "the infantry of the barbarians came on to the attack like a vast sea in motion." But the Romans won, killing 120,000 and selling into slavery more than 60,000 invaders (Plutarch, *Life of Marius* 26–7). The vast numbers and terrifying ferocity of these northerners are repeatedly emphasized in the literary sources.

Julius Caesar, the War against Gaul, and Citizenship Issues

Rome moved decisively into temperate Europe during the war against Gaul led by Julius Caesar from 58 to 51 BCE, and in his contemporary seven-book *War against Gaul* he describes his opponents and expresses admiration for them even while consistently justifying Roman aggression. The hostilities began against the Gallic Helvetii (whose home was near modern Lake Geneva, Switzerland) so as to protect Roman allies and to avenge an earlier defeat (in 107), but by the end of seven years of war Caesar had swept through all of Gaul, crossed the Rhine into what he calls "Germania," and traversed the English Channel to invade Britain (Fig. 14). The Romans won a conclusive battle in 52 BCE at Alesia (modern Alise-Sainte-Reine, France), despite being outnumbered five to one at one point and themselves surrounded while besieging the fortified hilltop town. Caesar is very positive about some of the Gallic leaders and warriors he fought, especially the heroic Vercingetorix, who almost beat him at Alesia (e.g., *War against Gaul* 7.14, 7.20, 7.29). Caesar's narrative includes a notable ethnographic digression on the Gauls and the Germans (*War against Gaul* 6.11–28). There he speaks admiringly of the Druids, an elite Gallic priestly caste overseeing religion and sacred verses; he notes that they did not record such verses, and that Gauls used

14. Map of Gaul, indicating many of the Gallic hill forts (□, small hollow squares), Graeco-Roman towns (●, dots), and Gallic and Germanic tribes at the time of Caesar's campaigns (58–51 BCE) detailed in *War against Gaul*. Map © 2011, Ancient World Mapping Center (www.unc.edu/awmc). Used by permission.

Greek, not a native language, for their public and private transactions (*War against Gaul* 6.13–14). Caesar's campaigns enslaved one million and killed another million of the three million then inhabiting Gaul, and by 50 BCE the Romans controlled all the land to the Rhine River. Prisoners of war were marched in Caesar's fourfold triumphal procession held in 46 BCE, and some fought in the arena during festivities for the dedication in Rome of Caesar's Temple of Venus Genetrix that same year. (See the coin of Caesar illustrated in Fig. 5a.)

Caesar is also linked to issues of political assimilation and enfranchisement of Gauls, although these were quite contentious. We have already seen that he granted Roman citizenship to Cisalpine Gauls in 49 BCE. After the civil war ended in 46 BCE, he enrolled in the Roman senate some individuals from Cisalpine Gaul, and probably some from Narbonese Gaul as well. The new senators were undoubtedly the descendants of colonists who had enjoyed Roman citizenship for generations. But Caesar was mocked for introducing as senators "half-barbarians" and Gauls "whom he had just led in triumph in their breeches" (Suetonius, *Life of Caesar* 76.3, 80.2). The ridicule denigrates Caesar himself, whom many considered increasingly despotic, but it also expresses anxiety about a too-rapid rate of cultural change. Similar concern may echo in the remark made by Pliny the Elder when reporting the triumph of Lucius Cornelius Balbus in 19 BCE over African tribes – namely, that Balbus, born in Gades (modern Cadiz, Spain), had himself just been granted Roman citizenship (*Natural History* 5.36). The desire to distance former enemies and subjects is also evident in a speech the Augustan Livy puts in the mouth of the Roman general Marcus Popilius Laenas before a battle against the Gauls in 316 BCE. Popilius is supposed to have spurred on his troops by asking: "Why are you standing about, soldiers? We are not dealing with a Latin or Sabine enemy who, once conquered, you make an ally in arms rather than an enemy. We have drawn our swords against wild beasts, and blood must be shed either on our side, or on theirs" (Livy 7.24.4–5). Assimilation of northerners was obviously a controversial subject.

The Lyon Tablet of 47/48 CE and Gallic Senators

Similar conflict emerges in a senatorial discussion of 47/48 CE about allowing individual Roman citizens from Gallia Comata north of the Mediterranean to serve as Roman senators. The emperor Claudius spoke for the proposal in a speech that has been preserved in two versions. One is a verbatim copy on a bronze inscription originally exhibited in Lugdunum (where Claudius had been born); this is now called the Lyon Tablet from the modern name of this French city (translation in Lewis and Reinhold 1990: II, 54–55). We also have a paraphrase that Tacitus made over sixty years after the speech was given (see *Annals* 11.22–25); some have attributed his favorable stance toward the issue to his own possible origins in Narbonese or Cisalpine Gaul.

In both versions Claudius emphasizes the continuing acceptance of "foreigners" as fundamental to Rome's history and strength. Tacitus' account introduces Claudius' speech with anonymous objections to the proposal. These included protests that Italy was not so weak as to have to import senators and complaints that Veneti and Insubres (Cisalpine groups) had earlier "burst" into the senate. Tacitus' unnamed senators also raise the specter of the Gallic Sack, more recent Gallic victories over Rome, and the siege of Julius Caesar at Alesia. But Claudius responds that his own genealogy (his ancestors were Sabines) urged Rome to take to itself whatever outstanding was found elsewhere, and that Roman history demonstrated continual expansion of the Roman citizenship and acceptance of other races (Tacitus, *Annals* 11.23–4). When on the Lyon Tablet Claudius mentions that Gallia Comata engaged Caesar for ten years, he immediately contrasts the period to the following century of peaceful support for Roman action against Germans farther north. Claudius' view prevailed. Gauls from this area were admitted to the senate, a right ultimately granted to Roman citizens from all the provinces (except, perhaps, Egypt; see Chapter 4). In fact, however, throughout Rome's history only a few senators are known to have come from European Gaul, Germany, and other northern provinces.

Both versions of Claudius' speech reveal a ready recourse to loose stereotypes and prejudices, as well as the shifting location of "barbarism." This latter point is also clear in a slightly earlier Claudian monument. In 43 CE Claudius was celebrated for conquering Britain. The Roman arch commemorating his triumph, which was erected over the main road entering the capital city from the north, included a monumental inscription boasting that "he received the surrender of eleven kings of the Britons, defeated without any loss, and first brought barbarian peoples across the Ocean into the dominion of the Roman people" (see Lewis and Reinhold 1990: II, 36-7). Although it actually took until the 80s CE to control the island, and even then its northernmost part remained autonomous, in Rome Claudius was fêted for subjugating northern barbarians and defeating Britons without loss of Roman life. Similar arches celebrating his victory were set up in Cyzicus, Asia (modern Kyzikos, Turkey) and in Gesoriacum, Gallia (Boulogne, France).

Germans and Others Farther North (and Northwest and Northeast)

On the Lyon Tablet of 47/48 CE, Claudius justifies acceptance of the Gauls partly by contrasting them to the farther Germans, peoples with whom the Romans were by then familiar, although they feared them (see Fig. 1). Augustus had extended Roman territory north of the Rhine all the way to the Elbe River (in modern northern Germany). But in 9 CE the new Roman general in the recently conquered region, Publius Quinctilius Varus, was ambushed, losing three legions and his own life in an area now identified as Kalkriese. The sources generally scapegoat Varus for being too trusting of a barbaric people. Contrasting (barbarian) force to (civilized) law, the Roman historian Velleius Paterculus says: "Varus foolishly thought that the Germans, who had not been able to be subdued by the sword, could be soothed by the law" (*Roman History* 2.117.3). In Rome the disaster resulted in deporting to islands all Germans and Gauls, including those serving as Augustus' bodyguards (Cassius Dio, *Roman History* 56.23; cf. Suetonius, *Life of Augustus* 49). We have no idea how many were sent away in 9 CE, or for how long. Nor do we know how the Gauls and Germans were identified in Rome – by language and appearance? or simply by others' denunciations? (Similar difficulties must have been encountered when identifying Christians for scapegoating after the Great Fire of 64 CE; see Chapter 6.) The deportation underscores Roman tendencies to lump northerners together: here Gauls were also expelled from Rome although it was Germans who plotted and accomplished the ambush in Germany, 700 miles away. The incident also reveals Roman ambivalence toward the Germans, who were trusted enough by Augustus to serve as bodyguards of his family but also seen as threatening.

Varus' disaster is credited with limiting Roman ambitions in north-west Europe to the Rhine River (rather than farther north and east at the Elbe), but Rome continued to expand over Europe's northwest and northeast into the second century of the Empire. After Caesar's death in 44 BCE Roman conquests and diplomatic negotiations had steadily annexed "northern" territories and peoples as new provinces or as expanded areas of preexisting provinces. These acquisitions included northwestern Spain (19 BCE), a large chunk of the northwestern Alps (under Nero), Britain (43–47 CE, though insecure until the 80s, as we have seen), and Thrace (46 CE). Under Augustus, the Romans had conquered central Europe up to the Danube River and over to the Black Sea, adding the provinces Moesia and Pannonia (6 and 9 CE) so as to control a northern route from west to east. Flashpoints along the winding inland route were the "Agri Decumates," the triangular-shaped land between the upper reaches of the Rhine and the Danube, and – by the end of the first century CE – Dacia, centered on the Carpathian Mountains east of the Danube. Domitian fought in both areas, bringing to Rome what seem to have been large numbers of German prisoners (Fig. 15). Trajan succeeded in conquering Dacia (101–102, 105–106 CE), importing into Rome immense booty that included numerous Dacian slaves (Fig. 16).

Northern Provinces and Resistance

Rome's northern provinces tended to be large, rural, and relatively sparsely populated, with few cities and scattered concentrations of Roman troops. During the first century of the principate their loose political organization, combined at times with a general resistance to Rome sharpened by appalling Roman misrule, incited various conflicts and insurrections, such as Boudica's rebellion in Britain in 60–61 CE. The ancient historians who detail this rebellion, Tacitus (*Annals* 14.31–37) and Cassius Dio (*Roman History* 62.1–12), stress its leadership

15 (left). Remains of a marble statue showing a bound barbarian (life-sized). Part of his thick, flowing beard remains, and his stance emphasizes his snug breeches (or trousers) that contrasted Roman tunics and togas. This was probably part of a statuary group decorating a garden or a formal eating room, and apparently dates to the end of the first century CE, when Domitian had renewed hostilities in Germany. It comes from the Roman resort spa town Baiae (modern Baia on the Bay of Naples), and is now in the Museo Archeologico dei Campi Flegrei, Bacoli, Italy. Photo by permission of the Soprintendenza Speciale per i Beni Archeologici di Napoli e Pompei.

16 (right). Head of a statue of Dacian prisoner from the Forum of Trajan in Rome. This massive Forum was paid for by Trajan's Dacian Wars of 101–102 and 105–106 CE, and the ornate decoration of its porticoes and the Basilica Ulpia that closed its western side featured numerous statues of subjugated Dacians (some ca. 3 m H; others ca. 2.40 m H). The non-Romanness of the Dacians was often emphasized by the use of a colored marble for their "northern" fringed cloaks and long trousers, and white marble for their hands and heads, as here. From the Archivio grafico e fotografico della Sovraintendenza ai Beni Culturali di Roma Capitale, Mercati di Traiano, Stefano Castellani. Published by permission of the Sovraintendenza ai Beni Culturali di Roma Capitale.

by a woman, Queen Boudica of the Iceni tribe. Both also contemptuously mention Druidic rites or specifically local religious acts, reflecting Rome's greater stress on religion as a mark of difference in the first century CE and later. Other native uprisings occurred in Germany (culminating in the disaster of Varus in 9 CE) and in the Balkans (9 BCE–2 CE, again early 20s), in Gaul (in 21 and 68–69 CE), and in Britain (sporadically into the 80s). Romans reacted savagely. For example, in the Balkans in 9–12 CE they virtually decimated the indigenous population. In 15 CE, Tiberius' adoptive son Germanicus spread fire and devastation across the Rhine as the Romans quelled opposition and avenged Varus' disaster (Tacitus, *Annals* 1.49–71). In the Julio-Claudian period, thirteen of Rome's legions were stationed in the provinces along the Rhine and Danube, with three other legions in Spain, and such stationing would continue throughout the Empire.

Rome's northernmost frontiers were often troubled even when rebellions were suppressed or absent. Concentrations of troops on the borders often caused problems upon the death of an emperor, when new allegiances were called for; in 68–69, for example, the uncertainties surrounding Nero's death helped trigger a Germano-Gallic revolt of auxiliary troops and provincials against Rome. Furthermore, northern areas saw a constant admixture of non-Romans. Rome increasingly incorporated into its frontier provinces large groups of non-Roman persons who had requested permission to settle on Roman land: among other instances, we know that some 40,000 Germans were moved to the Roman bank of the Rhine in 8 BCE, and some 100,000 trans-Danubian Germans were allowed to settle across the Roman bank of the lower Danube ca. 60 CE. Such migrations became more frequent after 166/167, when repeated invasions crossed the central Danube River. The emperor Marcus Aurelius responded not only by going on the offensive in the Marcomannic Wars (166/167–180) but also by accommodating trans-Danubian settlers at least in Pannonia, Moesia, and Thrace.

Problems intensified in Britain, Noricum, Germany, Pannonia, and elsewhere. In the third century, Marcus Cassianus Postumus, then governing Upper and Lower Germany, refused to acknowledge the leadership of Rome. Acting independently to protect Roman territory along the Rhine and refusing to deliver the area's taxes to Rome, Postumus ultimately gained the allegiance of all Gaul, as well as much of Spain, Britain, and Raetia (the latter province roughly comprising modern eastern and central Switzerland, southern Germany, and part of Lombardy, Italy). It took more than ten years for Rome to reestablish control in its northwest provinces (260–274 CE). In the northeast, the emperor Aurelian (270–275) decisively abandoned most of the province of Dacia north of the Danube. Such fragmentation of Rome's territories presaged the division of the empire a century later by the Western Roman Emperor Honorius and the Eastern Roman Emperor Arcadius (395 CE).

Romans and Northerners, in the North and in Rome

On Rome's heavily militarized and sparsely populated northern edges it must always have been difficult to distinguish "Roman" from non-Roman, and in many places a hybrid culture thrived. Roman soldiers often formed families with indigenous provincial women while serving twenty years (or more), even though they were barred until around 200 CE from contracting legal marriages. The visual and epigraphic evidence from Rome's northern provinces reveals a mixed culture in which indigenous customs and traditions, such as family names and women's adornment, and Roman ones, such as symbols of Roman marriage, flourished simultaneously (Fig. 17). Differences in dress, customs, and the like could be accommodated on Rome's northern frontiers, with their mixed populations of indigenous peoples, traders, and Roman soldiers. Especially since Rome's troops sometimes came from very different parts of the empire, like the thousand-man equestrian force from Emesa (modern Homs or Hims, Syria) that served in the Danube fort of Intercisa (modern Dunaujvaros, Hungary), "ethnic" distinctions must have been quite blurred. More significant commonalities for identity must have been the Latin language and educational system, the imperial cult, and Roman taxes and other obligations, which were shared by

17. Funerary monument of the Ennius family (2nd c. CE), found along a Roman road near Celeia, Noricum (now Sempeter, Slovenia), and now in the Archaeological Park Roman Necropolis Sempeter, Slovenia. The tomb is in the form of a shrine. The niche contains representations of the deceased, with the parents in the upper register and their young daughter (flanked by mourning figures) below. The mother, Ennia Oppidiana, wears what is known as the "Norican cap," a hair covering often found on images from this Roman province; she also has elaborate jewelry and a heavy cape. The father, Quintus Ennius Liberalis, wears a Roman toga, and is pointing to a scroll to indicate his Roman citizenship status. On the front of the base is a relief showing Europa as she is seduced by Zeus in the form of a bull; this perhaps indicates belief in rebirth, but certainly shows familiarity with Greco-Roman mythology. Other decorative elements, such as the thick vines with grapes and birds carved in relief on the base's lower pilasters, are similarly common in Roman art. Local marble; 2nd c. CE. Published by permission of the Regional Museum Celje, Slovenia.

those few scattered in cities and military camps along Rome's northern borders. Such cultural, religious, and political bonds could tie people to Rome more readily than individual origins, serving for an alternative but subordinate identity.

Yet in Rome itself, and in other Mediterranean centers, provincials and citizens from Rome's northern territories seem to have retained a marginalized status and threatening reputation, at least into the fourth century CE. Until that time epigraphic evidence and scant literary remarks locate in Rome only a few Gauls, Germans, Dacians, Thracians, and others from the north. (The fourth century saw the flowering of Roman Gaul, including the rise of noted rhetors and poets like Ausonius, but that phenomenon is outside the limits of this book.) Men from Pannonia, Thrace, Moesia, and similar northern locales were prized as soldiers, as we have seen, but often doubted as virtuous generals and leaders.

Only in the third century CE, in the period after 235 that is commonly thought to have begun the "fall" of the Roman empire, did men from Thrace, Pannonia, and other Balkan provinces become emperors. (Individuals from these areas are often now described as "Illyrian" from an early designation of the Balkans, especially the western territories, as Illyria.) Maximinus, for instance, who rose through the ranks to rule as emperor from 235 to 238 after probably having had a hand in the assassination of the previous emperor, was decried by Herodian as being "from the innermost Thracians and mixed savages" (*Roman History* 6.8.1; this gave him the name by which he is now usually called, "Maximinus Thrax" or Maximinus the Thracian, although he likely was from Moesia). Such "soldier-emperors" were usually acclaimed emperor by their troops, and when one did not even bother to turn to the Senate and the People of Rome for ratification of his imperial power in 282, the civil basis of the Roman empire seemed irrevocably undermined. A half-century of internal political and military turmoil was ended when Diocletian took control in 284 to reorganize Rome's political and provincial system as the "Tetrarchy," which lasted until his retirement in 305. Diocletian and his corulers also came from the Balkans, and although they successfully

18. The Tetrarchs. This group portrait of the four tetrarchs (ca. 300 CE) originally topped a column in Constantinople but was brought to Venice during the Middle Ages and cut into two pieces to adorn a corner of St. Mark's Basilica. It shows four almost undistinguishable men in military costumes, similarly clutching their eagle-headed swords. The two with raised arms and beards are identified as Diocletian and Maximianus, the two more senior and powerful rulers in the tetrarchy (see also Chapter 6). The headgear all four wear, and which fourth-century authors identify as a Pannonian cap that could serve both in warfare and ceremonially, have central holes, presumably once intended to hold gems or a differently colored stone. The dense red marble of the sculpture was by now reserved for images of individuals belonging to the imperial court. Erich Lessing / Art Resource, NY.

reestablished Roman rule and Rome's frontiers, they were distrusted by the elite of Rome. They did not disguise the military basis of their power or offset it by emphasizing their civil role as first citizens, as had the *princeps* Augustus (see Fig. 2). Rather, they were portrayed most frequently in military costume, and rich new clothing and jewelry displays were devised to demonstrate their eminence over all others, high and low (Fig. 18). Rome's traditional elite – the senators and other highly placed individuals who are responsible for Rome's literature and monumental art – rarely included or accepted individuals from the most northern provinces.

Another Sack of Rome (410 CE), and Rome's Enduring Anxiety about Northerners

The strength and longevity of the northern barbarian stereotype are underscored by accounts of the Sack of Rome in 410 CE at the hands of the Visigoth Alaric and his men. The Visigoths, usually classified as Germanic or Scandinavian peoples, had settled along the lower Danube and above the Black Sea, and by the fourth century were mentioned as troublesome in the Balkans. They then moved west, ultimately into Italy and beyond. The Visigothic Sack of Rome in 410 was the first time the city had fallen to a foreign invader since the Gauls sacked Rome in 390/386 BCE. About a century after the astonishing event in the early fifth century (CE), the Byzantine historian Zosimus provided a description of it. His account includes particulars reminiscent of those describing Brennus and the Gauls some eight centuries earlier. The derision and greed of the boorish leader – in this case the Visigoth Alaric – are underscored in reported speech, for example:

> When Alaric heard that the [Roman] people were trained and ready to fight, he said that thicker grass was easier to mow than thinner, and he laughed broadly at the ambassadors. But when they turned to discuss peace he used expressions excessive even for an arrogant barbarian: he declared that he would not give up the siege unless he got all the gold and silver in the city, as well as all movable property and the barbarian slaves. When one of the ambassadors asked what he would leave for the citizens if he took these, he replied: "Their lives." (Zosimus, *New History* 5.40; trans. Ridley)

Zosimus also stresses the great numbers of barbarians pouring into the city, an element we saw in Livy's description of the Gallic Sack of

Rome: it was as though, in their eyes, Rome could be overpowered only by being completely outnumbered.

But in another reference to the calamitous event, a famous letter of Saint Jerome written in Jerusalem slightly after the sack itself, we see the familiar use of northerners to reflect the Romans themselves. Upon hearing the news, Jerome lamented, "The city [Rome], which had taken captive the whole world, was itself taken" (*Letters* 127.12). We will see such reversals in Roman thinking also about the Greeks, the subject of the following chapter.

SUGGESTED FURTHER READING

Aillagon, J.-J. (ed.). 2008. *Rome and the Barbarians: The Birth of a New World*. Milan: Skira, and New York: Rizzoli.

Bowman, A. K. 1994. *Life and Letters on the Roman Frontier: Vindolanda and Its People*. London: Routledge.

Burns, T. S. 2003. *Rome and the Barbarians: 100 B.C.–A.D. 400*. Baltimore, MD: Johns Hopkins Press.

Carr, G., and Stoddart, S. (eds.). 2002. *Celts from Antiquity*. Cambridge: Antiquity Publications.

Ebel, C. 1976. *Transalpine Gaul: The Emergence of a Roman Province*. Leiden: Brill.

Ellis, P. B. 2001. *The Celtic Empire: The First Millennium of Celtic History, 1000 BC–AD 51*. New York: Carroll and Graf.

Ellis, P. B. 2003. *A Brief History of the Celts*. Rev. ed. London: Robinson.

Fishwick, D. 1987–2005. *The Imperial Cult in the Latin West. Studies in the Ruler Cult of the Western Provinces of the Roman Empire*. 4 vols. Leiden: Brill.

Green, M. J. (ed.). 1995. *The Celtic World*. London and New York: Routledge.

Haywood, J. 2001. *Atlas of the Celtic World*. New York: Thames and Hudson.

http://www.maryjones.us/ctexts/index_classical.html: A site for specific "Greek and Roman References to the Celts." With links to translations and commentary; some documents are included in the original language.

James, S. 1993. *The World of the Celts*. London and New York: Thames and Hudson.

King, A. 1990. *Roman Gaul and Germany*. Exploring the Roman World 3. Berkeley: University of California Press.

Lewis, N., and M. Reinhold (eds.). 1990. *Roman Civilization Selected Readings*. I: *The Republic and the Augustan Age*. II: *The Empire*. New York: Columbia University Press.

Wells, C. M. 1972. *The German Policy of Augustus: An Examination of the Archaeological Evidence*. Oxford: Clarendon Press.

Wells, P. S. 1999. *The Barbarians Speak: How the Conquered Peoples Shaped Roman Europe*. Princeton, NJ: Princeton University Press.

Wilkes, J. 1992. *The Illyrians*. Oxford: Blackwell.

Woolf, G. 1998. *Becoming Roman: The Origins of Provincial Civilization in Gaul*. Cambridge: Cambridge University Press.

Zosimus. 1982. *Zosimus, History: A Translation with Commentary by R. T. Ridley*. Sydney: Australian Association for Byzantine Studies.

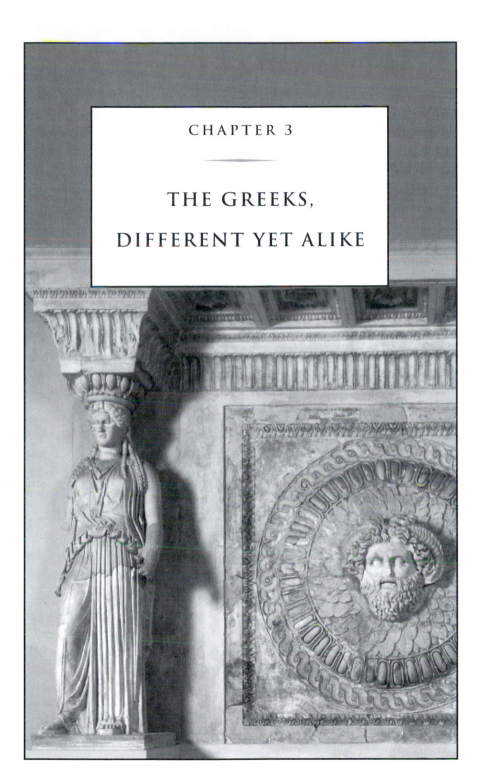

CHAPTER 3

THE GREEKS,
DIFFERENT YET ALIKE

Introduction

Whereas the Romans stereotyped northerners as barbarians who were innately inferior to them even while possessing admirable fighting capacities, a quality Romans valued in themselves, they were even more ambivalent about the Greeks. The situation of Greeks in Rome is one of striking polarization on the one hand and beneficial symbiosis on the other. This comes in part from the history of Rome's cultural and political involvements with Greece as a region and in part from frequent Roman labeling as "Greek" anyone who spoke Greek, regardless of the wide geographical range of Greek speakers after the conquests of Alexander the Great (d. 323 BCE; Fig. 19). By the beginning of the Empire this tension had been expressed numerous times in literature. Horace, for example, famously wrote:

> Captured Greece [*Graecia capta*] has taken its fierce captor and brought the arts to rustic Latium. Thus that crude Saturnian meter [a native Italian one] has become obsolete, and dainties have driven away the heavy stench of the farm. But traces of the field lingered nonetheless for long and remain even today. For only recently has the Roman moved his wits to Greek writings and, at leisure after the Punic Wars, has he begun to inquire what [the great Greek playwrights] Sophocles, and Thespis, and Aeschylus have usefully offered. (*Epistles* 2.1.156–63; 14 BCE)

Most prominent in this quotation is its opening, "Graecia capta," that emphasizes Rome's conquest of Greece. But these same lines stress Greece's "victory" over its conqueror by the importation of Greek arts and literature into Latium and Rome. Horace goes on to point out the greater literacy, aesthetics, and sophistication of Greece relative to Rome, as well as the many profits to be gained from Greece – once warfare is over

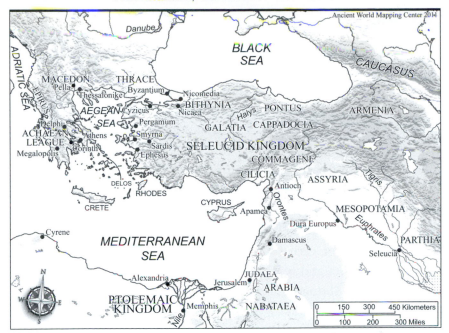

19. Map of the Eastern Mediterranean world around 200 BCE. The area in which Greek was commonly used for official purposes and literature is known as the Greek East. The largest kingdoms – that of the Seleucids centered at Syrian Antioch on the Orontes; that of the Ptolemies with its capital at Alexandria, Egypt; and Macedon, ruled from Pella – were established by Alexander's generals and successors, and Greek was the language of diplomacy, administration, and literature. Pergamum, which gained power as a kingdom in the third century, also used Greek. Parthia, far to the east, moved steadily westward and started coming into conflict with Rome in the first century BCE. Map © 2011, Ancient World Mapping Center (www.unc.edu/awmc). Used by permission.

for the Romans. Thus, even these few Latin lines simultaneously express feelings of cultural inferiority vis-à-vis Greeks and boast of Rome's military superiority over Greece, Carthage, and other powers. Such thoughts and ambivalences recur in other Roman writings about "Greeks."

Cultural Distinctions between Romans and Greeks

There were few obvious distinctions between Greeks and Romans and, at least until the end of the Republic, Romans seem usually to have grouped together all Greek speakers regardless of their location in Macedonia, the Peloponnese, Syria, or any of the other eastern Mediterranean areas now known as the Greek East (thus called because Greek was the common administrative and literary language there after Alexander the Great's conquests and death in 323 BCE). As opposed to some other "peoples" of the Roman world, such as northerners who could be typified as large, disorderly, and differently clothed (if clothed at all), Greeks were seen as looking much like Romans. The majority of Greeks and Romans daily wore tunics and other clothing befitting the climate and geography of Italy, the lower Balkans, and the Mediterranean coast. The elite Greek male's outer garment, the himation, had squared edges rather than rounded ones and was arranged differently than the Roman toga, but both were voluminous, heavy pieces of cloth whose special draping marked a man's status and standing (Fig. 20; compare Fig. 2).

Yet, as with other possible marks of distinction, Greek clothing was important in cases of disputed allegiance or citizenship. When in 41/40 BCE Mark Antony became infatuated with the Egyptian queen Cleopatra VII, a Macedonian Greek, in Alexandria, Egypt (for the Greek nature of this city, see Chapter 4), he was charged with neglecting his Roman duties and habits: "[Antony] had laid aside his commitments and his general's escort; he wore the square Greek garment instead of his native Roman one, and the white Attic shoe of the Athenian and Alexandrian priests" (Appian, *The Civil Wars* 5.11; written early second century CE). Once, when the emperor Claudius (r. 41–54 CE) was hearing arguments that a Greek man had illegally claimed Roman citizenship, he made the man wear a himation when he was accused but a toga when defending his claim of Roman citizenship (Suetonius, *Life of Claudius* 15.2). We have already seen in Chapter 1 that Augustus promoted the toga as the special mark of a Roman citizen; his ruling helped to proclaim publicly his successful establishment of a peaceful and well-ordered Roman empire after the chaos of the late Republic.

Religion and religious practices did not sharply differentiate Greeks from Romans. By the late Republic the Roman state religion included many "Greek" gods such as the Dioscuri (Castor and Pollux) as well

20. The Greek himation. In this marble statue, Julian, Roman emperor 361–363 CE (see also Chapters 5 and 6), is shown in a Greek himation with squared corners rather than the rounded Roman toga (cf. Fig. 2). He also wears a full Greek-style beard, the first emperor to do so after Constantine reintroduced the clean-shaven style at the beginning of the fourth century. Not only do these obvious changes distinguish Julian from his immediate predecessors, but they also publicize his stance as a Greek philosopher. Marble; 1.83 m H without plinth. Now in the Louvre, Ma. Nr. 1121, brought to France from Italy in 1787. Photo Credit: Erich Lessing / Art Resource, NY.

as those we think of as the Olympian deities (Jupiter = Zeus; Juno = Hera; Minerva = Athene; and the like). Many Roman rituals, such as civic processions and animal sacrifice, were broadly similar to those in Greek-speaking areas, and Greeks could easily accommodate themselves to Roman public cult. The earliest organization of the imperial cult occurred in the Greek East when, in 19 BCE, Pergamum in Asia (modern Bergama, Turkey) and Nicomedia in Bithynia (modern Izmit, Turkey) each successfully petitioned the Roman senate for permission to build a temple to Rome and Augustus, and to perform annual rites overseen by provincial elite.

Romans also had long associations with Greek religious sites. Even before the establishment of the Republic in 510/509 BCE they allegedly went to Delphi to consult the Panhellenic oracle; and they continued to be attracted to the Panhellenic sanctuaries, perhaps in part for religious reasons but surely also for the broad draw of the religious sites and their related sacred games. For example, at the conclusion of the Second Macedonian War in 196 BCE, Titus Quinctius Flamininus chose the celebrated Panhellenic Games at Isthmia (on the eastern isthmus between Athens and Corinth in modern Greece) for his staged proclamation that all Greek cities would be free and autonomous rather than subject to Rome or a Roman ally, to Philip V of Macedon, or to another Hellenistic king. The joyful cheering of the assembled multitudes reportedly knocked out ravens flying over the games' stadium and could be heard ten miles away (Plutarch, *Life of Flamininus* 10.3–6). Some thirty years later, after leading Roman forces to victory in the Third Macedonian War in 168 BCE, Lucius Aemilius Paullus erected a large monument near the corner of Delphi's famous Temple of Apollo (Fig. 21). In the next generation Lucius Mummius, the Roman conqueror of Achaia who had destroyed Corinth in 146 BCE in the aftermath of the Fourth Macedonian War, made dedications at Olympia and other sites. Such gestures demonstrate Romans' recognition of the sanctity and power of Greek religious sites and the importance of acting respectfully toward the Greeks, especially after armed hostilities.

The Romans and Greek Language and Literature

Romans did not normally refer to language when distinguishing themselves from the Greeks, in part because Greek was perceived as the fundamental language of literature and erudition and many Romans spoke, read, and wrote it. In contrast, for Greeks in the fifth century BCE, if not before, Greek language was a defining element of civilization. The term and concept "barbarian," derived from the Greek, originally referred to those who could not speak Greek but only languages whose sounds in Greek ears resonated like "bar-bar." By the fourth century BCE the increasingly pejorative term was also often leveled at those who could

21. Monument of Lucius Aemilius Paullus, as reconstructed. This was once adjacent to the Temple of Apollo at the Sanctuary of Delphi and over 9.58 m H. After the Roman leader's victory in 168 BCE over King Perseus and the Macedonians, he repurposed an unfinished commemorative pillar intended for a portrait of Perseus. Although the capping (bronze) statue of a rearing horse and rider resembled victorious depictions of Alexander and subsequent Hellenistic kings, and the frieze immediately underneath it similarly used conventional Hellenistic forms to portray fighting Romans and Macedonians, the dedicatory inscription on the base's front proclaimed in Latin, and with traditional Roman phrasing, "Lucius Aemilius, son of Lucius, set this up from the spoils which he took from King Perseus and the Macedonians." After H. Kähler, "Der Fries vom Reiterdenkmal des Aemilius Paullus in Delphi." *MARV* (1965), frontispiece.

speak Greek but not without grammatical mistakes or traces of a foreign accent. As we have seen in Chapters 1 and 2, however, some Romans considered behavior, not language, a critical indication of barbarism (see Cicero in *On the Republic*, quoted in Chapter 1).

From Rome's earliest historical contacts with Greece, and even more after the third century BCE, elite and other Romans knew Greek and frequently employed the language for literature and diplomacy. (We see an instance of this in Chapter 4, in Rome's dealings with Ptolemaic

Egypt.) Rome's earliest literary author, Livius Andronicus (ca. 285–204 BCE), wrote a Latin version of the *Odyssey* after coming to Rome probably as a slave from Tarentum (modern Taranto) in Greek-colonized southern Italy. The earliest Roman history by a Roman was actually written in Greek (around 200 BCE). Its author, Quintus Fabius Pictor, was a Roman senator who had fought against Gauls in northern Italy in 225 and against the Carthaginians in the Second Punic (or Hannibalic) War, in the midst of which he had participated in an official Roman embassy to consult the Delphic Oracle. The plays of Plautus, from the end of the third and the beginning of the second century BCE, incorporate many Greek words as well as evoke Greek plays: his audiences of all social levels must have understood and routinely used at least some Greek. Precedents and exemplars of Greek literature were always elemental to Latin authors and Latin literature: understanding and enjoyment of Vergil's *Aeneid*, for example, are infinitely enhanced by a knowledge of the *Iliad*, the *Odyssey*, and other Greek epic and poetry.

In the last century of the Republic, Cicero famously bridged both languages. In his youth he practiced oratorical exercises more frequently in Greek than in Latin, because he felt his skills would benefit more with Greek than with Latin training, and because he considered the best teachers to be Greek (Cicero, *Brutus* 310). By his day Greek oratory had been "perfected," expounded in rhetorical treatises, and elaborated for over four centuries. In contrast, Cicero himself is the author of some of the earliest known Latin rhetorical treatises. At the end of his life he also strove successfully to develop Latin into a language capable of expressing philosophy, another genre and mode of thought that also had been developed by the Greeks: Cicero translated Greek terms into Latin, used Latin words with new meanings, and even adopted Greek words.

Despite modern debate about the extent and depth of Greek-Latin bilingualism, it is plain that by the first century BCE elite Romans knew Greek as well as they did Latin, and most inhabitants of the city of Rome understood some Greek. Cornelius Nepos (d. 24 BCE) wrotes that Titus Pomponius Atticus, Cicero's friend and correspondent, "spoke Greek so well that he seemed to have been born at Athens, yet there was such sweetness in his Latin that it was clear he had innate charm, not rote skills. Likewise, he read poems in Greek and Latin so well that nothing could have been added" (Nepos, *Life of Atticus* 4). The emperor Nero (r. 54–68 CE) had decided appetites for Greek games, drama, music, and the like, and he built a Greek-style gymnasium in Rome. Hadrian (r. 117–138) acquired in his youth the nickname "Graeculus," or "the little Greek," because of his well-known preference for all things Greek; this continued throughout his life as emperor, when he was identified in the Greek East as Hadrianus Olympius (like Olympian Zeus) and sponsored a Panhellenic organization. Marcus Aurelius (r. 161–180) wrote his autobiographical *Meditations* in Greek. On the other hand, Marcus Aurelius' work was a philosophical one, Hadrian was derided for being too partial to Greeks, and Nero's gymnasium and its "decadent" associations were decried by traditionalists like Tacitus (Tacitus, *Annals* 14.47). It seems that even in imperial Rome, long after the Romans had "captured Greece," Greek and Greeks could be objectified as different and unsettling. This relates to the historical subjugation of the Greek-speaking world by Rome.

Rome's Conquest of the Greeks, and Greeks' "Conquest" of the Romans

Romans and Italians had interacted with Greeks from earliest times – Mycenaean shards from the fourteenth century BCE have been found at Rome – but contacts became more frequent in the latter part of the fourth century BCE, and more antagonistic in the third century BCE and following. Rome's expansion into southern Italy in the fourth century BCE took it into areas earlier colonized by various Greek city-states (Fig. 22). In 327 BCE Rome established a treaty with Neapolis (modern Naples), a Greek colony established around 600 BCE in south-central Italy. Farther south in Italy, Rome fought from 280 until 272 BCE against the Greek city of Taras (Latin Tarentum, modern Taranto), whose forces were led unsuccessfully from 280 to 275 by Pyrrhus of Epirus

22. Fish plate from Campania, ca. 350–325 BCE, seen from above. This wide, flat, footed platter (22.5cm or 8 7/8 in. diam.) slopes downward from the rim to a depression in the center, used to hold sauce. It depicts the particular fishes for which the plate is designed: an octopus, a bream, and a striped perch. Although made of Campanian clay, this is similar to the fish plates developed in Greece in the early fourth century and demonstrates the Greek background of the Bay of Naples. From the Boston Museum of Fine Arts, Henry Lillie Pierce Fund 01.8096. Photograph © 2011 Museum of Fine Arts, Boston.

(then a kingdom in what is modern northwestern Greece and southern Albania), a Greek "general for hire" and distant relative of Alexander the Great (Fig. 23). As involvements widened in the third century BCE, Rome struck a treaty in 273 with Ptolemy II, the king of Hellenistic Egypt (see Chapter 4). In the early stages of the First Punic War less than a decade later (264–241 BCE), Rome allied with Hieron II, leader of the great Greek kingdom of Syracuse in Sicily. This treaty was to last until Hieron's death in 215. But by that date Rome was embroiled in the Second Punic War (218–201 BCE), whose entanglements helped Rome toward domination of the Mediterranean world (see also Chapter 2). In both the First and Second Punic Wars Rome fought extensively in Sicily, ultimately acquiring as its first province most of this island that had been

23. Map of Southern Italy in the mid- to late Roman Republic. Both Sicily and Southern Italy (the latter region was often loosely termed "Magna Graecia" or "Great Greece") had many Greek colonies established along their shores in the eighth century BCE and afterwards; on Italy's western coast the colonies went as far north as Campania, the area around the Bay of Naples. Such colonies, like Tarentum (the Roman name for the Greek Taras, now known as Taranto), Neapolis (modern Naples), and Syracusae (modern Syracuse, off the map in Sicily), were flourishing cities in their own rights, extending their autonomous power into the Italian hinterland as far as they could, and supporting (Greek) literature and the arts. Rome's expansion into southern Italy and then the Mediterranean in the fourth and third centuries entailed political and military interactions with these and other Greek city-states. Map © 2011, Ancient World Mapping Center (www.unc.edu/awmc). Used by permission.

heavily colonized by Greeks beginning in the eighth century BCE. But Rome gained other resources and benefits through its early alliances and belligerencies with Greek states: as we have already seen, for example, Livius Andronicus, "Rome's" first poet, came to Rome apparently after being enslaved during the war against Taras.

Roman military might and, much less frequently, diplomacy caused the Greek East's kingdoms, including those of Macedon, Seleucid Syria, and Pergamum, and the free city-states (*poleis*) and leagues in the lower Balkans and other Greek-speaking areas, to fall to Rome in a succession of wars that began in 200 BCE. But the conquests were not wholly beneficial to Rome. Later Romans attributed what they saw as Rome's corruption by luxury to the time served in the East by Roman soldiers and generals: Livy, Sallust, and other historians and authors tie to specific campaigns and victories there the beginnings of a moral decline for Rome. Little distinction is drawn between "Old Greece" (Rome's new province of Achaia, roughly corresponding to modern Greece) and other Greek-speaking areas, and the starting date of the decline is given variously. For example, Livy remarks, at the triumph of Gnaeus Manlius Vulso over (Celtic) Galatians in central Asia in 187 CE, an immediate consequence of Rome's war against the Syrian King Antiochus (192–189/188):

> The beginnings of foreign luxury were introduced into the City by the troops that served in Asia. They imported into Rome for the first time couches made of bronze, valuable robes for coverlets, tapestries and other textiles.…Then female lute-players … and other festal delights were added to banquets …; the cook, to the ancient Romans the most worthless of slaves both in their estimation and in the use they made of him, began to have worth. (Livy 39.6.7–9)

(Many of the goods paraded in Vulso's triumph were ones the Galatians had seized while plundering cities in the kingdoms of Pergamum and Syria, in what is now Turkey and the Middle East.) Some seventy years after Livy, Pliny the Elder asserted, "The victory over the Achaean League [146 BCE], from which statues and paintings came to Rome, had great importance in the decline of morality" (*Natural History* 33.149).

Such thinking may have been influenced by the ideas of geographic and climatic determinism that concluded the East was "soft" (see Chapter 1). But Rome's conquests in the Greek East in the second and first centuries BCE did thoroughly affect Rome's economy. Large numbers of slaves and vast quantities of booty are reported as coming from Rome's nearly constant wars against "Greeks." Even if we cannot take literally all of the quantities cited, such as the 150,000 men enslaved in one day in 167 under Lucius Aemilius Paullus' command in western Greece at the end of the Third Macedonian War (Plutarch, *Life of Aemilius Paullus* 29.3), they do suggest the vast scope of Rome's gains from the Greeks. Paullus' subsequent triumph in Rome is said to have lasted for three days, of which the first was devoted solely to a parading of statues, paintings, and colossal images carried on 250 wagons. Under the leadership of Paullus and others, art objects, furniture, educated and uneducated slaves, and whole libraries were seized and brought to Rome; veritable slave markets and traders of various portable goods met with Roman armies before they ever made it home and developed in Rome and Italy as well. "Greek" plunder increased the personal wealth of generals and soldiers, and sculpture and other art enriched the public buildings both of the capital city and of cities of important Roman allies. Many Romans, especially among the educated, seem to have increasingly appreciated Greek aesthetics, goods, and even opinion.

Rome's Duplicity toward Greece and Greeks in the Later Republic

But Romans' public attitudes toward Greeks and Greek culture vacillated widely in the second and first centuries. The same Aemilius Paullus who so brutally brought the Third Macedonian War to an end in 167 BCE is also the man responsible for the monument at Delphi here illustrated (Fig. 21). In the mid-second century BCE, Cornelia, the widowed mother of Tiberius and Gaius Gracchus, was courted by the Greek "Ptolemy the King," a Macedonian Greek king of Egypt (see Chapter 4). She also surrounded herself with Greeks and other literary men (Plutarch, *Life of Gaius Gracchus* 19.2). But many attributed her son Tiberius' radical ideas, which led to his murder by Roman conservatives, to his education by Greek philosophers and teachers such as Blossius of Cumae and Diophanes of Mytilene (Plutarch, *Life of Tiberius Gracchus* 8.4–5; Cumae, a Greek colony, is modern Cuma above the Bay of Naples in Italy; Mytilene still has the same name as the modern capital of the Greek island Lesbos). During the wars of the early first century against King Mithridates of Pontus (on the south shore of the modern Black Sea), Sulla was responsible for the brutal sack of Piraeus and Athens in 86 BCE. For his self-congratulatory memoirs, however, he wrote in Greek. It would appear there was no consistent Roman stance toward the Greeks.

The one exception seems to have been the statesman and orator Cato the Elder of the first half of the second century BCE, although even he turned to Greek models for his oratory and writing. Nonetheless, Cato emphatically assumed a public posture against Greeks and Greek influence. He often charged that Greek intellectuals, doctors, and others were corrupting Rome by "slick talking and snake medicine," that is, by teaching rhetoric and medically attending to the sick. In 161, and perhaps again in 154, there were even expulsions of Greek rhetors and philosophers from Rome. But Cato was waging a losing battle against the Greeks. In the early second century CE the Greek intellectual Plutarch wrote with satisfaction:

And, while seeking to prejudice his son against Greek culture, [Cato] indulges in an utterance all too rash for his years, declaring, in the tone of a prophet or a seer, that Rome would lose her empire when she had become infected with Greek letters. But time has certainly shown the emptiness of this ill-boding speech of his, for while the city was at the zenith of its empire, she made every form of Greek learning and culture her own. (*Life of Cato the Elder* 23.2–3 [Loeb trans. by B. Perrin]; see also 12.4)

Many elite Romans personally knew Greeks more fortunate than the Greek slaves they were purchasing for their own households and farms. By the middle of the second century BCE, Greek intellectuals were coming to Rome for extended stays. Some arrived as ambassadors from Greek cities: for example, in 155 BCE two philosophers, Carneades "the Academic" and Diogenes "the Stoic," came to Rome as envoys from Athens to appeal a Roman judgment against the Athenians. After concluding their business, however, they remained in Rome and held philosophical discussions with young Romans (which Cato abhorred). In the 140s the Stoic philosopher Panaetius of Rhodes (who taught Posidonius, an early ethnographer of the Celts; see Chapter 2) stayed in Rome as a guest friend of Scipio Aemilianus. Even the brilliant historian Polybius, who came to Italy as a hostage from the Achaean League in 168/167 during the aftermath of the Third Macedonian War, ultimately found Rome more congenial than his ancestral Megalopolis (modern Megalopoli, Greece). He became friends with Scipio Aemilianus and other powerful Romans, and at Rome wrote (in Greek) his insightful *Histories* analyzing Rome's domination of the known world. By the first century BCE it was clear to many Greek intellectuals and other elite men that Rome was the center of power in the Mediterranean, and that association with individual Roman leaders could be personally rewarding.

Romans, too, could and did benefit from association with talented Greeks. Cicero makes this clear in *On Behalf of Archias*, a speech he delivered in 62 BCE to verify the Roman citizenship of Aulus Licinius Archias. Archias, who had been born around 120 BCE in Syrian Antioch (modern Antakya, Turkey), had lived much of his life in Italy, and with the sponsorship of the Licinius family had become a Roman citizen around 93 BCE. But the many difficulties with Rome's citizen lists from the 80s into the 60s, a consequence of Rome's Social War of 91–88/87, allowed Archias' citizenship status to be challenged. In advocating for

Archias, Cicero claimed that no great poet is alien to any city, and that poets can do nothing barbarian. Furthermore, because poetry and epic works brought undying and widespread glory to Roman deeds and arms, Archias and other Greek poets deserved Roman citizenship (Cicero, *On Behalf of Archias* 19; here "barbarian" is defined by cultural norms, not language or behavior). Cicero was not completely disinterested: he wanted Archias to memorialize what he himself had done as consul in 63 BCE in suppressing the Catilinarian conspiracy.

Rome's Evolving Discrimination among Greeks

Although in *On Behalf of Archias* Cicero categorized together all Greek intellectuals regardless of their origins in Antioch, Athens, or some other city in Syria, Achaia, Asia, or another Greek-speaking land, in other Ciceronian speeches and in later literature distinctions among various types of "Greeks" were made. In 59 BCE, when defending Lucius Valerius Flaccus against charges of embezzlement and mismanagement as governor of Asia, Cicero lauds the Greeks of Athens for their humanity and culture:"Here are men from Athens, which we consider the origin of humanity, learning, religion, grain, rights and laws, for all lands ... [Athens] has such renown that the now shattered and weakened name of Greece is supported by the name of this one city" (Cicero, *On Behalf of Flaccus* 62). This praise comes, however, as a result of Cicero's attempt to bolster the credibility of Athenian character witnesses for Flaccus. Elsewhere in the same speech he repeatedly maligns Greeks from Asia so as to undermine their case against his client (e.g., *On Behalf of Flaccus* 66). Three years later, in his speech of 56 BCE *On the Consular Provinces* (5.10), Cicero excoriates Syrian Greeks, grouping them with Jews to condemn both as "nations (*nationes*) born to slavery." Syrian and Asian Greeks are later damned together as "the most vile types of men, and born for slavery," in a speech that Livy attributes to Manius Acilius Glabrio, who was instrumental in 191 BCE in the War against Antiochus (Livy 36.17.5). The disparagement of Greeks from areas east of Rome as "characteristically servile" or possessing some other flaw may reflect the widespread concept of the impact of climatic influences on character (see Chapter 1). But such statements also disclose the ambivalence, even hypocrisy, with which Romans could consider and treat Greeks, including those like Archias who had obtained Roman citizenship.

Perhaps because we have more writings of Cicero than of other late Republican Romans, his words loom large in our evidence. When writing to his brother Quintus as the latter set off for Asia to replace Flaccus as governor in 60/59 BCE, Cicero privately expresses uncertainty about what seem to be *all* provincial Greeks. On the one hand Cicero warns his brother:

> And even among the Greeks themselves certain close intimacies must be diligently avoided except from a very few, if there are any who are worthy of old Greece (*vetus Graecia*); for thus indeed the great majority are false, fickle, and schooled by their habitual subservience to be simply "yes men." (Cicero, *Letters to His Brother Quintus* 1.5.16; here he privileges Athens as "Old Greece," and raises the stereotype of easterners' slavishness.)

On the other hand Cicero also extols Greek culture in general, contrasting it to "barbarians" elsewhere under Rome's control:

> If the luck of the draw had sent you to govern savage, barbarous tribes in Africa or Spain or Gaul, as a civilized man you would still be bound to think of their interests and devote yourself to their needs and welfare. But we are governing a civilized race, in fact the race from which civilization is believed to have passed to others, ... Everything that I have attained I owe to those pursuits and disciplines that have been handed down to us in the literature and teachings of Greece. (Cicero, *Letters to His Brother Quintus* 1.9.27–28)

His words clearly reveal both the shifting boundaries of "barbarism" and a sense of Rome's intellectual inferiority to the Greeks.

Greece and the Greek East as Roman Retreats

Respect for Greek literature, history, and the arts was among the motivations for Romans in the late Republic to travel to famous Greek sites and even to contribute to Greeks' material welfare, and under the Empire such visits and patronage continued and intensified. Atticus, Cicero's great friend, went to Athens first in the 80s BCE expressly to escape Rome's civil turmoil. Captivated by the city's "antiquity, culture, and learning," Atticus became its great patron, and the Athenians reciprocated both by offering him Athenian citizenship and by erecting statues to him (Nepos, *Life of Atticus* 2–4). When Sulla brought Roman troops to lay siege to Athens in 86 BCE during Rome's war against Mithridates of Pontus, he razed relatively few buildings. (In contrast, Piraeus, Athens's port, was largely destroyed; both cities, however, experienced massacre and looting.) Plutarch explains Sulla's comparative moderation toward the city of Athens: "after some words in praise of the ancient Athenians, ... [Sulla said] that he forgave a few for the sake of the many, the living for the sake of the dead" (Plutarch, *Life of Sulla* 14.3–6; Loeb trans. by B. Perrin). The "many" and the "dead" must have included Herodotus, Plato, and others of Athens's glorious fifth- and fourth-century BCE past.

Despite the devastation wrought by Sulla, Athens still continued to function as an intellectual center, and by the late 50s more Romans had begun to emulate wealthy kings and other non-Athenians, including the prototypical Atticus, who donated buildings and created endowments there. Soon after 80 BCE, Cicero visited Athens, a city he always cherished; subsequently his brother, and then his son, similarly went there to study with philosophers and orators. Some thirty years later Claudius Appius Pulcher, the Roman governor of Cilicia, contributed a gateway for the Sanctuary of Eleusis, a world-renowned sanctuary 15 miles (22 km) distant from Athens but under its control (Fig. 24). Cicero comments on

24. A fragment of Appius Pulcher's Gateway for Athens's Sanctuary of Eleusis, ca. 50 BCE. Mixed Doric and Ionic entablature from the inner entrance at Eleusis, with the Eleusinian motifs of wheat, rosette, and pyxis carved on the frieze and Appius Pulcher's dedicatory inscription in Latin on the architrave below. This is one of the few instances of the use of Latin in the Roman Republican province that included Athens; most inscriptions are in Greek even when made by Romans. One wonders whether Appius was aiming precisely at a Roman audience like Cicero. Photo Credit: Scala / Art Resource, NY.

the gesture in a letter to Atticus of 50 BCE: "There is one thing I wish you to consider. I hear that Appius is putting up a ceremonial gateway at Eleusis. Shall I look a fool if I do so at the Academy [a philosophical school in northwest Athens]? You'll say, 'I think so!' But you should write me that very thing. Indeed, I am very fond of the city of Athens. I should like it to have some memorial of myself; I hate the fabricated inscriptions on others' statues" (Cicero, *Letters to Atticus* 6.1.26).

Other highly placed Romans apparently shared Cicero's mixture of philanthropy and self-interest regarding Athens and other Greek centers, which provided some compensation for the depredations of Rome's wars of conquest and the exploitation perpetrated by countless Roman governors and provincial staffs. Julius Caesar contributed to the rebuilding of Athens by endowing what is now called the Roman Agora or Market of Caesar and Augustus, a large peristyle building finished by

Augustus and dedicated in 11–9 BCE (Plate I). Wealthy and influential Romans continued to visit Athens and other Greek centers: from 6 BCE to 2 CE, for example, the future emperor Tiberius studied philosophy on the island of Rhodes, celebrated for its teachers and intellectuals, and in 18 CE Tiberius' adopted son Germanicus visited the oracular sanctuary at Claros (near modern Ahmetbeyli, Turkey). Athens, Aphrodisias (near modern Geyre, Turkey), and some other city-states shrewdly used diplomacy and their glorious histories to improve their economic, political, and physical relations with their Roman overlords, particularly after the great Roman general Pompey had reorganized the provinces and areas of Asia, Syria, and other eastern locales in the 60s BCE.

Greeks in Rome in the Late Republic and Early Empire

In turn, Greek writers, intellectuals, and artists came to Rome in increasing numbers during the late Republic and first century of the Empire, when the ancient world's wealth, power, and distinction were centered in Rome's capital city and its rulers. From Caesar's supremacy in the 40s BCE through the Augustan age, Diodorus Siculus, Dionysius of Halicarnassus, and Strabo are just a few of the authors originally from Sicily, Asia, Pontus, and other Greek-speaking provinces and regions whose histories, ethnographies, and other writings in the capital city contributed to the reshaping of Rome's past and the articulation of its future. (We saw in Chapter 1 how Dionysius of Halicarnassus depicted Rome's founding, for instance.) Greek artists and architects came to Rome to work on the Augustan building program (Fig. 25) and on privately funded construction spurred by Augustus' own example and the Augustan peace. Tiberius was particularly fond of sculptural groups that are now (misleadingly) termed "baroque" because of their expression of pathos and movement and their large scale; Greek sculptors from Rhodes created many of these (Fig. 26).

Roman public taste for Greek art, or at least for individual precious pieces, increased. There was a general outcry, for example, when

25. Caryatid from the reconstructed attic of the portico of the Forum of Augustus,
Rome. This is from a reconstruction, now in the House of the Knights of Rhodes,
made in the 1940s and including original fragments of the figures of the different
caryatids on their own bases. This over-two-meter-high (including plinths and
cushion) classical marble caryatid, like its counterparts, is an exact, to-scale copy
of an Athenian Acropolis's Erechtheum caryatid (from ca. 415 BCE). From the
Archivio grafico e fotografico della Sovraintendenza ai Beni Culturali di Roma
Capitale, Mercati di Traiano. Published by permission of the Sovraintendenza ai
Beni Culturali di Roma Capitale.

Tiberius appropriated for his own dwelling a nude male athlete statue
by the famed fourth-century sculptor Lysippus that had been on public exhibition in front of the Baths of Agrippa in Rome (Pliny, *Natural
History* 34.62; the statue type is called Apoxyomenos). One grand gesture
Vespasian made to mark his distinction from Nero was to place on public exhibit in Rome prized works of Greek art that Nero had kept for
himself: the area of Vespasian's Temple of Peace in Rome has revealed
bases with Greek inscriptions indicating the subject of the piece and the
name of the sculptor, including the famed Polykleitos and the Athenian
Praxiteles. Pliny the Elder, Quintilian, and other Latin authors of the era

26. Part of the decoration of Tiberius' villa at Sperlonga, Italy, that apparently confirms Tiberius' predilection for dramatic Hellenistic "Greek" sculpture. This, a (marble, 2" 1.25' H) head of Ulysses (the Romans' name for Odysseus) as he was directing his companions in the blinding of Polyphemus, is one of a group of finely carved pieces relating Odyssean themes appropriate for the seaside grotto in which they were displayed. They were carved in the same fine-grained marble (probably from Asia Minor) and by the same workshop. Some of the work was signed by Athanodoros son of Hagesandros, Hagesandros son of Paionios, and Polydoros son of Polydoros – all identified as Rhodians. Two of these artists are further identified by Pliny the Elder as responsible for the renowned Laocoön group (now in the Vatican; Pliny the Elder, *Natural History* 36.37). The deep undercutting and wild hair contrast with the smooth surface treatment of the skin, adding drama to the greatly expressive face. Photo Credit: Scala / Ministero per i Beni e le Attività Culturali / Art Resource, NY.

revealed themselves as familiar with Greek sculptors, architects, painters, and other artists when they discussed the relative merits of Phidias and Praxiteles (the "best" Greek sculptors of the fifth and fourth centuries BCE, respectively), thereby securing a canon of Greek aesthetics that is influential even now. The mixture of Graeco-Roman aesthetics and culture is evident in the poem by Horace that opened this chapter.

By the end of Trajan's rule (98–117 CE) Greeks from Asia, Syria and other Greek-speaking provinces, as well as from "Old Greece" (Achaia), were part of the Roman senate and state. Good examples of this development are Gaius Julius Epiphanes Philopappus and Julia Balbilla, his sister. These siblings were descendants of the family that had ruled Commagene, a small fertile kingdom in what is now eastern Turkey, from the second century BCE until its annexation by Rome in 72 CE. At that point the ruling family, which claimed descent from the Persian king Darius as well as from the Seleucid kings of Syria, moved first to Sparta (modern Sparti, Greece) and then to Rome. Philopappus himself, whom his friends called "king," attained high offices in Rome that included serving among the Arval Brethren (an elite religious priesthood there), admission to patrician rank by Trajan, and a consulship in 109 CE. But he also cherished Athens, where he was an honorary citizen and served as archon in the city's highest position. Although not a native Athenian, he is the first known Roman senator from Athens. The location of his magnificent tomb on Athens's Museion hill, across from the Athenian Acropolis, indicates that he died in Athens rather than Rome (probably around 115 CE). The design, architectural sculpture, and inscriptions of his tomb refer to Philopappus' achievements in the capital city of Rome, as well as to his "Greek" and ancestral identities (Fig. 27).

Philopappus' sister Balbilla, too, became prominent in the Roman world while also asserting a "Greek" identity. Balbilla was a close friend of Sabina, wife of the emperor Hadrian. Along with Hadrian, Sabina, and others in the imperial entourage (including Antinous; see Chapter 4), Balbilla traveled to Upper Egypt to view the Colossus of Memnon, a damaged seated statue that "sang" (or hummed) when touched by the dawn's rays. There she engraved four poems on the Colossus's legs. In a deliberately archaic Greek dialect – Aeolic, which the famous poet Sappho had used in the sixth century BCE – Balbilla declared her ancestors' and her own piety even while recording her deference to "Lord Hadrian" and the "lovely Queen Sabina." Balbilla and Philopappus clearly had no problem reconciling their Greek as well as Roman and, in Philopappus' case, Syrian and other identities from the Greek East.

27. Tomb of Philopappus, from the Mouseion Hill in Athens. On the remains of this curved tomb of Pentelic marble (9.80 x 9.30 m, on a base 3.08 m H), we can still see (on the lower register) Philopappus depicted in a toga and in a chariot procession that attests to his position as consul in Rome in 109 CE. The design recalls triumphal processions featuring the Roman emperor and members of the imperial family, such as that on the Arch of Titus in Rome. The upper register once held, in alternating rectangular and arched niches, seated statues of Philopappus (in the center) and his royal ancestors, King Antiochus IV of Commagene and King Seleucus Nicator, founder of the Seleucid dynasty that ruled Syria. The inscriptions, in both Greek and Latin, allow us to date Philopappus' death to 114–116 CE. Photo published by permission of the American School of Classical Studies at Athens: Agora Excavations.

Greek Romans, Roman Greeks, and the Second Sophistic

Overlapping identities seem also to have been the norm for other elite "Greeks" in the Roman Empire, high-placed families from Sparta, Ephesus, Smyrna, Antioch, and other storied cities of Achaia, Asia, and Syria (but not Egypt, as we shall see in the next chapter).

Some of these individuals reached the senate as early as the later first century CE, and the numbers of "Greek" senators rose to peak in the early third century (see Chapter 1). This was also the heyday of the "Second Sophistic," a literary movement that boasted a connection to the past greatness of Greek literature and history. Many Greek cities in Asia, Achaia, and elsewhere in the Greek East claimed to have had mythological founders as a way of bolstering their cultural and political standing.

Great orators and philosophers spoke stunningly and regularly – at times to enhance their own reputations, at others to convince emperors to shower benefactions on a city. For example, the sophist Marcus Antonius Polemo "so entirely converted Hadrian to the cause of Smyrna [from that of Ephesus] that in one day the emperor lavished on Smyrna [so much money that with it] were built a corn market, a gymnasium – the most magnificent of all those in Asia – and a temple that can be seen from afar, the one on the promontory" (Philostratus, *The Lives of the Sophists* 531; Smyrna and Ephesus are modern Izmir and Selçuk, Turkey). Some sophists also became Roman senators and politicians, like Athens's Tiberius Claudius Herodes Atticus, who attained the position of consul in 143 CE (Fig. 28). Other sophists devoted themselves primarily to literary and rhetorical studies and teaching. One of the most famous sophists of the early second century, Favorinus of Arelate (modern Arles, France), summed up his life in three paradoxes: although a Gaul he spoke Greek; although a eunuch he was charged with adultery; and he had quarreled with an emperor [Hadrian] yet was allowed to live. Favorinus can be seen as exemplifying the power exerted in this period by academic and intellectual pursuits, which were conducted primarily in Greek. This was a real change from the end of the Roman Republic, which was dominated by military success, civic leadership, and family – all centered in Rome and Italy.

Similarly, in contrast to earlier times, in the second century CE Rome itself was less of a magnet for intellectuals, whose circuits through the empire took them to other places as well as to the capital city. Although Plutarch, Aelius Aristides, and other writers and intellectuals

28. Tiberius Claudius Herodes Atticus, consul in 143 CE, as depicted on a marble head now in the British Museum (Reg. no.1990, L01.1). Herodes Atticus was a confidant of Hadrian and Antoninus Pius; a renowned orator, he instructed both Marcus Aurelius and Lucius Verus. In his villa in Kephisia near Athens he hosted the author Aulus Gellius. Herodes Atticus was also a generous benefactor to Athens and other cities. London: British Museum. © The Trustees of the British Museum.

visited Rome, they did not move there permanently as had, for example, Dionysius of Halicarnassus in the Augustan era. The decentering of the city of Rome and a concomitant emphasis on its cities and provinces are often attributed to Hadrian, who traveled outside of Italy for more than half the period of his rule (from 117 to 138 CE) and who was famously interested in local customs and traditions. But the change – much more gradual than could be assigned to the influence of one person – demonstrates different understandings of power and merit than had held true at the end of the Republic. Analogously, the magnificent monuments of Tiberius Julius Celsus Polemaeanus, Herodes Atticus, and others in Ephesus, Athens, and other cities throughout Rome's empire confirm that material resources could be expended elsewhere than at Rome (Fig. 29). At this distance from the "high empire" of the second century CE it may seem that Greeks, the Greek past, and Greek erudition and aesthetics were valued just as much as Rome's "own" traditions, and that the concept of what was Roman itself had changed.

29. Library of Celsus, Ephesus (now Selçuk, Turkey). This elaborate structure, constructed at the head of a prominent street in Ephesus ca. 115–120 CE, served as tomb or hero's tomb for Tiberius Julius Celsus Polemaeanus (consul in 92 CE and governor of the province of Asia ca. 106), as well as a library for the city. It was given by his son Tiberius Julius Aquila, who served as Roman consul in 110. The marble façade displayed personifications of four of Celsus' virtues – Wisdom (Sophia), Knowledge (Episteme), Good Sense (Ennoia), and Excellence (Arete) – as well as a statue of Celsus' son Tiberius Julius Aquila. As did the Tomb of Philopappus, this highly decorated building had inscriptions in both Greek and Latin. Photo Credit: Vanni / Art Resource, NY.

Anxieties about Roman and Greek Interaction

Some have argued, however, that besides ignoring the complexity of the question of what *is* Roman, this impression is too simplistic and ignores the discomfort and misgivings expressed by many Greeks who compared an idealized "Greek" past to their "Roman" present. For example, at the end of the first century CE, Plutarch advised a fellow Greek entering local politics never to forget "the boots of the Roman governor poised above your head" (Plutarch, *Precepts of Statecraft* 813e). Statements like this, just like recurrent notices concerning Roman destruction of Greek monuments in the works of the second-century Greek travel writer Pausanias, indicate that the self-identity of at least a few Greek intellectuals included distancing themselves from Rome despite their own Roman status and acceptance (Plutarch, for example, became a Roman citizen and was granted consular honors by Trajan). And on the other side were the continuing sneers and slights on the part of "Romans from Rome." Greeks still were occasionally branded as being overly clever and facile, and as too interested in aesthetics, superficial goods, and transient pleasures rather than in adopting the traditional Roman military and civic discipline and organization. Hadrian's nickname "the little Greek" was not meant to be flattering. And Trajan grumbled at one point, "Oh, those little Greeks love their gymnasia!" when fielding a letter from Pliny about building problems in Bithynian Nicaea (Pliny, *Letters* 10.40; Nicaea is modern Iznik, Turkey).

Trajan's aside may just have been a result of the exasperation of an overworked administrator. But it does evoke Vergil's characterization of Romans as those who put the stamp of custom on law and by arms brought down the proud while sparing the humble, but left such niceties as sculpture, oratory, and astronomy to others (Vergil, *Aeneid* 6.847–53). Trajan's words also resonate with one of the most abusive outbursts against "Greeks" now extant, Juvenal's *Satire* 3. In this tirade from the Trajanic period the satirist has his speaker Umbricius complain about a Greek takeover of Rome (hyperbolically called a Greek capital city, *Graecam urbem*). Portraying a deplorable flow of Greeks into Rome as the Syrian Orontes River flowing into the Tiber, Umbricius first defines the intrusive Greeks as Syrians from Antioch on the Orontes. But he ends by scorning Asian Greeks as well, and even Athenians. The archaic flavor of the following translation of Juvenal's *Satire* 3 (lines 60–80), based on William Gifford's version of 1817, emphasizes the anachronism of such stereotypes:

> I cannot rule my spleen, and calmly see, citizens,
> A GRECIAN CAPITAL, IN ITALY!
> Grecian? O, no! with this vast sewer compared,

The dregs of Greece are scarcely worth regard:
Long since, the stream that wanton Syria laves,
Has disembogued its filth in Tiber's waves,
Its language, arts; o'erwhelmed us with the scum
Of Antioch's streets, its minstrel, harp, and drum.
Hie to the Circus! ye who want to prove
A barbarous mistress, an outlandish love.
Hie to the Circus! There in crowds they stand,
Tires on their head, and timbrels in their hand ...;
while every land,
Sicyon, and Amydos, and Alabanda,
Tralles, and Samos, and a thousand more [cities in the Roman
    province of Asia],
Thrive on this indolence, and daily pour
Their starving myriads forth: hither they come,
And batten on the genial soil of Rome;
Minions, then lords, of every princely dome!
A flattering, cringing, treacherous, artful race,
Of torrent tongue, and never-blushing face;
A Protean tribe, one knows not what to call,
Which shifts to every form, and shines in all:
Grammarian, painter, augur, rhetorician,
Rope-dancer, conjuror, fiddler, and physician,
All trades his own, your hungry Greekling counts;
And bid him mount the sky – the sky he mounts!
You smile – was't a barbarian, then that flew?
No, 'twas a Greek; 'twas an ATHENIAN, too!

Juvenal seems to be aiming, not at "Greek" senators like Philopappus or Celsus, but at a much lower echelon in Rome, individuals of Greek descent in Rome's general populace. Throughout Rome's history Greek-speaking slaves were imported into the capital city, where they were regularly manumitted. Greek was a common language in the East: not only did the Jewish intellectuals Philo and Josephus (from Alexandria,

Egypt, and Judaea: see Chapter 4) write in Greek, but Paul and other Christians contributing to the New Testament used Greek for their works. Epigraphic evidence suggests a steady migration of free Syrians, Jews, and Asian Greeks to Rome, Italy, Africa, Gaul, and Spain, where they engaged in commerce, crafts, and other occupations. Romans relied upon Greek skilled labor even while scorning those who provided it. We may see this in some of the criticisms of nurses and child-care givers from the principate. In such critiques Plutarch held that hiring nurses would inhibit bonding between mother and child, and Tacitus stressed the potential harm of "frivolous Greek nurses" (*Graecula aliqua ancilla*) who imparted their own carelessness to their charges. On the other hand, learning the Greek language was essential to the elite (e.g., Quintilian, *Institutes of Oratory* 1.1.12–14). Greek appears in perhaps a small but appreciable number of epitaphs from Rome (Fig. 30), where its use signals the appearance of erudition and also suggests that at least some "Greeks" maintained their Greek language among family and community. If so, such separatism may have galled traditionalists even though they prized Greek as the language of literature and ensured that it was taught to their descendants.

Synthesis of Greeks and Romans in the Later Empire

By the time of the Severan dynasty (193–235 CE) it must have seemed as futile as it was difficult to separate "Greece" from Rome. Septimius Severus' wife, Julia Domna, was from Syria, as were most of the imperial women from this era. Septimius Severus himself was praised for his sophistication in Latin and Greek literature and was said to be ashamed of the poor Latin spoken by his sister Leptitana. The great Roman historian Cassius Dio – who scorned the "barbarization" of Rome's troops in the early third century CE (see Chapter 1) – was from Nicaea in Bithynia and wrote in Greek. His continuing preference for his homeland Nicaea, which he called "his home" in contrast to the villa near Rome that

30. Funeral monument of Quintus Sulpicius Maximus, who died at age eleven after winning first prize for his Greek poem delivered at the Capitoline Games in Rome in 94 CE. The poem is inscribed on the monument, as are two funerary epigrams, also in Greek, and his epitaph in Latin. The marble monument (1.61 m H), with its over-life-sized and togate portrait of Sulpicius in a central niche, was found outside the Porta Salaria of Rome. The monument forms part of the Musei Capitolini collections and is exhibited in the Centrale Montemartini, Rome. Photo by permission of the Sovraintendenza ai Beni Culturali di Roma Capitale.

31. Map showing location of Constantinople, the city Constantine had built up in 324–330 CE as his center of power in the Greek East. Within a century it was the new capital of the Roman empire. Popular tradition likened Constantinople to Rome, the earlier *caput mundi* ("head of the world"), holding that both had seven hills and fourteen regions. Constantine's city replaced the Greek city Byzantium on the Straits of Bosphorus, whose strategic location on the sea routes into the Black Sea and on a major east–west crossing had repeatedly brought it both riches and destruction. Constantine's city was larger in area and protected by city walls. Its location would prove opportune in the empire's subsequent struggles with non-Romans from across the lower Danube and from farther east. Map © 2011, Ancient World Mapping Center (www.unc.edu/awmc). Used by permission.

he termed "my residence in Italy," demonstrates how Rome's empire allowed the maintenance of multiple, nuanced identities for Greeks in the Roman world.

The fundamental connections of Rome and "Greece" are nowhere more marked than in Constantine the Great's decision to make his center of power, not in Rome or Italy, but in the East. In 324–330 CE he rebuilt and renamed the Greek city Byzantium, Constantinople (modern Istanbul, Turkey; Fig. 31). Thereafter more and more official business was transacted in Greek. But the inhabitants of Constantinople, and indeed of the now diminishing Roman empire, were known as *Romaioi*, Greek for *Romani*, or the Romans.

SUGGESTED FURTHER READING

Adams, J. N., Janse, M., and Swain, S. (eds.). 2002. *Bilingualism in Ancient Society: Language Contact and the Written Word*. Oxford: Oxford University Press.

Alcock, S. E. 1993. *Graecia capta: The Landscapes of Roman Greece*. Cambridge: Cambridge University Press.

Arafat, K. W. 1996. *Pausanias' Greece: Ancient Artists and Roman Rulers*. Cambridge: Cambridge University Press.

Badian, E. 1958. *Foreign Clientelae, 264–70 B.C.* Oxford: Clarendon.

Birley, A. 1997. *Hadrian: The Restless Emperor*. London: Routledge.

Camp, J. M. 2001. *The Archaeology of Athens*. New Haven, CT: Yale University Press.

Bowersock, G. W. 1969. *Greek Sophists in the Roman Empire*. Oxford: Clarendon Press.

Goldhill, S. (ed.). 2001. *Being Greek under Rome: Cultural Identity, the Second Sophistic, and the Development of Empire*. Cambridge: Cambridge University Press.

Gruen, E. S. 1992. *Culture and National Identity in Republican Rome*. Ithaca, NY: Cornell University Press.

Kleiner, D. E. E. 1983. *The Monument of Philopappos in Athens*. Rome: Bretschneider.

Morgan, T. 1998. *Literate Education in the Hellenistic and Roman Worlds*. Cambridge: Cambridge University Press.

Price, S. R. F. 1984. *Rituals and Power: The Roman Imperial Cult in Asia Minor*. Cambridge: Cambridge University Press.

Scheid, J. 1995. "*Graeco Ritu*: A Typically Roman Way of Honoring the Gods." *Harvard Studies in Classical Philology* 97: 15–31.

Swain, S. 1996. *Hellenism and Empire: Language, Classicism, and Power in the Greek World, AD 50–250*. Oxford: Clarendon Press; New York: Oxford University Press.

Wallace-Hadrill, R. 2008. *Rome's Cultural Revolution*. Cambridge: Cambridge University Press.

Whitmarsh, T. 2001. *Greek Literature and the Roman Empire: The Politics of Imitation*. Oxford: Oxford University Press.

Woolf, G. 1994. "Becoming Roman, Staying Greek: Culture, Identity and the Civilizing Process in the Roman East." *Proceedings of the Cambridge Philological Society* 40: 116–43.

Yarrow, L. M. 2006. *Historiography at the End of the Republic: Provincial Perspectives on Roman Rule*. Oxford: Oxford University Press.

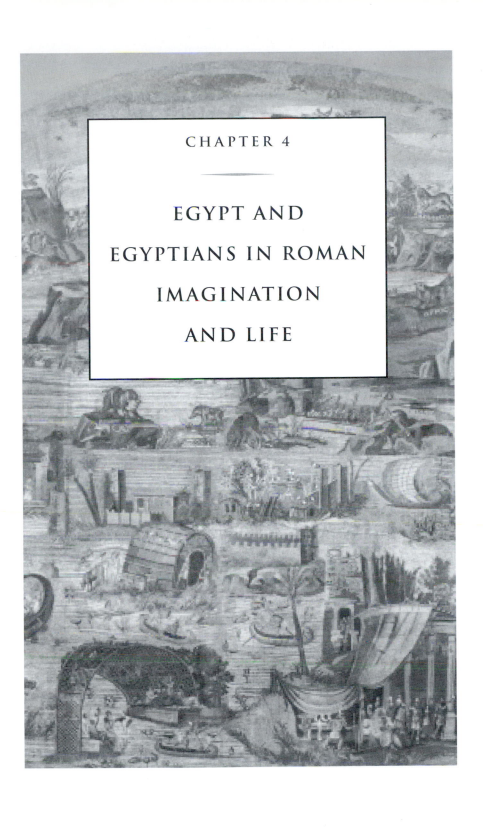

CHAPTER 4

EGYPT AND
EGYPTIANS IN ROMAN
IMAGINATION
AND LIFE

Introduction

For the Romans, as for the Greeks, Egypt was both a mysterious ancient realm of exotica and power and a wealthy, strategic land that influenced the rest of the Mediterranean (Fig. 32). Although often serving as the "other" to highlight what was "normal" and normative in Greece and Rome, Egypt played an important role in both Greek and Roman history. Herodotus devoted to Egypt the second of the nine books of his *Histories*, opening Book 2 with the conquest of Egypt and its pharaoh Psamtek III by the Persian king Cambyses (525 BCE). His ethnography portrays Egypt as the reverse of Greece (see, e.g., *Histories* 2.35) even as he admits Greece's debts to Egypt and its marvels (e.g., 2.4, 50, 124–8). In Rome some four centuries later, the historian Diodorus Siculus devoted to Egypt the opening book of his *Library of History*, similarly sketching an age-old religious and political system that possessed many wonders and departures from Graeco-Roman norms (e.g., 1.50, 69). Many other ancient writers and artists were awestruck by the verdant Nile River valley surrounded by uninhabitable deserts; by Egypt's pyramids, sphinxes, obelisks, temples, hieroglyphs, and zoomorphic (animal-formed) gods; and by the concept of *truphe*, luxurious plenty and bliss, that was associated with this fruitful land. Romans also were particularly fascinated by Egypt's famous Cleopatra VII, who seemed to threaten Rome itself when she seduced two of the empire's most powerful men, Julius Caesar and Mark Antony.

In addition, the unique political situation of Egypt, which Augustus added to the Roman empire not as a province per se but as his own personal property, seems to have influenced the perceived remoteness from Rome of Egypt and Egyptians. Egypt's anomalous position persisted until the late third century CE, as did the emperors' restriction of access to the country, but for convenience's sake, in this chapter I refer to Egypt as a province. In Rome, Italy, and during most of the Empire,

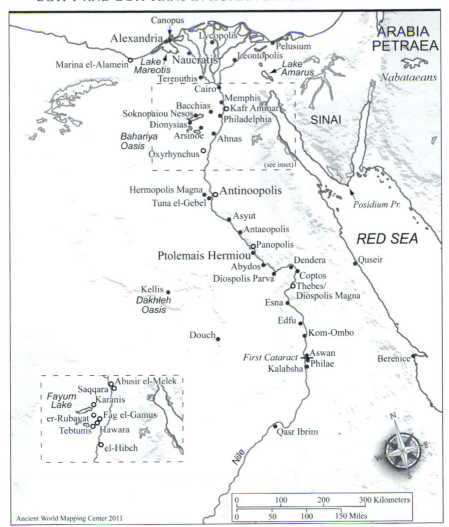

32. Map of Roman Egypt. Cities in which mummy portraits have been found are noted by a circle (○) rather than the dot (●) used for other cities. Roman Egypt's four "Greek" cities are indicated in larger font than the other cities. (The dense inhabitation around the Fayum Lake precludes duplicating all toponyms in the inset and the general map.) Map after S. Walker (ed.), *Ancient Faces: Mummy Portraits from Roman Egypt* (New York: Metropolitan Museum of Art and Routledge, 2000), 8. Map © 2011, Ancient World Mapping Center (www.unc.edu/awmc). Used by permission.

exoticism is often in the forefront of textual and visual references to Egypt, and relatively few Egyptians can be identified by names or other features. Yet Egypt was absolutely integral to the Empire, since from the time of Augustus grain shipped from Alexandria supplied most of the produce for the capital city Rome, and from the early third century CE it also provided for many of Rome's troops in the East.

Information from Roman Egypt itself, which we explore at the end of this chapter, can balance the general exoticism of many Roman reports about this vital part of Rome's world. Some nine hundred "mummy portraits" from Egypt's Roman period are now known. These portraits, like Egypt's Roman-era mummies, derive from Egypt's funerary traditions and attest to the persistence of indigenous customs in Roman Egypt. In contrast to clichéd literary prejudices, many of which I also discuss later in this chapter, Egypt's mummy portraits offer us apparently familiar and affecting visages. Like portraits from elsewhere in the Roman world, these portraits can frequently be dated by similarities in their hairstyles and clothing to imperial preferences, or by likeness of portrayed jewelry to excavated and dated finds. The abundant visual material for Roman Egypt lets us see beyond the words of Romans in Rome. This is true also for the papyri of Roman Egypt, which document the men, women, and children of this region. Although papyri are usually short and formulaic, and many record legal transactions such as petitions to magistrates and tax returns, in their aggregate and detail they enable much more insight into local lives and material circumstances than is available for peoples in other provinces, or indeed in Rome itself.

Ptolemaic Egypt during the Roman Republic

When the Romans encountered Egypt in the early third century BCE it was no longer a sovereign Egyptian state; those who dealt with the Romans were not native Egyptians, although they boasted of some continuities with the Pharaonic past. After the Persian king Cambyses had defeated Pharaoh Psamtek III in 525 BCE, Persians intermittently ruled Egypt until Alexander the Great conquered it in 332 BCE. It was then that Alexander founded Alexandria as his new ruling city and was declared "pharaoh" in Egypt. After his death in 323, first his Macedonian general Ptolemy (I Soter), and thereafter Ptolemy's descendants, collectively called the Ptolemies, controlled Egypt until 30 BCE. They, too, adopted the guise of pharaohs and were depicted in conventional Egyptian ways (Fig. 33).

The Ptolemies turned to Greek and Macedonian personnel for their administrative and military needs and used Greek for official purposes. Many Greeks were settled in Alexandria, where they had special civic status. Numerous Greek soldiers were given land in the fertile area of the Fayum Lake, and they and their descendants retained legal and civic distinctions (some as belonging to "the 6,475 Hellenes of the Arsinoite nome"). Two other Greek cities – the old Greek colony Naucratis on the Nile delta and Ptolemais Hermiou in Upper Egypt – also enjoyed extraordinary privileges; their inhabitants were called *astoi* (Greek for "citizens"). Lesser concentrations of Greeks lived elsewhere in Ptolemaic Egypt, particularly in the capitals of the administrative units (or nomes). In all these cases the term "Greek" encompasses individuals who may not have been considered "pure" Greeks: indeed, the fourth-century (BCE) Athenian Demosthenes had scorned Macedonians as "barbarians" who supposedly spoke Greek poorly in their northern kingdom (see Chapter 2 for the importance of language in Greek conceptions of barbarism). But Ptolemaic Egypt distinguished the native population of Egyptians from all others, considered "Greeks." The colonizing newcomers to Ptolemaic Egypt used Greek as their common language. Jews also played significant roles here, notably in Alexandria where they too enjoyed some privileges. Some had immigrated in the sixth century BCE when Persia first conquered Judaea; more came during Ptolemaic control of Judaea in the third century; and more again in the early second century BCE, when Jews fled Syrian invasions into Judaea. The Jewish immigrants, too, used Greek for formal purposes (Philo is an example; see later in this chapter, and Chapter 5).

33. Relief of Cleopatra VII, the last of the Ptolemies and the last Pharaoh (d. 30 BCE), from the outer wall of the Hathor Temple in Dendera, Egypt. In front of Cleopatra the small "ka" or protective spirit of her son Ptolemy XV Caesarion, whose parentage from Caesar was widely touted, wears pharaonic costume including an elaborate headdress/crown. Photo Credit: Erich Lessing / Art Resource, NY.

The extent of interaction between the "ruling Greeks" and others in Egypt is controversial. By 30 BCE Egypt's Greeks, including Alexandrian Jews, numbered perhaps one million out of a total population estimated as having been above four million, and they are usually thought to have been deeply divided from the majority they ruled. Most who lived within the Ptolemaic kingdom were Egyptian, along with some immigrant Libyans, Nubians, and other neighboring peoples. The vast majority of non-Greeks lived in villages and engaged in subsistence agriculture under the Ptolemies and later the Romans, in addition often tilling soldiers' plots and the estates of the kings, and later of the emperors. A few highly placed Egyptians controlled Egyptian temples and religion, and some "Hellenized Egyptians" may also have held top positions in the Ptolemaic administration. In the countryside and on temple reliefs, the Ptolemaic rulers presented themselves as Egyptian successors to the pharaohs. But the language of administration was Greek, and Greek was the dominant culture of the capital city, Alexandria.

The Ptolemies built up Alexandria and its famous Library/Mouseion into one of the great cultural centers of the Greek Hellenistic world, an eminence that continued through Roman rule. Alexandria thrived even after its legendary library burnt down during Julius Caesar's stay in Alexandria in the winter of 48/47 BCE. After Rome's takeover of Egypt eighteen years later (30 BCE; see later), Alexandria was the port city for the enormous quantities of grain that were shipped to Rome, at first via Puteoli (modern Pozzuoli on the Bay of Naples), and then also through Ostia at the mouth of the Tiber River. Alexandria became one of the four major cities of the Roman Empire, along with Syrian Antioch, north African Carthage, and Rome itself. It was an intellectual and cultural center with a mixed and dense population estimated at more than three hundred thousand. The mix fostered the growth of philosophical schools and various religious communities, including Christian ones by the third century CE.

Early Diplomatic and Other Interactions between Rome and Egypt

When in 273 BCE the Romans formed a treaty of friendship with Ptolemy II, their first treaty with a Hellenistic kingdom, the negotiations were conducted in Greek. From that time until the 30s BCE, official relations between Rome and Egypt were like those between Rome and other Greek Hellenistic kingdoms, although much less antagonistic, as no wars were waged. Elite Romans apparently considered and treated Ptolemaic kings and ambassadors like they did other elite Hellenistic Greeks. Plutarch's report of the refusal by Cornelia, the mother of the Gracchi, to marry "Ptolemy the king" (probably Ptolemy VIII Euergetes, or perhaps Ptolemy VI Philometor, sometime in the mid-second century BCE) significantly omits any allusion to Egypt, stressing instead Cornelia's admirable modesty (Plutarch, *Life of Tiberius Gracchus* 1.4; see also Chapter 3). Starting in the mid-second century BCE, various royal claimants of the Ptolemaic kingdom sporadically turned to Rome for support. But the Romans did not engage militarily with Egypt until 55 BCE, when a Roman army entered Egypt to back Ptolemy XII Auletes in his successful struggle for power.

Seven years later Pompey fled to Egypt after losing to Caesar in the Battle of Pharsalus (in August 48 BCE), because he expected to find a haven in Alexandria in return for his earlier support of Ptolemy Auletes; instead, he was treacherously slain. Caesar, who arrived too late in pursuit of his rival, became involved with Ptolemy Auletes' daughter, Cleopatra VII, and in her ultimately successful struggle for power against her husband and younger brother, Ptolemy XIV. Caesar stayed in Alexandria over the winter, fathering a child with the twenty-one-year-old Cleopatra. One of his innovations in Rome upon his return to Italy was the introduction of a solar calendar modeled on the Egyptian one. When Cleopatra came to Rome to visit Caesar in 44 BCE, Cicero bitterly railed against her, but merely as an arrogant queen, including no "ethnic" slurs about Egypt or Egyptians (*Letters to Atticus* 15.15.2).

"Egyptomania" in Italy

At the same time, however, Romans and Italians – particularly in and around the capital city and the Bay of Naples – evinced such growing fascination with Egypt, the Nile, and Egyptian gods that some have now called it "Egyptomania." The famous Nile Mosaic from Praeneste (modern Palestrina, Italy), usually dated to the end of the second century BCE, shows a bird's-eye view of Egypt during the Nile's annual flooding from May to October (Fig. 34). The mosaic once decorated a large, apsed hall in this city twenty-three miles east–southeast of Rome. Its multiple scenes are arranged to suggest a north–south movement up the Nile from Alexandria to Ethiopia. In the lowest section scenes from Alexandria and

34. Overall view of the Nile Mosaic, found in Praeneste where it once decorated the floor of a large, apsed hall associated with Praeneste's Sanctuary of Fortuna. The mosaic is usually dated to the end of the second century BCE. This overall photo reveals the "seams" of where the mosaic was dismantled and reconstructed in the seventeenth century. Although at that time some material may have been lost, the current configuration of twenty-one scenes is generally accurate, as it suggests a north–south movement up the Nile from Alexandria to Ethiopia. Now 5.85 m W, 4.31 m H, in the Museo Nazionale Prenestino, Palestrina, Italy. Photo credit: Nimatallah / Art Resource, NY.

its famously luxurious suburb, Canopus, include Greek soldiers, some near a temple (Fig. 35) and others at a feast; at another feast, women and men recline and drink together at leisure. In the middle register appear Egyptian temples, one fronted by two obelisks and another built up like a fortress (Fig. 36). Farther away from the viewer (i.e., to the south) the scenes become more fanciful, with sphinxes, rhinoceroses, leopards, and other unusual animals and landscape, including pygmies fighting cranes. The Nile in flood unites all, offering abundance, mysticism, exotica, and even some isolated "realia" in the soldiers.

35. Greek/Macedonian soldiers in front of a shrine of Greek design, as depicted on Praeneste's Nile Mosaic. Now in the Museo Nazionale Prenestino, Palestrina, Italy. Photo credit: DeA Picture Library / Art Resource, NY.

The purpose of Praeneste's Nile Mosaic is unknown, but discussion and images of Egypt were quite popular in late Republican and Imperial Rome as the Romans interacted ever more frequently with the fertile and wealthy area. The first book of Diodorus Siculus' *Library of History*, written slightly before Caesar's death in 44 BCE and perhaps reflecting Caesar's interest in Egypt, attempts to present respectfully Egyptian history and myth to Roman readers. Stressing the longevity of Egyptian rule, Diodorus focuses on pre-Ptolemaic Egypt, offering numerous examples of its good government and pious relations with the gods (e.g., Diodorus Siculus, *Library of History* 1.49). He accentuates the odd animal forms of Egyptian gods as well as Egyptians' veneration of animals, noting that he had personally witnessed the mob murder of a Roman who had accidentally killed a cat (Diodorus Siculus, *Library of History* 1.83.8). Other marvels the historian describes

36. Sacred buildings, and hunting, along the Nile, as depicted on Praeneste's Nile Mosaic. In the lower center is depicted a large fortress-like temple in the Egyptian style, raised on a platform. Its central entrance is flanked by two large pylon towers characteristic of Egyptian temples, and in front of each of them are two statues that may represent Osiris with his arms crossed over his breast. On their heads the statues have lotus leaves, symbolizing regeneration. Farther in the distance are hunters with various wild and fanciful animals, some of which are named in Greek ("Lynx" and "Crocodilopardalis" or "crocodile-leopard"). Now in the Museo Nazionale Prenestino Barberiano, Palestrina, Italy. Photo credit: Nimatallah / Art Resource, NY.

in this book include the great Egyptian pyramids and other engineering feats, and the spontaneous generation of life in pools left after the Nile's annual flooding. Strabo, the geographer and historian of the Augustan and early Tiberian period, also thought highly of Egypt's great past and monuments (e.g., *Geography* 17.1.46), although he could be dismissive in the book of his *Geography* devoted to Egypt (e.g., Strabo 17.1.16–17).

Material culture also reveals Roman interest in Egypt. In the capital city, the "Aula Isiaca" (Hall of Isis), a wealthy house on the Palatine hill later built into the substructures of the imperial palace, was redecorated

37. The Pyramid of Cestius in Rome, commemorating a Roman senator and constructed ca. 18–12 BCE. The marble-sheathed tomb was later incorporated into walls of Rome built in the late third century (CE), whose "Porta San Paolo" (or Porta Ostiensis) is visible in the left background. The pyramid (base 28.5 m²; H 36.8 m) is actually taller than it looks in this photo, since the ground level has risen around it in the last twenty centuries. We do not know why Gaius Cestius or his heirs chose an enormous pyramid as his memorial. Photo credit: Alinari / Art Resource, NY.

around 25 BCE with wall paintings alluding to the Egyptian gods Isis and Serapis (discussed later): at the very least it shows delight in Egyptian exotica as decoration. The famous "Pyramid of Cestius," a Roman senator's tomb dated to 18–12 BCE, is one of at least four pyramidal tomb structures known from the capital city (Fig. 37). The later eruption of Vesuvius in 79 CE preserved about forty paintings and mosaics depicting the Nile and other Egyptian scenes on Pompeii's walls, floors, and outdoor spaces, again revealing wealthy Romans' fascination with Egypt (Plate II). Hadrian's famous Villa at Tibur (modern Tivoli, Italy) included many statues and other artifacts from and evoking Egypt, presumably in remembrance of his beloved Antinous, who drowned in the Nile in 130 (see later; Fig. 38). We cannot tell, however, how far down the social and

38. Antinous as Osiris. This over-life-sized standing statue comes from Hadrian's Villa in Tibur (now Tivoli, Italy; statue dates to after 130 CE). The presentation of Hadrian's young lover combines Egyptian elements, such as the frontal pose, the kilt, and the headdress, with Graeco-Roman realism in the treatment of the slightly fleshy body and face, and the slight displacement of the feet. Marble, 2.41 m H. Now in the Vatican Museums, Museo Gregoriano Egiziano, inv. 22795. Photo Vatican Museums.

political scale such "Egyptomania" extended in the late Republic and early Empire.

Egyptian Cults in Rome

Whether Egyptian scenes and objects in Roman houses and villas were merely decorative or had religious significance is hard to discern, but it is certain that Egyptian cults were worshipped in Italy by the later second century BCE. The worship centered on Serapis, Isis, and Harpocrates, "hybrid" Egyptian gods in anthropomorphic forms fostered by the Ptolemies from the later third century BCE. These cults seem to have come to Italy not directly from Egypt but via the great trade center of the Aegean island Delos, perhaps brought by Italian and Roman traders and/or Egyptian slaves. But without doubt the structures for these cults, such as the Serapeum (shrine to Serapis) dating to 105 BCE in Puteoli and the Iseum (shrine to Isis) originally built around 100 BCE in Pompeii, primarily served not enslaved or free native Egyptians but wealthy Romans and Italians. By the first century BCE, Isis, Serapis, and other "Egyptian" gods were known and being worshipped in Herculaneum and Capua, and in Rome itself (see, e.g., Catullus 74.4; 10.26). Rome's temples and images of Isis and Serapis may have been officially restricted in some way during the 50s BCE, and they certainly came under governmental control with Augustus. The earlier restrictions may indicate a general Roman suspicion of non-state cults within the capital city or disquiet caused by Ptolemy Auletes' scheming to be restored to power in Egypt. The repression under Augustus fits anti-Egyptian sentiment that arose during the period of the Second Triumvirate (43–33 BCE) and continued for some time beyond it, as well as the first emperor's push to "restore" ancestral values and religion (see, e.g., Vergil, *Aeneid* 12.834–40, and Augustus' law that Roman citizens must wear the toga on specific occasions).

Romans of the 50s and 40s BCE knew about Egyptian religion that included worship of animals as well as of the anthropomorphic Isis and Serapis. Although Cicero scornfully referred to "the [religious] madness of the Egyptians" (*On the Nature of the Gods* 1.43; 45/44 BCE), both he and Diodorus Siculus recognized the pure intensity of Egyptians' devotion to zoomorphic gods (recall the rioting caused by the Roman who accidently killed a cat). But "animal-headed gods" were also fundamental to stock prejudices about Egypt. Egyptians' "peculiar" veneration for animals was a favorite target of Greek and Roman commentators, from Herodotus (*Histories* 2.65) through the

39. Cleopatra and Antony. Silver denarius from an unknown mint, from 32 BCE, showing Antony with an Armenian tiara behind him (*obverse*) and Cleopatra with a diadem and small earrings (*reverse*). Although this impression may be simply due to the die cutter's style, the two rulers resemble one another in their noses, chins, and forceful expressions. The legends are in Latin (including "Queen of kings and of her sons who are kings" on the reverse), and the coin itself is a Roman type rather than one more usual in Alexandria. Antony's public image offered Octavian the opportunity to claim that Antony wanted to move Rome's capital to Alexandria. London, British Museum, CM 2002,0102.4863. © The British Museum.

Roman period (e.g., Juvenal, *Satire* 15) to Christian polemicists (e.g., Lactantius, *Institutes* 1.20).

Cleopatra and Rome

Rome's general lack of warfare with Egypt, and the great distance separating the two places, may help to explain the relatively late appearance in Rome of prejudice against Egypt and Egyptians and even against Egyptian zoomorphic gods. It was only during the last civil war of the Republic that Roman opinion grew actively hostile toward Egypt and Egyptians, when Mark Antony's increasing involvement with Cleopatra VII after 41 was seized upon by his rival Octavian (the later Augustus; Fig. 39). By the late 30s in Rome and Italy, Octavian had successfully cast his power struggle with Antony, then based in Alexandria and supported by Cleopatra, as pitting Rome – the West and rationality – against Egypt – the East and irrationality (see, e.g., Augustus, *The Achievements of the Divine Augustus* 25; also Chapter 3). When the Second Triumvirate dissolved completely in 33 BCE, it was Cleopatra, not Antony, against whom the senate declared war. Her demonization was a way of mitigating, at least in Rome and the West, the bloody civil strife through which Octavian came to power.

The Battle of Actium, at which Octavian decisively gained the upper hand, was fought in 31 BCE at sea off Actium, a small promontory on the western coast of Greece (modern Punta, Greece). Cleopatra and Egypt figure in Horace's famous *Odes* 1.37, written soon after the battle, and in Vergil's description of the Battle of Actium as it was depicted on the shield of Aeneas in *Aeneid* 8. The assembled forces of Antony and Cleopatra were so outmaneuvered by Octavian and his admiral Agrippa that the Egyptian queen and Antony sailed back to Egypt, relinquishing their claims to power in Rome. In Horace, Antony does not appear, just as he is not named in the *Achievements of the Divine Augustus* written by Augustus (known as Caesar Octavian before 27 BCE). Horace contrasts Cleopatra and her supporters to Roman tradition. He celebrates the restoration of ancestral "Salarian" banquets, ritual brotherhoods, and Italian wine libations – traditional marks of respect to Rome's gods – by depicting the maddened queen as she fled from Caesar (Octavian) as a "fatal monstrosity" (*fatale monstrum*) drunk on Egyptian wine and surrounded by a crowd of degenerate men. Yet the poem ends in admiration for the courage of the queen, termed "a woman not submissive" and "courageous," who acted "rather nobly" when she chose suicide rather than capture and exhibition in a Roman triumph.

In Vergil's *Aeneid*, composed a few years later, Vergil specifies Augustus Caesar, Agrippa, Antony, and the "appalling Egyptian wife" (*Aeneid* 8.688). He also describes the Battle of Actium (8.671–713) as one pitting traditional Roman gods – Neptune, Venus, Minerva, and others – against Egypt's "monster gods," headed by the "baying Anubis" (*omnigenumque deum mostra et latrator Anubis*, 8.698). As Actian Apollo threatens from above, all of the "East" flees, terrified: Egypt, India, Arabia, and the inhabitants of southernmost Arabia. In any case, after Octavian's arrival in Alexandria in 30 BCE, only minor skirmishes preceded the suicides of Antony and Cleopatra. With the murder of Ptolemy XV Caesarion, the son of Cleopatra and Julius Caesar, Egypt was left without a ruler and open to Roman takeover.

40. "With Egypt Captured," or *Aegupyo Capta*, coin. Denarius of Octavian (still called Caesar), struck in 28 BCE. On the reverse is a crocodile facing right, with the Latin legend reading (*above*) AEGVPTO and (*below*) CAPTA ("On the Conquest of Egypt," or "With Egypt Captured"). The crocodile represents Egypt, which had now been "captured" after the Battle of Actium in 31 and the deaths of Antony, Cleopatra, and Caesarion in 30. British Museum, Coins and Medals: CM.1487–1963. © Trustees of the British Museum.

Rome's Occupation of Egypt, and Egyptians in Rome in the Early Empire

Despite his boast in the *Achievements of the Divine Augustus* (chap. 27) that Egypt was added "to the rule of the Roman people," Augustus made Egypt his own property. Cassius Dio says his decision was motivated by the populousness of cities and country alike, by the "facile, fickle character of the inhabitants," and by Egypt's extensive grain supply and wealth (Cassius Dio, *Roman History* 51.17.1). Octavian (the later Augustus) stationed three legions there under an equestrian administrator, the *praefectus Aegypti* he directly supervised. He commemorated the capture of Egypt profusely, including the minting of coins showing crocodiles and the transport of two obelisks to Rome at huge expense and trouble (Figs. 40 and 41). Egypt differed from other areas under Roman control. No Roman senators or highly placed equestrians could enter it without the emperor's permission, and Augustus reportedly forbade Egyptians entrance into the Roman senate. Thus it was difficult for "ruler and ruled," Romans and Egyptians, to develop the personal interaction and social and political mobility that so benefited Rome in the principate, when a large proportion of the second- and

41. The Obelisk of Psamtek II from Heliopolis (7th c. BCE; ca. 31 m H with base), which Augustus had brought to Rome to commemorate the Roman capture of Egypt in 10 BCE. The obelisk, which fell sometime after the eighth century CE, was restored and moved in 1792 to its current place in front of the Parliament Building in Rome's Piazza di Montecitorio. Some of the hieroglyphs are missing from the restoration. The Augustan inscription repeated on two sides of the obelisk's base celebrates the submission of Egypt to the power of the Roman people and Augustus' donation of the obelisk as a gift to the sun; see also Strabo, *Geography* 17.805; Pliny, *Natural History* 36.71. Photo Credit: Vanni / Art Resource, NY.

third-century (CE) senate came from outside Italy (see Chapter 1). Scholars have been able to identify at most four senators from Egypt, and these tentative examples, from the second and early third centuries, seem to have been Alexandrians (see later).

Egyptians lower on the socioeconomic scale similarly seem to have left the province but rarely. Egyptians could not join the more prestigious and higher-paying army legions, although they could serve in the imperial fleets. Naval service for twenty-five years earned one Roman citizenship, an attraction for provincials (and for freedmen in Italy and Rome). Rome's fleets were stationed at Misenum and Classis (modern Miseno on the Bay of Naples, and near Ravenna, respectively), with smaller units in other Mediterranean ports, squadrons in the North and Black seas, and detachments on the Rhine and Danube rivers. Occasionally Egyptian sailors from the Italian fleets were used for temporary service in Rome, as we saw in Chapter 1. There were always fewer sailors than legionaries and other types of soldiers, and even from Italy only fifty-some Egyptian sailors can be identified. Overall, the general restrictions on Egypt established by Augustus and perpetuated by later emperors kept this area and its inhabitants estranged from the rest of the Roman world.

Complexities of Status and Identity in Roman Egypt

Roman Egypt, the most densely populated of Rome's provinces, maintained many of the social and civic divisions that had evolved over the Ptolemaic period. Although by the middle of the second century CE such categories seem to have had little effect, the divisions must have contributed to internal instability when the country first fell to Rome. Alexandria saw numerous struggles between Jews and Greeks during the early Empire, and such ethnic divisions were especially lethal to Jews outside of the Egyptian capital during the Second Jewish Revolt of 115–117 (see Chapter 5). The most privileged inhabitants of Roman Egypt were Roman citizens. This very small group included Roman administrators, Roman veterans, Roman soldiers from the three legions stationed in the province, and individuals granted Roman citizenship. Next came "Alexandrians," individuals affiliated with the "Greek cities" Alexandria, Ptolemais (Hermiou; where now the Egyptian city of El-Manshah is located), and Naucratis (72.5 km southeast of the Mediterranean), which owed fewer burdens to Rome than the rest of the province. Alexandria's Jewish populace also enjoyed many rights, although perhaps not full Alexandrian citizenship. The majority of Egypt's inhabitants remained peasants tied to the land.

Alexandria supplied most of the renowned "Egyptians" of Rome's first two centuries CE, although total numbers were never high. In the first century Alexandrian Jews such as Philo and Tiberius Julius Alexander attained positions of great importance (see Chapter 5). An Alexandrian Greek, Chaeremon, was summoned to Rome as Nero's tutor after overseeing Alexandria's library. The historian Appian was born and raised in Alexandria, where in 116/117 he experienced the rioting associated with the Second Jewish Revolt there (see Chapter 5). Once granted Roman citizenship, he went to Rome to become a lawyer associated with the imperial court (around 120 CE), served as an equestrian procurator (high official), and wrote his *Roman History*. Alexandria seems to have had such high standing that for Roman administrative purposes it was not regarded as part of Egypt. Nonetheless, Augustus forbade the city to have a self-governing assembly (Greek: *boule*), so most Alexandrians were prevented from gaining the political experience vital to social and political mobility into Rome's elite.

Some select Greeks, like "the 6,475 Hellenes in the Arsinoite nome," enjoyed lesser but important privileges that generally raised them above native Egyptians but not as high as Alexandrians (or as citizens of the other two Greek cities Ptolemais Hermiou and Naucratis). "Egyptian" Greeks could also reach positions of eminence in the Roman world: a good example is Athenaeus of Naucratis, whose *Learned Banqueters* (published in Rome in the early third century CE) offers many learned anecdotes about philology, literary figures, earlier customs, music, and even cooking. By Athenaeus' time the inhabitants of Egypt apparently enjoyed more mobility in Egypt and the rest of the empire than they had before: the influential Neoplatonist philosopher Plotinus (b. 204 CE), for instance, came from Lycopolis in the southern part of the Nile Delta.

The various civic distinctions in Roman Egypt could cause confusion, at least before the *Constitutio Antoniniana* (212 CE) granted Roman citizenship to free inhabitants of the empire. When Pliny the Younger asked Trajan for Roman citizenship for his masseur, Harpocras, whom he credited with saving his life during an illness, he found that this Egyptian (earlier freed by an Egyptian woman) had to be registered as an Alexandrian citizen before he could obtain it. Pliny's and Trajan's letters about the case incidentally reveal that imperial grants even of Alexandrian citizenship were deliberately rare at the beginning of the second century CE (Pliny, *Letters* 10.5, 6–7, 10).

A generation later, the foundation of Antinoopolis by Hadrian in 130 indicates both the importance of privilege in Roman Egypt and increasing ambiguity among "ethnic" categories. Hadrian established Antinoopolis where his young lover, Antinous, had drowned as the imperial entourage was visiting Egypt and making its way up the Nile. Undoubtedly to attract settlers from elsewhere in Egypt, Hadrian granted many privileges to the Antinoites (the inhabitants of the new city Antinoopolis). These included the right to enroll in the Roman legions, the right to be tried in Antinoopolis if they became involved in a judicial proceeding elsewhere in Egypt, exemption from the property purchase tax, and public provision for grain supply. Particularly interesting is Antinoopolis's unusual marriage law according to which children of Antinoite and Egyptian spouses became citizens of Antinoopolis regardless of which parent was a citizen of the city. This remarkably inclusive policy – Roman law (as Greek law before it) normally relegated children to the civic status of their mothers – is one reason to regard Antinoopolis as a vibrant mixture of Roman, Greek, and Egyptian elements. Another is the prominence in the new city of Egyptian-style temples and obelisks, imperial Roman urban elements such as a theater and colonnaded streets, and characteristic Greek urban amenities. These last included a gymnasium and baths for the training and care of Antinoopolis' youths and competitors for games. Mummy portraits from Antinoopolis provide us with visual images of some of the cultured inhabitants of the city (Plate IV).

Negative Early Imperial Attitudes
toward Egypt and Egyptians

Earlier in Imperial Rome, however, the issue of integration of Egypt and
Egyptians was often controversial. In Egypt itself in 30 BCE, Octavian
enunciated a long-standing prejudice when he expressed contempt for
traditional Egyptian religion, refusing to view the sacred Apis bull at
Memphis because "he was accustomed to worshipping gods, not cattle"
(Cassius Dio, *Roman History* 51.16.5; the ruins of Memphis are south
of modern Cairo). On the other hand, on numerous temples in Egypt
Octavian had no qualms about being depicted as a pharaoh and being
associated with Egypt's traditional zoomorphic gods (Fig. 42). Cassius
Dio also attributes the Roman leader's earlier decision to spare the
inhabitants of Alexandria in 30 BCE to his respect for their (anthropomorphic) god Serapis and for Alexander (Cassius Dio, *Roman History*
51.16.3–4). Thus, Augustus was selective about which aspects of Egypt
to pointedly reject and which to accept. In Egypt he aimed to slip
smoothly into the roles Cleopatra and the Ptolemies had earlier filled
as Egypt's rulers.

In Rome and Italy, however, the demonization of Cleopatra
and Egypt persisted after Cleopatra's death in 30 BCE. Horace's and
Vergil's depictions of the Battle of Actium were among the first of
many negative portrayals of Egypt and Egyptians. The Roman ele-
giac poet Propertius focused on Cleopatra in various poems, at times
scathingly insulting her for unbridled sexuality, association with animal-
headed gods, faithlessness toward Romans, and drunkenness (e.g.,
Elegies 3.11.29–56; 4.6.15–60; written after 23 BCE). In the mid-first
century CE, the poet Lucan labeled Egypt as an "unfaithful" land
because Pompey had been murdered there and depicted Cleopatra and
the denizens of Canopus as shameless and degenerate (e.g., *Pharsalia*
10.58–60; 8.539–43; ca. 65 CE). Pliny the Younger described Egypt as
an insolent, blowhard nation (*ventosa et insolens natio*) that had prided
itself on its indispensability to Rome's grain supply until a year without the Nile's flooding (99 CE) made it properly subservient to its

42. The Temple of Dendur, dedicated to Isis and two local deities but featuring Augustus as Pharaoh. On the outer walls Augustus is depicted multiple times in the likeness of a pharaoh, making offerings to Isis, Osiris, Horus (their son, depicted with a falcon head in the upper left), and other deities. In the first room Augustus is depicted praying, again in pharaonic guise. He is identified by cartouches, although some simply identify him as "pharaoh." The temple, built ca. 15 BCE, was 24.60 m (82 ft.) long from gate to rear of temple. Originally at Dendur (about 77 km south of Aswan), it was moved in the 1960s to the Metropolitan Museum of Art in New York after the Nile was dammed and the area flooded. Photo credit: © The Metropolitan Museum of Art / Art Resource, NY.

conquerors (Pliny, *Panegyric* 31.2–5). Plutarch's *Life of Antony*, written around the same time, revivified the image of the seductive Cleopatra who had weakened the Roman general in decadent Alexandria. A few years later the satirist Juvenal disparaged "maddened" (*demens*) Egypt and Egyptians with accusations of riotousness, degeneracy, monstrous superstition, and even cannibalism (see especially *Satire* 15, apparently written after 127 CE). Juvenal mocked the followers of Isis in his *Satire* 6, which scorns people from Asian Phrygia, Jews, and others as well as Egyptians.

Alongside such insults, however, can be found more neutral or even positive references to Egypt, including some from early in the principate. The poet Tibullus (d. 17 BCE) praised the fertile Nile and the Egyptian god Osiris, whom he presented as an inventor of agriculture and viticulture. More than a century later Tacitus expressed two different judgments about Egypt. Summarizing the status of the Roman world in 68/69 CE, he explained Augustus' appointment of equestrians to rule Egypt and its Roman forces as reasonable, "since it has been thought expedient thus to keep under home control a province difficult of access and productive of grain, distracted and excitable owing to its superstition and license, ignorant of laws and unacquainted with magistrates" (*Histories* 1.11, written ca. 100–110 CE). (This short description presages the important role Tiberius Julius Alexander, prefect (or governor) of Egypt from 66 to 69, played in Vespasian's rise to power; see Chapter 5.) Later in the *Annals* Tacitus reported more positively on the marvels and ancient power of Egypt as he recounted an impromptu visit made to the country in 19 CE by Germanicus, a member of the imperial family (*Annals* 2.59–61). Here he even declared that the tribute rendered Ramses II (ca. 1250 BCE), whose depiction Germanicus saw at Thebes (a capital of Pharaonic Egypt 800 km up the Nile), was scarcely less than the magnificence commanded in his own day by "the violent force of Parthia [Rome's long-time enemy to the east] or by Roman might" (a passage written after 117 CE). To view such sights and other vestiges of Egypt's earlier supremacy was one reason that highly placed Romans toured Egypt. Germanicus, Hadrian, Balbilla (see Chapter 3), and others came to see Alexandria, the pyramids and temples farther south, and the "singing" statue of Memnon, the broken seated colossal statue at Thebes that could emit a noise when the sun's morning rays struck it. Some Roman observers may have prided themselves on having conquered such an impressive culture; others may have seen in Roman Egypt a striking reminder of the variability of fortune; and still others may have simply been awed by the exotic sights.

Isis and Serapis

Before the discussison in this chapter turns to Egyptians' words and portraits, the continual attraction for Romans of the Egyptian gods Isis and Serapis should be pointed out. Egyptian gods were worshipped in Rome until Octavian (later Augustus) excluded them from Rome's *pomerium* or sacred boundary in 28 BCE. Although in 19 CE Tiberius expelled Egyptian and Jewish worshippers from Rome (see Chapter 5), his successor, Caligula, may have monumentalized a sanctuary to Isis and Serapis in Rome's Campus Martius. The Flavians were more obviously supportive of Egypt, and with reason. Vespasian had cemented his bid for the imperial power in Alexandria in 69/70. Domitian escaped mortal danger during civil strife in Rome in 69 by disguising himself as a priest of Isis. In fact, it was under Domitian's patronage that the great "Isaeum," or sanctuary to Isis and Serapis, was built in Rome's Campus Martius and decorated with Egyptian artifacts (Fig. 43), including what seem to have been the first obelisks with hieroglyphs carved in Rome.

The cult of Isis and Serapis also spread elsewhere: for example, an important shrine with obelisks, sphinxes, and other Egyptian artifacts has been found in Beneventum, central Italy (dated to 88/89 CE by its obelisk's hieroglyphs; Beneventum is modern Benevento); and a huge shrine, four times the size of the better-known one from Pompeii, was found in Savaria, Pannonia (modern Szombathely, Hungary). The prolific Plutarch wrote a treatise on Isis and Serapis around the turn into the second century CE. The personal attraction of Isis is beautifully depicted in *The Golden Ass*, a Latin novel written in the later second century by Apuleius of Madaurus (modern M'Daourouch, Algeria; Fig. 44). Its final book (Book 11) centers on the protagonist's conversion and devotion to Isis, depicted as a loving, maternal, and redemptive goddess who cares for all regardless of social standing. The novel indicates that by mid-second century CE priests and devotees of Isis, Serapis, and other Egyptian deities were not all Egyptians: the nurturing goddess drew many to her worship.

43. Basalt sphinx, apparently once exhibited in the Isaeum of Rome as reconstructed by Domitian after 80 CE. The royal sphinx (now restored) names the Pharaoh Hachoris (393–380 BC), of the Twenty-ninth Dynasty, on its base and was carved at that time. 78 cm H, 44 cm W, 1.51 m D. Now in the Louvre, accession number A 27. Photo Credit: Réunion des Musées Nationaux / Art Resource, NY.

Information from Roman Egypt Itself

Offsetting Roman insults about "alien" Egyptians, some of which (especially regarding their lack of discipline) echo criticisms directed at other peoples of Rome, Roman Egypt offers modern students the extraordinary opportunity to appreciate its inhabitants from their own perspectives. Mummy portraits and papyri from Roman Egypt are ever more accessible to the nonspecialist. Albeit somewhat formulaic and stylized, both types of evidence come from Roman Egyptians themselves rather than from "Roman" observers like Tacitus and Juvenal. Underscoring the persistent importance of Greek as one of Rome's official languages, up through the third century CE Roman Egypt's papyri are usually written in Greek despite the fact that most daily transactions in the countryside, perhaps even in cities, must have been in the native Egyptian language. Most extant papyri – whether penned or dictated by a Greek,

44. Isis. Marble statue of Isis (1.795 m H), from ca. 117–138 CE. In her right hand she holds the *sistrum*, the rattle used in rites, and in her left, an *urceus*, or single-handled jug, which would have carried Nile water in religious processions and other contexts. Her fringed cloak is gathered between her breasts in the "Isis knot," which accentuates her fertility, but her head is modestly veiled. From the Hall of the Galatian in the Musei Capitolini (Albani Collection; inv. MC0744). Photo by permission of the Sovraintendenza ai Beni Culturali di Roma Capitale.

a Hellenized Egyptian, or an Egyptian – document legal transactions, but many are personal letters, school exercises, books from personal libraries, and the like, illuminating everyday life in the province (Fig. 45). We see, for example, that travel within Egypt seems not to have been uncommon, especially to visit shrines and temples or for personal reasons such as childbirth or a relative's illness, and that it could be dangerous even though much of the activity undertaken by Roman soldiers in Egypt was police work. Brother-sister marriages comprise about one-sixth of all documented marriages.

Other than this last practice, which is thought to go back to Pharaonic Egypt, it is hard to determine which of the customs and situations documented by Egyptian papyri were common throughout the Roman empire, and which are characteristic of Egypt alone. One aspect of the

45. Woman's letter (recto) from Roman Egypt. This papyrus letter (illustrated and translated in Rowlandson 1998, 326–27, Doc. 6.259, Pl. 41; P.Corn. inv. I 11), dated July 7, 59 CE, was written by the woman Thermouthis to her husband Nemesion, a tax collector in Philadelphia (east of Lake Fayum). In it Thermouthis reports on various matters at home to her husband, who is away on business. The handwriting is somewhat awkward, perhaps a sign that the writer did not often use pen and ink; spelling and grammar are shaky, also suggesting relative inexperience with writing. On the other hand, Thermouthis seems very much in charge of affairs in her husband's absence. Her closing greeting is written in the same hand as the rest of the missive, suggesting that she wrote the entire letter rather than dictating it to a scribe and then adding a farewell. Image digitally reproduced with the permission of the Papyrology Collection, Graduate Library, University of Michigan at Ann Arbor.

papyrological evidence that directly relates to the aims of this book is the difficulty of distinguishing ethnicity by names or other criteria, especially by the second century CE. Many individuals have Egyptian theophoric names (names that embed the name of a god, such as Isigenes, "born from Isis"), even if that individual was one of "the 6,475 Hellenes in the Arsinoite nome" (one of the most "Greek" groups in Egypt, as already noted). We also find that within a single family sons' names can be "Greek" but daughters' names "Egyptian." Intermarriage seems to have occurred regularly, even if Antinoopolis' marriage law is the only known special provision made for it. The assembled evidence indicates that legally recognized ethnic designations were not so important in the second century and afterwards as they might have been when first established in Egypt. Much of the elite population – those with the resources to write and document their lives and property – seems to have had both Greek and Egyptian identities.

Roman Egypt's portraits similarly underscore the difficulty, even futility, of trying to categorize Roman Egyptians by ethnic distinctions. Such portraits are often called "Fayum" portraits, because many of the earliest ones discovered came from the fertile Fayum region in northern Egypt; "mummy" portraits is a better term, both because it acknowledges that such portraits come from numerous areas of this Roman province, and because it signals the function of these likenesses. A bust-length portrait, painted on a thin sheet of wood, was often placed inside the cloth wrappings of the mummified corpse (Plate III). The dry climate of Egypt has also preserved some full-length portraits painted directly on linen or other cloth wrappings (Fig. 46). These can seem remarkably fresh and direct, like the portrait of a woman from Antinoopolis dating to when the city was first founded (Plate IV). Her wide eyes, sideways glance, and jewelry are comparable to other portraits from the Roman world. What seems distinctly Egyptian, however, is the gold leaf added to the portrait below her face. This has been related to the long-standing Egyptian belief that gold was "the flesh of the gods" and thus ensured immortality and divinity when applied to an image or the corpse of the dead.

Another portrait, the shroud for a young man perhaps from Memphis, combines elements scorned by Juvenal and others (Plate V). Standing on a boat in the painted shroud's center is a bearded man. The two (dark-red or purple) stripes (*clavi*) on his long white tunic indicate in Egyptian portraits affiliation to Rome, as do his hair and beard, which resemble those of the reigning emperor, Marcus Aurelius. But the portrait is otherwise very "Egyptian." The deceased steps toward Osiris, offering him a libation from a small flask. Behind him is the jackal-headed Anubis, who

46. Painted mummy shroud from Roman Egypt. Full-length portrait of a boy painted in tempera on a linen shroud, which was wrapped around his mummy and then placed in a painted wooden coffin (ca. 230–250 CE). In his painted left hand he holds a bunch of myrtle leaves. The portrait's four tufts of hair have analogies with other portraits of boys from Roman Egypt. This mummy is only 85 cm H, ca. 21.5 cm W and 18.5 cm thick, and CAT scans of it suggest that the boy died between the ages of eight and ten. The provenance is unknown, but the coffin and mummy were formerly in the collection of Henry Salt. British Museum: EA 6715. Courtesy of the Trustees of the British Museum.

protectively guides him. The background of the shroud shows other Egyptian motifs: souls of the dead rendered as stick figures (upper-left edge), a *uraeus* (a cobra identified with the goddess Wadjit), an ibis, and more. The whole blends together disparate elements, just as mummy portraits themselves combine Graeco-Roman portraiture with Egyptian funerary practices.

Roman Egypt reveals the difficulties Rome could encounter in attempting to integrate the peoples it conquered. Egypt had an imperial past that long preceded the foundation of Rome, and memorials and memory of that history and culture continued throughout Roman occupation. "Roman" literary and visual material often exoticized Egypt and the Egyptians, revealing the fascination many Romans felt for this mysterious and powerful land, and even for its gods. As we know, Egypt's

Queen Cleopatra notoriously seduced two of Rome's most powerful leaders from their "disciplined" Roman ways of thought and behavior. Egypt's agricultural wealth and strategic position convinced Augustus to isolate it and its native inhabitants from the rest of the Roman world, ensuring that those outside of the province would have little experience of Roman Egyptians. Portraits and documentation from Roman Egypt itself, however, indicate a generally harmonious integration of Greek, Roman, and Egyptian elements, at least among the literary and wealthy elite. The assembled evidence reveals how difficult it is to categorize "Roman" during the Empire, particularly when the viewpoint is not that of the elite inhabitants of the city of Rome itself.

SUGGESTED FURTHER READING

Alston, R. 1995. *Soldier and Society in Roman Egypt: A Social History.* London: Routledge.

Arnold, D. 1999. *Temples of the Last Pharaohs.* New York: Oxford University Press.

Ashton, S.-A. 2008. *Cleopatra and Egypt.* Malden, MA: Blackwell.

Bagnall, R. S., and Cribiore, R. 2006. *Women's Letters from Ancient Egypt.* Ann Arbor: University of Michigan Press.

Burstein, S. M. 2007. *The Reign of Cleopatra.* Greenwood Guides to Historic Events of the Ancient World. Norman: University of Oklahoma Press.

Clarke, J. R. 2007. *Looking at Laughter: Humor, Power, and Transgression in Roman Visual Culture, 100 B.C.– A.D. 250.* Berkeley: University of California Press.

Erdkamp, P. 2005. *The Grain Market in the Roman Empire: A Social, Political and Economic Study.* Cambridge: Cambridge University Press.

Gruen, E. S. 1986. *The Hellenistic World and the Coming of Rome.* Berkeley: University of California Press.

http://www.egyptomania.org/bib/biblioant.html is an ongoing, annotated, and online bibliography for "Egyptomania" and related matters.

Kleiner, D. E. E. 2005. *Cleopatra and Rome.* Cambridge, MA: Belknap Press of Harvard University Press.

Lewis, N. 1983. *Life in Egypt under Roman Rule.* New York: Oxford University Press.

Matthews, R., and Roemer, C. (eds.). 2003. *Ancient Perspectives on Egypt.* London: University College London Press.

Meyboom, P. G. P. 1995. *The Nile Mosaic of Palestrina: Early Evidence of Egyptian Religion in Italy.* Leiden: E. J. Brill.

Roullet, A. 1972. *The Egyptian and Egyptianizing Monuments of Imperial Rome.* Leiden: Brill.

Rowlandson, J. (ed.). 1998. *Women and Society in Greek and Roman Egypt: A Sourcebook.* Cambridge: Cambridge University Press.

Scheidel, W. 2001. *Death on the Nile: Disease and the Demography of Roman Egypt.* Leiden: Brill.

Smelik, K. A. D., and Hemelrijk, E. A. 1984. "Who Knows Not What Monsters Demented Egypt Worships? Opinions on Egyptian Animal Worship in Antiquity as part of the Ancient Conception of Egypt." *Aufstieg und Niedergang der römischen Welt* II.17.4.1852–2000.

Versluys, M. J. 2002. *Aegyptiaca Romana: Nilotic Scenes and the Roman Views of Egypt.* Leiden: E. J. Brill.

Walker, S. (ed.). 2000. *Ancient Faces: Mummy Portraits from Roman Egypt.* New York: Metropolitan Museum of Art and Routledge.

CHAPTER 5

THE JEWS –
POLITICAL, SOCIAL, OR
RELIGIOUS THREAT,
OR NO THREAT AT ALL?

Introduction

The incorporation of Jews and Judaea into the Roman Empire was even more problematic than that of other peoples in the Roman world. The status of the Jewish homeland, Judaea, vacillated among various forms of political dependency upon Rome from 63 BCE until 44 CE, with a Roman legion installed after 6 CE in the port city of Caesarea Maritima (roughly halfway between the modern cities of Tel Aviv and Haifa, Israel; Fig. 47). Despite the reduction of most of the area to provincial status in 44 CE, Judaea flared up into Rome's most obstinate provincial rebellion, the First Jewish Revolt (66–70/73 CE). Although this ended in 70 CE with the destruction of the Temple of Jerusalem, a site immensely important to Jewish religion and life, eventually Judaea again blazed up in the fearsome Third Jewish Revolt, also called the Bar Kokhba War after its charismatic leader (132–135 CE). The area went into revolt yet again, but much less extensively, in 351–352 CE. Jews in Judaea seem to have resisted assimilation into the Roman provincial system more than the other groups we have discussed, even though Judaea was irrevocably part of Rome's world after the late Republic.

Jewish resistance and adjustment occurred in other areas and also on the individual level. Beginning in the biblical period and long before the Romans knew of Judaea and its inhabitants, Jews had begun to settle outside their homeland of Judaea. This process, the Diaspora, continued and intensified through our period. Sizable Jewish groups lived in Egypt, especially in Alexandria (see Chapter 4); in Mesopotamia (including parts of modern Turkey, Syria, and Iraq), Cyrenaica (roughly modern northeastern Libya), Asia (roughly modern Turkey), and neighboring provinces; in Achaia and the Balkan region; in Rome; and elsewhere. By the end of the Republic, Roman authorities treated Jews – the usual terms for whom, *Iudaei, Ioudaeoi, Ebraei*, and *Hebraioi* sometimes nuanced religious, geographical, or some other identity – as a distinct group in

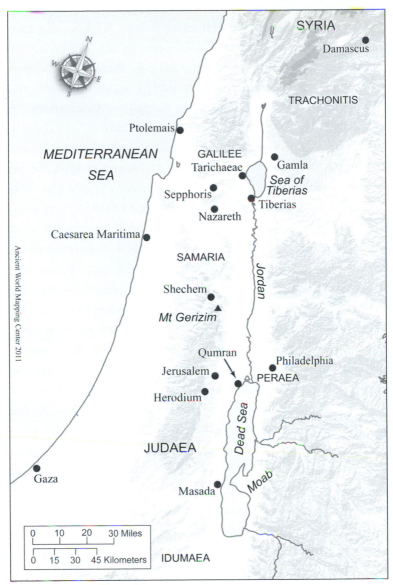

47. Map of Judaea during Rome's late Republic and early Empire, showing regions (e.g., Idumaea, Galilee), cities (e.g., Gaza, Jerusalem, Shechem, Caesarea Maritima), and sites (e.g., Masada). With the Third Jewish Revolt (the Bar Kokhba War) of 132–135 CE, Jerusalem was renamed Colonia Aelia Capitolina, and Judaea was renamed Syria Palaestina. The Sea of Tiberias is also known as the Sea of Galilee. Map © 2011, Ancient World Mapping Center (www.unc.edu/awmc). Used by permission.

Rome and in other cities as well as in Judaea. Jews in the Diaspora maintained a Jewish identity and allegiance to the important Temple of Jerusalem even as they gained citizenship in their local communities and/or Roman citizenship. During the early Empire Philo, the philosopher who came to Rome to advocate for fellow Alexandrian Jews in front of Caligula, held that Jews could be distinguished by "the particularity of their exceptional customs, not mixing with others to alter the ancestral ways" (*On the Life of Moses* 1.278). Indeed, during the Second Jewish Revolt, which broke out in Cyrenaica and elsewhere in 116–117 CE, Jewish identity was stronger than local and Roman commitments in many places in the Diaspora (although not in Rome, and perhaps not in Judaea). Romans often remarked as alien Jews' monotheism (usually depicted as separatism); the importance of Moses, and of Jerusalem and its Temple; the practice of the Sabbath; their dietary restrictions, especially abstinence from pork; and male circumcision.

The beliefs and practices contributing to the covenant between Jews and their god were tenacious, and Roman law often made exceptions to accommodate them. But Jews followed their religion and customs in a Judaea subject to Rome or as minorities in cities scattered throughout a Roman world. Tension between maintaining a traditional Jewish identity and assimilating to the dominant Roman and/or local customs was often a flashpoint, as is suggested by the recurrence and ferocity of the three major Jewish revolts. But more often these obligations were balanced and compromises made as Jews and Romans reacted to changing historical circumstances locally and throughout the empire. Although it is clear that Jews constantly renegotiated their identity, and that that identity was often not considered in ethnic terms, it is just as clear that they succeeded in maintaining distinctiveness throughout the Roman period.

Sources

There is much more extensive literary evidence for the history of the Jews in the Roman world than for that of other peoples. Particularly significant is the historian Titus Flavius Josephus, an aristocratic Jewish priest and rebellion leader who deserted to the Romans early in the First Jewish Revolt. He then gained from Vespasian Roman citizenship (and his Roman name) and a life in Rome, where he wrote *The Jewish War, Jewish Antiquities*, and other works. His details about Judaea and Jewish history quote or paraphrase relevant Roman laws, as well as provide other information. His writings also furnish insight into the intellectual makeup of a historian from Rome's eastern boundaries who had to deal with his non-Roman religion and his more mainstream, and profound, Hellenic education. This tension also applied to Philo, mentioned earlier, whose works are an invaluable historical source. Slightly later, the Roman historian Tacitus articulated a plainly "Roman" perspective when he gave an extensive ethnography of the Jews (*Histories* 5.1–13) before turning to the First Jewish Revolt (this latter narrative is now largely lost). Tacitus and other writers, from Cicero through Juvenal to Cassius Dio and beyond, also provide sporadic, mostly negative remarks, with this type of information peaking in the early second century CE (within generations of the major Jewish revolts). Laws and other documents supplement literary information, and epigraphy is particularly valuable for our knowledge of Jews in third- and fourth-century (CE) Rome and the Diaspora. Some evidence also comes from rabbinic texts from the second century CE and after. Finally, despite the traditional Jewish prohibition against the worship of icons or images that is stated in the Second Commandment, scholars are beginning to investigate the art and archaeology of Jews living under Roman rule, allowing us some perspectives that diverge from those commonly voiced (Fig. 48).

The resulting picture is layered and nuanced, in keeping with the imprecise Roman definition of Jews. Although Romans often singled out Jews as a group or a stereotype, the criterion for this identity could be geography, ethnicity, or religion. This is often confused by the Roman tendency to focus on politics and war. The combination could result in such statements as that of Cicero in *On Behalf of Flaccus*, a speech

48. The "Seasons Sarcophagus with Menorah" front from Rome (dated stylistically to the late 3rd c. CE; marble, 70 x 126 cm), now in the Museo Nazionale Romano, Terme di Diocleziano (inv. 67611). The central medallion, which contains a seven-branched menorah rather than the usual portrait bust of the deceased, is supported by two winged Victories. Winged nude males originally represented the Four Seasons, but now only one, Autumn, is fully visible. Under the medallion three boys or *eros* figures tread grapes in a basin; two others near Autumn play with animals. The iconography and design are traditionally "Roman" for its period, with the exceptional appearance of the menorah rather than a portrait. Published by permission of the Ministero per i Beni e le Attività Culturali – Soprintendenza Speciale per i Beni Archeologici di Roma.

given in a trial of 59 BCE (see Chapter 3 for its negative depiction of Greeks):

> Even while Jerusalem was standing and the Jews were at peace with us, the practice of their sacred rites was at variance with the splendor of our empire, the dignity of our name, the customs of our ancestors. But now all the more so, because that nation has shown what it thinks of our rule by armed warfare [during Pompey's conquest of the region in 63 BCE]. It has revealed how "dear" it was to the immortal gods by the fact that it has been conquered, let out for taxes, made a slave. (*On Behalf of Flaccus* 69)

Judaea and the Jews in the Second-Century Mediterranean World

Like other small states in the eastern Mediterranean, Judaea and the Jews caught Rome's notice initially through diplomacy. From 722 to 333 BCE parts of Judaea had fallen under the control of Assyrians, Babylonians, and Persians, and then, fleetingly, of Alexander the Great and his Ptolemaic successors in Alexandria (see Chapter 4). After 200 BCE the Seleucid kings of Syria seized the region. Throughout these years the Jews in Judaea, led by a high priest and aristocratic families, struggled to maintain their traditions and religion in the face of the cultural practices, physical structures, and religions imported and imposed by alien overlords. By 516/515 BCE they had rebuilt the great Temple of Jerusalem that had been destroyed by the Babylonians in 586 BCE; the significance of the religious building gives its name to the Second Temple Period of Jewish history (which lasted until the destruction of the Temple by the Romans in 70 CE). Jews who had settled outside of Judaea as slaves or in less miserable capacities also adhered to their traditions, especially in Babylonia, Mesopotamia, and Egypt. But some assimilation occurred even in Judaea. By the second century BCE Jerusalem and, despite the persistence here of Jewish law, some cities along the Gaza Strip and a few others seem to have publicly recognized Greek deities and to have accommodated Greek gymnasia and Greek organizations for the cultural and military/athletic training of male youths.

Such Greek practices and ideology contributed to the Revolt of the Maccabees in 168/167 BCE. Jewish resistance to assimilation helped bring to power the indigenous Hasmonean dynasty (also known as the Maccabees), which finally expelled the Syrians and their Jewish collaborators in 142 and established the Hasmonean Kingdom. During the struggles the Maccabean leaders sent embassies to Rome for support, establishing political connections between Judaea and Rome. This period incidentally marks increasing Roman involvement in the East (see Chapter 3), where Rome often allied with smaller polities like Judaea against larger ones like the Seleucid empire in Syria.

The later second century BCE was also a time of escalating unrest in Rome itself, caused in part by the many changes associated with its phenomenally successful warfare and conquest of land, peoples, and other resources (see Chapter 3). This is probably the best context in which to view a brief and problematic note from Valerius Maximus, a writer of the early Empire. The passage has unfortunately been preserved only in two summaries. The fuller one, from the late fourth century CE, states:

> Gnaeus Cornelius Hispalus, *praetor peregrinus* [in 139 BCE; a magistrate with jurisdiction over non-Romans at Rome], ordered by edict the Chaldaeans [astrologers] to depart from the city and Italy within ten days, because by their deceptive interpretation of the stars they confused frivolous and foolish minds and made a profitable living by their lies. The same praetor compelled the Jews, who had tried to infect Roman customs with the cult of Jupiter Sabazius, to return to their homes. (*Memorable Deeds and Sayings* 1.3.3, trans. Whittaker 1984, 85)

Although the association of Jews with the cult of Jupiter Sabazius, a Phrygian or Thracian deity, is implausible, Valerius Maximus' information indicates that Jews were identified as a group by late second-century (BCE) Romans, and that the basis for that identification was religious practices and/or beliefs rather than ethnicity or language.

However, this alleged expulsion of Jews from Rome was unique in the second century BCE. It seems to indicate not so much anti-Jewish sentiment as the strains of a city rapidly filling with immigrants and the destitute. Only six years later the popular Roman leader Tiberius Gracchus was clubbed down along with three hundred of his followers. In 126 Rome expelled Italian non-Roman citizens who had settled in the city. In 114/113 BCE two Gauls and two Greeks were ritually buried alive in Rome's Forum Boarium (along the Tiber) as a charm to avert disaster. (When reporting another instance of this rite at the calamitous beginning of the Second Punic War, Livy with horror calls it a "completely un-Roman sacrifice.") We saw in Chapter 3 the expulsion of Greek rhetors and philosophers from Rome in 161 and perhaps 154. And to return to the reported expulsion of Jews from Rome in 139 BCE, we have no way of knowing whether any Jews traveled at that time from Rome back to Judaea or some other "home."

Meanwhile the Hasmoneans, the new leaders in Judaea, used Greek for diplomatic and literary purposes regardless of their stance against assimilation. By now the Pentateuch, the first five books of the Bible, and other parts of what we consider the Bible, had been translated from Hebrew into Greek, and Greek was increasingly used in Jewish services and study. (In Judaea, however, the common spoken language was Aramaic.) Perhaps to bolster their Mediterranean standing, the Hasmoneans even alleged they had ancestral ties with Greeks in Achaia. Thus, in Rome's first interactions with Jews, limited though those dealings may have been, those in Judaea may have been treated as "Greeks." Nonetheless, the notice of Jews' expulsion in 139 suggests Roman recognition of Jewish religious distinctiveness.

Judaea and Rome in the Late Republic and Early Empire

When Pompey and his troops conquered the eastern Mediterranean in 66–63 BCE (Fig. 49) they encountered no one clearly defined Jewish population in a tightly bordered Judaea, but rather a diverse and shifting number of Jewish groups, such as Idumaeans and Samarians, living with one another and with other ethnic groups in the area and in cities in Asia. This fragmentation shaped Rome's immediate interactions with Jews. After Rome's annexation of Syria in 63 BCE, Judaea was organized into five districts as a subdivision of the new province. Many inhabitants were enslaved and sent to Rome and other cities. But as was the case with most Roman conquests, after the initial brutalities some accommodations were made so as to prevent insurrections. When in power in the 40s BCE, Julius Caesar established or reaffirmed important privileges: Jews were exempted from military service; they had freedom to send their traditional Temple tax to Jerusalem and to worship on the

49. Pompey the Great, in a first-century CE copy of an original of ca. 55 BCE (marble; 24.8 cm H). Upon taking Jerusalem and Judaea in 63 BCE, Pompey set a precedent for Roman dealings with the Jewish religion by respecting the Temple of Jerusalem and not entering it. Head from Rome; now in the Ny Carlsberg Glyptotek, Copenhagen. Photograph by Ole Haupt published by permission of the Ny Carlsberg Glyptotek, Copenhagen.

Sabbath (a day upon which they were not to be summoned to attend law courts); they had the right to assemble for religious meetings; and they could settle internal legal disputes by their own authority (see, e.g., Josephus, *Jewish Antiquities* 16.27). These rules were maintained by later rulers, with the exception of Jewish control of the tax for the Temple (Josephus, *Jewish Antiquities* 18.81–84); as we shall see when further discussing Cicero's *On Behalf of Flaccus* of 59 BCE, Jews' rights with the Temple tax seem to have predated Caesar.

Perhaps the most famous Jewish leader of the Roman era was Herod the Great, although even he was not considered completely Jewish because he was from Idumaea and had a non-Jewish mother from Arabian Nabataea. At the end of the 40s BCE, much of Rome's Judaean territory had fallen to invaders from the east (the Parthians), but the general Herod (later called Herod the Great) helped to regain it for Rome by 37 BCE (Fig. 50). His support of Rome, and an opportune marriage to the Hasmonean princess Mariamne, garnered him the position of king of Judaea from 37 to 4 BCE. During his thirty-three-year rule he was responsible for pro-Roman policies and Roman-style buildings. One of his most remarkable building projects was the creation of

50. Bronze coin of Herod I (later called Herod the Great), struck in Samaria as Herod was coming to power with the backing of Rome (40–37 BCE). On the obverse stands a tripod with a bowl, with the encircling Greek legend "Of Herod the King." On the reverse is a helmet with cheek pieces and a star on top, flanked by two palm branches. The tripod imitates a design found on several Roman coins from 44 to 40 BCE, as does the star on the top of the helmet flanked by two palm branches: Herod was thus making his allegiance clear. SNG.195, ANS 1944.100.62798. © American Numismatic Society.

a deepwater port city at Caesarea Maritima (Fig. 51), which thereafter served as a Roman center in Judaea; another was the sumptuous embellishment of the Temple of Jerusalem, supposedly including an image of a golden (Roman) eagle over the entrance gate. But his palace intrigues (he married ten times in all), non-Jewish buildings and decoration, high taxes, and "Greek" and "Roman" practices undercut his local support.

The division of Herod the Great's kingdom among three sons at his death in 4 BCE precipitated internal turmoil suppressed in time only by the intervention of the Roman governor of Syria and three Roman legions. When Judaea was reduced to a Roman province in 6 CE, a Roman equestrian prefect was assigned as its governor and a legion stationed at Caesarea Maritima. The first Roman census of the province caused unrest. More followed during the governorship, ca. 26–36 CE, of the prefect Pontius Pilate (see Chapter 6). Judaea reverted to being an autonomous (though client) kingdom from 37 to 44, when Herod Agrippa I (also known as Herod Agrippa), the grandson of Herod the Great, ruled increasingly larger parts of the region with Roman support. At his death in 44, his son Agrippa II was too young to rule; Judaea again became a Roman province, now under the rule of

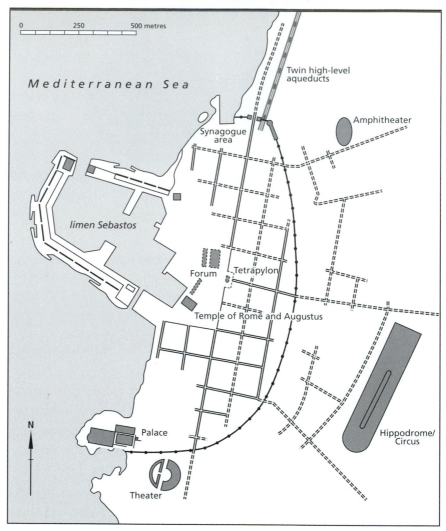

51. Plan of Caesarea Maritima, as built by Herod the Great in Judaea. The orthogonal layout with its wide city blocks, the use of high-quality Roman cement in the harbor works, and the inclusion of an amphitheater, theater, and circus (or hippodrome), are elements shared with the most up-to-date Roman cities of the Augustan period. The placement of the Temple of Rome and Augustus at the head of the harbor emphatically proclaims Herod's allegiance to Rome. Plan after A. Raban and K. G. Holum (eds.), *Caesarea Maritima: A Retrospective after Two Millennia* (Leiden: Brill, 1996), Map 2.

a civilian procurator. Yet in 48 the Romans ceded to Agrippa II control of some land north of the Sea of Galilee. By the 50s Agrippa II's power had grown, and he was centered – apparently with his sister Berenice as coruler – in Jerusalem and Caesarea Maritima (about 120 km north of Jerusalem). Caesarea Maritima was also the residence of the Roman governor of Judaea, indicating the close relationship between the two authorities. Although the early history of Roman–Jewish interactions may have contributed to Roman feelings that the Jews were unpredictable, or *mobiles* (e.g., Tacitus, *Histories* 5.8.3), it was rather the Romans who vacillated regarding this region.

Jews in the Late Republic

Jews in eastern Mediterranean cities and in Rome received some special dispensations from Roman authorities by the end of the Republic and were otherwise identified as distinct, if we accept Valerius Maximus' report about Jews' expulsion from Rome in 139 BCE. Among the charges Cicero had to refute in his tendentious *On Behalf of Flaccus*, delivered in 59 BCE (see Chapter 3), was that, as governor of Asia, Lucius Valerius Flaccus had confiscated annual contributions made by Asian Jews to the Temple of Jerusalem. In his effort to exonerate Flaccus, Cicero objectifies Jews as potential threats. He alleges that enough were in Rome itself to form a bloc in political meetings, where they acted in unison: "You know how numerous they [the Jews] are, how united, what weight they have in assemblies....There are plenty who would incite them against me [as Flaccus' defender] and against all good citizens" (*On Behalf of Flaccus* 66). Cicero then went on to attack the Jews' annual gold contribution to Jerusalem, implying that provincial resources belonged to Romans alone. His remarks were certainly sensationalized for courtroom purposes. At this time most Jews in Rome were probably slaves imported after Pompey's conquest of Judaea in 63 BCE or individuals who were recently manumitted. They would almost certainly not have been accustomed to being granted free expression in Rome's political assemblies.

Cicero is playing to an "us-versus-them" mentality among his listeners. Fastening on the Jews' peculiar right to support a non-Roman institution, the Temple of Jerusalem, he claims that they pose a political danger and threaten separatism in Rome. As we saw in Chapter 3 Cicero also called Jews and Syrians "nations born to slavery" in a speech of 56 BCE: he was a master at playing to the prejudices and fears of his audiences.

Cicero's references joined with other information make it clear that Jews were an identifiable group in Rome by the mid-first century BCE, and continued to be so. Suetonius reports that in the mourning by foreign peoples (*exterae gentes*) over Caesar's assassination in 44 BCE, the Jews particularly stood out, crowding around his cremation site for nights on end (Suetonius, *Life of Caesar* 84.5). As we have already seen, Caesar had been instrumental in authorizing or reaffirming accommodations for Jewish traditions, such as sending money to Jerusalem's Temple. Two generations later, some eight thousand Jews in Rome eagerly awaited information about the succession to Herod in 4 BCE (Josephus, *The Jewish War* 2.80). Augustus continued and even expanded accommodations for Jews in the city, such as allowing them to pick up their grain dole on days other than the Sabbath.

The Early Empire

The general peace imposed by Augustus' rule encouraged population growth, travel, and communications throughout the empire, but also resulted in more conflict concerning Jews in Rome and cities of the Diaspora. Religion seems to have become a marker for various groups in this expansive period: we have seen the negative attention paid to Egyptian animal-headed gods (Chapter 4), for example, and the use of Druidism to stigmatize Celts (Chapter 2). At times it seems as though non-Italian rites were simply lumped together as "the other." Tacitus notes that in an attempt to rid Rome of Egyptian and Jewish rites (*sacra Aegypta Iudaicaque*) in 19 CE, the Roman senate conscripted and sent to Sardinia four thousand men descended from freedmen who "had been infected by that superstition," and it expelled from Italy others who did not renounce those rites (Tacitus, *Annals* 2.85). Although here Judaism is conflated with another non-Roman religion, some of the other sources for the expulsion of 19 suggest that Romans were concerned with growing numbers of Jewish converts.

Problems concerning Jews in Alexandria from 38 to 41 CE are much better documented (Fig. 52). Here conflict and rioting between Jews and Greeks caused numerous embassies from the two groups, including the Alexandrian Jewish philosopher Philo, to appeal to Caligula. Philo's political pieces, *Against Flaccus* and *Embassy to Gaius*, both written in Greek, illuminate the havoc that erupted in Alexandria under the Roman governor Aulus Avilius Flaccus. In *Against Flaccus* Philo tells of demonstrations in the Gymnasium and attacks on Jews in the Greek sector, the agora, and the theater, suggesting that Jews went everywhere in Alexandria, even into prototypically Greek buildings like the theater. He also describes an Alexandrian mob's breaking into Jewish synagogues to forcefully install images of Caligula and the torture of Jewish women in the theater (*Against Flaccus* 41–52, 95–96), disclosing the brutal violence wreaked on Jewish symbols and persons in this Diaspora community. But Philo's embassies to Caligula underscore the political respect accorded Jews in the early Empire, especially those inhabiting the great city of Alexandria. Nonetheless, the vulnerability of Jewish rights and privileges is clear in Caligula's megalomaniac decision to place his image in Jerusalem's Temple itself, a notion that Josephus holds was triggered by the problems in Alexandria (Josephus, *Jewish Antiquities* 18.257–61). Only Caligula's death in 41 prevented the anathema. Jewish awareness of their defenselessness against arbitrary decisions made in Rome must have contributed to the outbreak of the First Jewish Revolt in 66.

Overall, in the early Julio-Claudian period no consistent Roman policy toward Jews can be discerned in Judaea, the Diaspora, or even in Rome, and outside of Judaea it may have often been unclear to Roman authorities who was Jewish and who was not. Between 44 and 46, for instance, Claudius received an embassy from the Jews of Jerusalem over

52. Plan of Alexandria, Egypt, during the Roman period. One of the largest and most cosmopolitan of Rome's cities, it had a large Jewish population. This plan, adapted from M. El-Abbadi, *The Life and Fate of the Ancient Library of Alexandria* (Mayenne, France: Imprimerie Floch, 1990), places in the city some of the attested buildings, neighborhoods, and sites, including the Jewish quarter in the northeast sector. We cannot securely place the gymnasium, the Greek sector, and various synagogues. The Caesareum near the Great Harbor was a site for imperial cult; the Library (Mouseion) is west of it and the theater is east of it. The luxurious Canopus suburb (see Chapter 4) is off the plan to the east.

what seems to have been a local and fairly minor issue, the High Priest's vestments. But this same emperor seems to have prohibited Jews from assembling in Rome and even expelled them from the city because they were "constantly making trouble, with Chrestus as instigator" (Suetonius, *Life of Claudius* 25.4; perhaps to be dated to 49 CE). (In Chapter 6 we return to this notice, which reveals Roman ongoing confusion about Jews and Christians even when Suetonius wrote Claudius' biography some seventy years after the incident.) Saint Paul met numerous Jews in Rome (Acts 28:17–23). It has been estimated that perhaps forty thousand Jews, slave and free, lived in the early Imperial city of Rome; assuming a total population of seven hundred thousand at the time, that would be about 6 percent of the city's inhabitants. Such low numbers would have made it relatively easy to "blend in" while sustaining social or religious communities. Although it has been thought that Jews lived closely together in Rome's neighborhoods of Transtiberim and Subura (Fig. 53), the density of the population in these cheap residential areas of Rome argues against assuming that any groups lived in isolated enclaves. Elsewhere, several million Jews are estimated to have lived in Alexandria and other cities of the Diaspora during the first century CE, and Judaea had a population of perhaps one million (not all Jews). These numbers can be placed against the total estimated population of the Roman world in 14 CE, perhaps 45.5 million.

The First Jewish Revolt

In Judaea itself internal religious conflict combined with misrule on Rome's part, and perhaps also with resistance to assimilation, culminating in a widespread insurrection in 66 CE. There is little evidence of "Romanization" in Judaea before the revolt. Almost all the names found on ossuaries, limestone chests used as the final resting place of human bones, are not Roman but Hebrew ones like Simon and Mariamne, and little figurative decoration has been found outside of Herod's palaces. The First Jewish Revolt took four years to quell despite the transfer to Judaea of numerous soldiers and the competent general Vespasian, and some places, notably Masada, held out for three more years. Judaea was devastated. Josephus informs us that Gamla, north of the Sea of Galilee, lost more than 9,000 people to massacre and suicide when the Romans took the city in 67; in the same year the fall of Tarichacae (modern Magdala, Israel) resulted in 30,400 prisoners being sold as slaves and another 6,000 sent to work on the Corinthian Canal (*The Jewish War* 4.80, 3.540). During and even after the Judaean revolt, Jews in Diaspora cities were attacked by locals, notably in Cyrenaica and Syrian Antioch, and Vespasian had a Jewish temple at Leontopolis in Egypt destroyed.

When Vespasian, who had commanded the Roman forces since 66 CE, left Judaea for Alexandria in 69 to gather support for his own bid

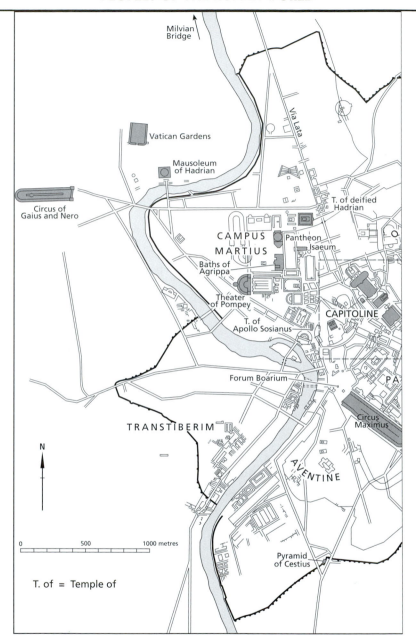

53. Plan of Imperial Rome, identifying monuments discussed in this book. For the legibility of the identifying labels, "T. of ..." stands for "Temple of ...". The Circus of Gaius and Nero area is where Constantine later located the Basilica of St. Peter. "The seven hills of Rome" are generally understood to have been the Capitoline, Quirinal, Viminal, Esquiline, Caelian, Aventine, and Palatine.

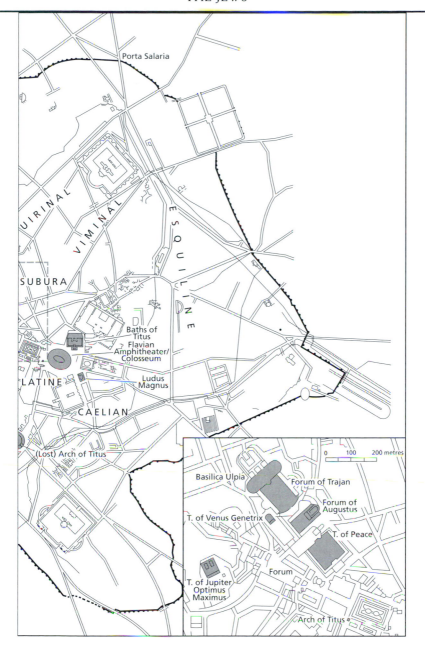

Porta Salaria

QUIRINAL

VIMINAL

ESQUILINE

SUBURA

Baths of
Titus

Flavian
Amphitheater/
Colosseum

PALATINE

Ludus
Magnus

CAELIAN

(Lost) Arch of Titus

Basilica Ulpia

Forum of Trajan

Forum of
Augustus

T. of Venus Genetrix

T. of Peace

Forum

T. of Jupiter
Optimus
Maximus

Arch of Titus

0   100   200 metres

54. Masada. View from the fortress of Masada (Israel), to the plain and the Dead Sea below (*to the middle right*). The fortress was developed by Herod the Great as a luxurious and self-sufficient palace complete with cisterns and gardens. It ended up being the last stand of the Jewish Zealots against Rome. When Jewish insurgents fled here after the Romans took Jerusalem in 70 CE, the Romans lay siege to the fortress on its high plateau, which they succeeded in taking only after three years and the construction of a massive ramp. Photo Credit: Erich Lessing / Art Resource, NY.

for imperial power (see Chapter 4), it was his son and lieutenant, Titus, who captured Jerusalem and burnt down the Temple in 70. Because the Temple had been the center of Jewish religious activity, its destruction profoundly impacted Jewish religious life: for instance, the requirement of ritual sacrifice now became obsolete, because sacrifices had previously been carried out only at the Temple. Despite the destruction, the revolt smoldered on until 73 in a few spots, most famously at Masada (Fig. 54). Josephus' dramatic version of Rome's siege and conquest of this fortress, once one of Herod's luxurious and self-sustaining palaces (Josephus, *The Jewish War* 7.163–215), has been adopted as a symbol of defiance against imperial forces. Given Josephus's own history as a defector, however, it may have been written to underline the futility of resistance against the Romans, who made sure to crush the rebellion in such a way that other provinces would not follow Judaea's example. Titus also broadcast this warning by exhibiting "costly spectacles in all the towns through which he passed [in Syria], and ... us[ing] his Jewish captives to act out their own destruction" (Josephus, *The Jewish War* 7.96). In Judaea, Rome established a permanent camp in Jerusalem for units of the Tenth Legion and hindered Jewish resettlement in the city.

The Aftermath of the First Jewish Revolt in Rome and Elsewhere

Although to our knowledge no measures were taken against Jews in Rome during the First Revolt, Vespasian and Titus did celebrate the suppression of the Jewish "war" with a lavish triumph in the city in 71 (Josephus, *The Jewish War* 7.123–57) and by raising more permanent memorials. This had been the most serious rebellion of Rome's subject peoples since the German and Pannonian revolts during Augustus' rule (see Chapter 2). But it is also true that by casting rebellious provincials as an alien group the Flavians masked Vespasian's rise to power during bloody civil strife in 68–69. (Compare the focus on the "alien queen" Cleopatra during and after the civil war by which Augustus came to power; Chapter 4.) On land in central Rome, Vespasian built the Temple of Peace to exhibit the spoils from Jerusalem that had been paraded in the Flavian triumph. Nearby he started construction of the great Flavian amphitheater (now known as the Colosseum), which a recent epigraphic discovery shows was paid for "from the war spoils." The original inscription may have left the origins of the spoils vague, since nothing seems to have been inscribed immediately after the traditional phrase *ex manubiis*. But the boastful expression must refer to money seized from the sack of Jerusalem as well as to enslaved Jewish laborers.

A triple arch, no longer extant, was raised in Rome's Circus Maximus in 80. In its last part its inscription claimed aggressively, and historically incorrectly: "The Senate and the People of Rome [raised this arch] to

55. Arch of Titus adjacent to the Roman Forum. Triumphal procession scene from Arch of Titus (constructed ca. 81 CE), on the eastern edge of the Roman Forum. The Roman soldiers, wreathed with laurel for the triumphal procession celebrating the Flavian suppression of the First Jewish Revolt, pass into the city through an arch carrying booty from Judaea, including the Table of Shewbread, the silver horns, and a menorah. Marble (2 m H). Archivi Alinari, Florence / Art Resource, New York.

the Emperor Titus Caesar Vespasianus, son of the deified Vespasian, ... its own leader, because in accordance with the instructions, counsels, and auspices of his father he conquered the race of the *Judaei* and destroyed the city of Jerusalem, either assailed in vain or completely untouched by all leaders, kings, and races before him." By 81 the better-known Arch of Titus had been built on the Roman Forum's eastern edge overlooking the western flank of the Colosseum. The visual message of this arch refers explicitly to the Jewish defeat, for its large and small reliefs depict the Flavian triumph that paraded the booty from Jerusalem's Temple in Rome (see also Chapter 1; and Fig. 55). Throughout Vespasian's rule numerous coins were struck showing "Captured Judaea" (Fig. 56). At least in Rome itself, and although no insurgency of Jews in Italy is known, the First Jewish Revolt resulted in Roman objectification of Jews and Judaea.

Such official distancing corresponds to the marked negativity toward Jews expressed by Pliny the Elder, Quintilian, Juvenal, Tacitus, and other Roman authors of the late first and early second centuries CE. Often their passages broadly criticize Jews rather than referring more specifically to the First Revolt. Pliny the Elder, for example, casually remarks that the Jews, "who are a people noted for their contempt of the gods," considered common a type of date palm that Romans used in religious rites (Pliny, *Natural History* 13.9.46). Among the many rhetorical tips in his *Institutes of Oratory* (3.7.21; ca. 95 CE), Quintilian says that a speaker can incite prejudice against an opponent by saying such things as: "We also hate those who have fathered evil. Founders of cities incur disrepute if they have produced a people pernicious to others, as for example the originator [Moses] of the Jewish superstition."

The First Revolt also resulted in tighter Roman control over the Jews. The tithe formerly paid to the Temple now had to go to Rome's Temple of Jupiter Optimus Maximus and was overseen by a new government department, the Fiscus Judaicus; only upon payment of this tax could Jews practice their religion legally. Thus their unique right to contribute to their own religion, thus perpetuating their links to their homeland and to one another, was taken away by Rome. A notorious story in Suetonius' *Life of Domitian* (12.2) portrays the emperor Domitian (r. 81–96) ordering a ninety-year-old man to be stripped in court and examined for circumcision. Suetonius recounts the incident to illustrate Domitian's avarice and cruelty, and he specifies that the emperor wanted all Jews to pay, not only "those who kept their Jewish origins a secret in order to avoid the tax, but ... those who lived as Jews without professing Judaism." The story may mark a new Roman identification of Jews by their religious practices rather than ethnicity or geographical origin: proselytes (new converts) as well as individuals born into the faith were considered Jews so that Domitian could exact the tax from as many as possible. This definition seems to have continued in force, although Domitian's successor, Nerva (r. 96–98), apparently put an end to such public humiliation of individuals (Fig. 57).

56. "With Judaea Captured," or *Iudaea Capta*, coin. The reverse of this coin of Titus shows Judaea (or Jerusalem) as a weeping captive woman to the right of the date-palm tree that symbolizes Judaea. A victorious Roman soldier rests his left foot on a discarded and useless enemy helmet. This *as*, a copper alloy coin of low denomination and thus presumably used by more people, was minted in Rome in 72 CE. It is now in the British Museum (Object no.: 1919,0214.17; CM RE2p131.607). © The Trustees of the British Museum.

Acceptance for Jews in Late First-Century Rome?

Undoubtedly because Vespasian came to power with some backing from Judaea and the East, a few Jews figured importantly in late first-century (CE) Rome. By the end of the century, however, they disappeared from Rome's highest circles, where their status seems to have been questionable in any case. Three individuals may serve to exemplify the equivocal situation: Josephus, Berenice, and Tiberius Julius Alexander.

The aristocratic Josephus, who arrived in Rome in 70 as a Roman loyalist after renouncing his duties as a leader of the First Jewish Revolt, resided in Vespasian's ancestral home on the Quirinal. (The Flavian emperors themselves moved to imperial dwellings.) As we have seen, Josephus's sophisticated works, written in Greek and following well-established literary genres, included investigation of the ancient Jewish traditions that perhaps earlier had prompted Roman respect for the faith; another focus was the devastating recent "war" or revolt. But Josephus apparently wrote in isolation from the capital's Romans, Greeks, and Jews alike before his death in the early second century; we have very little understanding of who read and responded to his works. Thus, despite his intimate connection with the most eminent family in Rome, the

57. "Reform of the Fiscus Judaicus." Bronze sestertius of 96 CE, issued to commemorate Nerva's reform of the Fiscus Judaicus. On the obverse is shown the emperor Nerva; on the reverse, a date-palm tree, which had become symbolic of the Jewish people and Judaea (compare the *Iudaea Capta* coin, on facing page). The reverse also carries the legend: FISCI IUDAICI CALUMNIA SUBLATA ("With the Malicious Accusations of the Jewish Tax Removed"), with S C ("By Consent of the Senate") flanking the palm tree. © Trustees of the British Museum.

ruling Flavians, he does not seem to have made much impression on contemporary society.

Much more notable in Flavian Rome was another Jew associated with the Flavians, Berenice, a descendant of Herod the Great. Berenice had coruled parts of Judaea with her brother Agrippa II before the First Revolt, but she had been humiliated in 66 while trying to curb Roman soldiers' attacks on Jews in Jerusalem:

> The mad rage of the soldiers vented itself upon the queen. Not only did they torture and put their [Jewish] captives to death under her eyes, but they would have killed her also had she not hastened to seek refuge in the palace.... She would come barefoot before the tribunal and make supplication to [Gessius] Florus [the Roman procurator], without any respect being shown to her, and even at the peril of her life. (Josephus, *The Jewish War* 2.312–14; Loeb trans. by H. St. J. Thackeray)

Berenice later became involved in an affair with Titus, and she supported Vespasian in his bid for imperial power. In 75 she went to Rome to live with Titus in the imperial palace, and there were expectations of marriage. She must have been extraordinarily fascinating, as she was then almost fifty and at least ten years older than he. We find some hints of her power in Rome – for instance, the rhetorician Quintilian says that he pled a case on her behalf and in front of her as judge (*Institutes of Oratory* 4.1.19). Titus broke off the relationship, supposedly when it became clear that "Romans were displeased by the situation" (Cassius Dio, *Roman History* 65.15.4). But the sources do not say whether it was Berenice's Jewishness that was objectionable, her status as a foreign queen (compare Cleopatra, Chapter 4), or something else.

Tiberius Julius Alexander, a nonpracticing Jew from Alexandria who was related to Berenice and to Philo (the philosopher and envoy to Caligula previously mentioned), unusually had risen through Roman equestrian ranks to become prefect of Egypt from 66 to 69 CE. In that position when the First Jewish Revolt broke out, he crushed Jewish unrest in his native city of Alexandria, and during the civil war of 68–69 he also provided key support to Vespasian. He then served in Judaea as Titus' chief of staff while Titus put down the rebellion for good. For his loyalty to Rome and the Flavians, Tiberius Julius Alexander was conspicuously honored by Vespasian, who installed in Rome's Forum of Augustus a bronze statue (or statues) of him. But we know this from the words of the satirist Juvenal, who scorned commemorating a "presumptuous Egyptian and Easterner" in this prestigious location (*Satire* 1.127–31). Interestingly, especially in light of Juvenal's frequent insults of Jews (discussed later), the satirist does not identify Tiberius Julius Alexander as Jewish. This suggests the fluidity of Jewish identity at this time, something already noted in connection with the Fiscus Judaicus. In any case, the examples of Tiberius Julius Alexander, Berenice, and Josephus may define the limits of acceptance of Jews in the capital city and Rome's elite. No Jews after them are known to have reached such heights.

Other Jews in the Empire

On the other hand, Roman vehemence against proselytes at the beginning of the second century suggests the attraction Judaism held for some polytheistic Romans. In his ethnography of the Jews Tacitus targets new converts and the reluctance of Jews to renounce their own religion:"For all the worst kind of [non-Jewish] people, abandoning their ancestral religion, heap up their dues and contributions; for this reason Jewish wealth has increased, as also because of their stubborn loyalty, their readiness to show pity [to each other], and their hatred and enmity toward all others" (*Histories* 5.5). Elsewhere he remarks on Jews' insistence on their religious beliefs (*Histories* 2.4). His notice of Jews' tenacity in holding on to their beliefs and their readiness to show pity to one another reveals one attraction of the religion – the creation of tight, supportive communities. Tacitus' contemporary Juvenal also insults recent converts, or at least the offspring of such converts, in his *Satire* 14:

> Some, whose lot it has been to have Sabbath-fearing fathers, worship nothing but clouds and the *numen* of the heavens, and see no difference between the flesh of swine and humans since their fathers abstained from pork; they then get themselves circumcised. They habitually condemn our Roman laws, preferring to learn, honor, and fear the Jewish commandments, all that Moses handed down in that mysterious tome of his – never to show the way to any but fellow-believers, never to lead to life-giving water any but the circumcised. (Juvenal, *Satire* 14.96–104; see also *Satire* 3)

Again Roman derision is directed against the perceived separatism, or nonassimilation, of Jews.

About a century later Septimius Severus outlawed conversion to Judaism. Despite the ban, inscriptions from third- and fourth-century Aphrodisias and other Asian cities name "god-fearers" and "god-worshippers" in such contexts as to make it plain that these are Jewish converts. The inscriptions document not only the attractions of the Jewish religion, but also greater public acceptance of Judaism and its adherents in this late period (see also Fig. 48). Conversion may have been particularly attractive to women, who did not have to undergo the difficult operation of circumcision. The practice of male circumcision, in fact, features importantly in the outbreak of the Bar Kokhba War, the later of the two second-century Jewish rebellions.

The Second and Third Jewish Revolts (115–117 and 132–135 CE)

The Second Jewish Revolt erupted in 115, with apparently simultaneous Jewish insurrections in Mesopotamia and Egypt (see Chapter 4). The revolt spread to Cyrenaica and Cyprus, and perhaps had some repercussions in Judaea as well, before it was suppressed in late 117. Its outbreak in Parthian Mesopotamia, which Trajan was invading, was particularly worrisome, because Jews there seem to have joined Parthian resistance to Trajan's expansionistic Parthian War in the East. As was the case with the First Jewish Revolt, there is no evidence of Jewish discontent or reprisals in Rome itself at the time. But in other parts of the Diaspora the Second Revolt was fought desperately and viciously (Fig. 58): later rebuilding inscriptions from the city of Cyrene (modern Shahhat, Libya), as on the Temple of Hecate, claim that reconstruction came after "burning and plundering in the Jewish tumult." If we can trust the eleventh-century epitome of Cassius Dio (himself writing a century after the events), the Jewish rebels were thought to have treated their opponents savagely, brutally killing over 220,000 in Cyrenaica alone (Cassius Dio, *Roman History* 68.32.1–3; Cyrenaica roughly corresponds to modern northeastern Libya). Jewish names virtually disappear from Egyptian papyri outside of Alexandria, suggesting that Jews were singled out throughout Egypt; further, tax receipts from after the Second Revolt was suppressed show merciless extortion of Jews. If and how the revolt was concurrently begun by Jews in the distant areas of Mesopotamia and Egypt, and then spread to other Diaspora sites, remain open questions. But such widespread outbreaks of Jewish dissatisfaction were not to reappear in Roman history: the Third Jewish Revolt, which was centered in Judaea in 132–135, did not expand to the Diaspora.

58. Menorah on Cyrene's road. This menorah was carved into the earlier rock-cut Roman road leading southwest from Cyrene to Balagrae and Cyrenaican Ptolemais (modern el-Beida and Khirbat al Yahud, Libya), undoubtedly by insurgent Jews in the Second Jewish Revolt. The city of Cyrene experienced particular devastation in the revolt, according to rebuilding inscriptions there. The large menorah carved into the road's surface strikingly symbolizes Jewish exasperation and determination to overthrow the status quo. Photo from G. Oliverio, *La stele dei nuovi comandamenti e dei cereali. Iscrizioni di Cirene (Gortina), El Gùbba, Ngàrnes, Gasr Barbùres, Gasr Taurgùni, Tòlméta*, Bergamo 1933 (= *Documenti antichi dell'Africa Italiana*, II, *Cirenaica, fasc. I*), pp. 128–29, tav. XLVI, fig. 106, through the kindness of Francesco Ziosi.

Ancient authors such as Cassius Dio (*Roman History* 69.12.1) attribute the Third Revolt to Hadrian's decisions to found at Jerusalem a Roman colony, Colonia Aelia Capitolina, and to construct a temple to Jupiter Optimus Maximus over the site of the Jewish Temple. Another

59. Silver coin restamped by the Jewish insurgents during the Third Jewish Revolt (132–135 CE), over a Roman coin with the head of Hadrian on its reverse. The restruck coin now shows on its reverse a *lulab* (palm branch, associated with the Jewish harvest festival of Sukkot) over the head of Hadrian (in profile). Here the insurgents also added a Jewish legend that partially obscures the Latin inscription originally encircling Hadrian's head. Even more prominent now is the new Jewish legend on the obverse, where can also be seen an *etrog* (citron fruit, also associated with Sukkot). The coin is now in the British Museum. © The Trustees of the British Museum.

affront was a ban of Jews from Jerusalem; still another, Hadrian's universal prohibition of circumcision. (The next emperor, Antoninus Pius, modified this to allow Jews to circumcise their own sons.) These decisions now look like an attempt to eradicate Judaism by destroying its origins, sacred locations, and customs. It took the Romans three years to suppress the hard-fought rebellion led by the messianic leader of the Jews, Simon Ben Kosiba, who was renamed Bar Kokhba, or "Son of a Star" (in Aramaic), once the revolt began. He featured the Temple on some of his coins, indicating a desire to rebuild it; on others other Jewish symbols appeared, supplanting Roman ones (Fig. 59). Bar Kokhba galvanized his followers. Hadrian had to send his best generals to fight him. The revolt resulted in the deaths of 580,000 insurgents and innumerable Roman troops, the destruction of almost a thousand villages, and the physical ruin of Judaea. A second legion was stationed in the province, which saw its name changed from Judaea to Syria Palaestina. Jewish slaves and exiles must have reached Rome and other large cities in the empire, although we have little direct evidence of this. The rebellion was so fierce as to cause Hadrian's omission of a customary opening to a communication to the senate during the fighting: "If you and your children are in health, it is well; I and the legions are in health" (Cassius Dio, *Roman History* 69.14.1–3).

Jews and Romans after the Third Jewish Revolt

The general dearth of information about Jews in the Roman empire during the rest of the second century may reflect the catastrophes and consequences of the Second and Third Jewish Revolts. Jews' greater visibility in the third century corresponds with the *Constitutio Antoniniana* of 212, which granted Roman citizenship to all free members of the empire without consideration of religious beliefs and practices. Around the same time Rabbi Judah (haNasi, or "the Prince") wrote down what is now known as the Mishnah (part of the later Torah). This preserved at least some of the Tannaim, originally oral debates among various rabbis who were influential in the period from the destruction of the Temple in 70 CE until around 200. The Mishnah provided guidance for Jews' practice of biblical laws and a commonality for Jews throughout the empire.

The evidence for the third century generally indicates peaceful coexistence of Jews with others in Rome and elsewhere. Since Jews were traditionally exempted from having to perform non-Jewish rites, they did not suffer during the third-century Christian persecutions that demanded Roman sacrifice from all within the empire (see Chapter 6). Epitaphs in Rome, Alexandria, and other cities allow us to identify individuals as Jewish because of their recorded name and/or religious position, and/or the appearance of Jewish symbols like the menorah, *lulab*, and *etrog* (festive palm branch and citron fruit), and shofar (the musical horn used in Jewish rituals). Some 14 percent of those identified as Jews in Rome's 530 Jewish inscriptions bear a Hebrew *cognomen*. Third- and fourth-century epitaphs in Rome identify members and leaders of the synagogues of the Augusteiani, Agrippeiani, Herodiani, Campenses, Suburenses, Verancoli, Hebrei, and others. Such distinguishing marks indicate acceptance of the Jewish "people" in the third- and fourth-century Roman world (see also Fig. 48), although we have no way of gauging the representativeness of our evidence. Although occupations are seldom recorded, Jews in Rome and elsewhere apparently held the same kinds of positions as other Romans. They did not cluster in banking, piece-good work, or other jobs similar to the ones post-antique laws forced upon them.

By the third century CE synagogues were common in Syria Palaestina and in other cities in the Diaspora, although no such building has been unequivocally identified in Rome. Already in the first century, however, literary evidence suggests that listening to Scripture on the Sabbath was both a common Jewish practice and considered an ancient command. In Sardis (modern Sart, Turkey) and some other cities, Jewish meetinghouses were adapted from preexisting structures; in others, such as Tiberias (on the Sea of Galilee, Israel) and Syrian Apamea (in northwestern modern Syria), they were specially built edifices. Floor mosaics in these structures often include Jewish motifs like the menorah and the date-palm tree. Occasional mosaic inscriptions list the contributors to the building's cost, allowing us to identify Jews and Jewish supporters, and to gain an idea of their financial standing. Dura Europus, a town on Rome's eastern frontier (now on the Syrian Euphrates) that was abandoned when captured in 256 CE, had numerous religious buildings including a well-painted Christian one, a Temple of Mithras, a Temple of the Palmyrene Gods, and a synagogue with narrative figured paintings (from 246 CE). The evidence, despite being scattered through various cities, argues for a third- and early fourth-century Roman world in which urban Jews lived side by side with others. Even in Judaea, where one might presume clear Jewish distinctiveness, we find the use of non-Jewish elements in decoration near signs of Jewish material culture and rituals (Plate VI).

The Breakdown of Accommodation in the Late Fourth Century

After the 313 (CE) Edict of Milan affirmed the right to practice all religions including Christianity (see Chapter 6), synagogues, churches, and temples to Rome's traditional gods could be found in the same city. But later changes in the fourth century would make life increasingly unpredictable for Jews. Reportedly because the Christians increasingly agitated against them without repercussions, in 351–352 CE Syria Palaestina witnessed a short-lived revolt against the eastern Roman emperor. Sepphoris (modern Zippori, Israel) and a few other places in Judaea that were briefly controlled by insurgents were destroyed. On the other hand, a decade later Jerusalem and the Jews were the intended recipients of imperial favor when the emperor Julian (r. 361–363) proposed to rebuild the Temple and to abolish the long-standing tax on Jews for Rome's Temple of Jupiter Optimus Maximus. Julian died in 363 before achieving either goal, but his plans seem to have been aimed more at discrediting and belittling Christianity than at strengthening Judaism per se. Jews' circumstances worsened irrevocably in the 380s. The emperor Theodosius I (379–395 CE) considered himself a scrupulous Christian. At first ambivalent toward other religions, even at the start he treated Christian heretics severely, and he became increasingly intransigent toward all "nonbelievers." In 388, Theodosius did not punish the Christian monks and others who were clearly responsible for burning down a synagogue in Callinicum, Mesopotamia (modern Ar-Raqqah, in northern Syria). He began actively to legislate against polytheism and Judaism. With this emperor, religion was reinstated as a distinguishing criterion for the rights and privileges of Roman subjects. Judaism was penalized throughout Rome's empire, and the modus vivendi that had existed – although often shakily – for Jews and Romans for over five centuries was destroyed.

SUGGESTED FURTHER READING

Barclay, J. M. G. (ed.). 2004. *Negotiating Diaspora: Jewish Strategies in the Roman Empire*. London: T&T Clark International.

Berlin, A. M., and Overmann, J. A. (eds.). 2002. *The First Jewish Revolt: Archaeology, History, and Ideology*. London: Routledge.

Chancey, M. A. 2006. *Greco-Roman Culture and the Galilee of Jesus*. Society for New Testament Studies Monograph Series, 134. Cambridge: Cambridge University Press.

Edmondson, J., Mason, S., and Rives, J. (eds.). 2005. *Flavius Josephus and Flavian Rome*. Oxford: Oxford University Press.

Fine, S. 2005. *Art and Judaism in the Greco-Roman World. Toward a New Jewish Archaeology*. Cambridge: Cambridge University Press.

Goodman, M. 2007. *Judaism in the Roman World: Collected Essays*. Leiden: Brill.

Goodman, M. (ed.). 1998. *Jews in a Graeco-Roman World*. Oxford: Oxford University Press.

Gruen, E. S. 2002. *Diaspora: Jews amidst Greeks and Romans*. Cambridge, MA: Harvard University Press.

Horst, P. W. van der. 2003. *Philo's Flaccus: The First Pogrom. Introduction, Translation, and Commentary*. Leiden: Brill.

Lewis, N. 1983. *Life in Egypt under Roman Rule*. Oxford: Clarendon.

Lieu, J. 1996. *Image and Reality: The Jews in the World of the Christians in the Second Century*. Edinburgh: T&T Clark.

Lieu, J., North, J., and Rajak, T. (eds.). 1994. *The Jews among Pagans and Christians in the Roman Empire*. London: Routledge.

Macdonald, C. 1976. *In Catilinam 1–4. Pro Murena. Pro Sulla. Pro Flacco*. Cicero Vol. X. Loeb Classical Library 324. Cambridge, MA: Harvard University Press.

Millar, F. 1993. *The Roman Near East, 31 B.C.–A.D. 337*. Cambridge, MA: Harvard University Press.

Noy, D. 2000. *Foreigners at Rome: Citizens and Strangers*. London: Duckworth.

Pucci Ben Zeev, M. 2005. *Diaspora Judaism in Turmoil, 116/117 CE: Ancient Sources and Modern Insights*. Leuven: Peeters.

Rajak, T. 1984. *Josephus: The Historian and His Society*. Philadelphia: Fortress Press.

Reynolds, J., and Tannenbaum, R. 1987. *Jews and God-fearers at Aphrodisias: Greek Inscriptions with Commentary. Texts from the Excavations at Aphrodisias Conducted by Kenan T. Erim*. Cambridge: Cambridge Philological Society.

Schäfer, P. 2003a. *The History of the Jews in the Greco-Roman World: The Jews of Palestine from Alexander the Great to the Arab Conquest*. Rev. ed. London: Routledge.

Schäfer, P., ed. 2003b. *The Bar Kokhba War Reconsidered: New Perspectives on the Second Jewish Revolt against Rome*. Tübingen: Mohr Siebeck.

Schürer, E. 1973. *The History of the Jewish People in the Age of Jesus Christ (175 B.C.–A.D. 135)*. Rev. and ed. G. Vermes, F. Millar, and M. Goodman. Edinburgh: Clark.

Sievers, J., and Lembi, G. (eds.). 2005. *Josephus and Jewish History in Flavian Rome and Beyond*. Leiden: Brill.

Smallwood, E. M. 1976. *The Jews under Roman Rule: From Pompey to Diocletian*. Leiden: Brill.

Thackeray, H. St. J. 1927. *Josephus. The Jewish War. Books 1–2*. Josephus Vol. II. Loeb Classical Library 203. Cambridge, MA: Harvard University Press.

Whittaker, M. 1984. *Jews and Christians: Graeco-Roman Views*. Cambridge Commentaries on Writings of the Jewish and Christian World 200 BC to AD 200, vol. 6. Cambridge: Cambridge University Press.

Plate I. Gate of Athena Archegetis, the western entrance into Athens's Roman Agora (or Market of Caesar and Augustus), as depicted from the west by James Stuart, *View of the Gate of Athena Archegetis, Athens 1750–60* (30.5 x 46.5 cm; now in the Victoria and Albert RIBA Library Drawings Collection, SD145/1). The structure is now less well preserved than when Stuart drew it in the eighteenth century. The dedicatory inscription on the entablature (not visible here) proclaims that the building was paid for with money provided by Caesar and Augustus, and that it was dedicated to Athena Archegetis (Athena the Leader) in the archonship of Nikias (11–9 BCE). The pedestal above the pediment once carried a statue of Augustus' grandson and presumed heir, Lucius Caesar. The gate opened into a massive civic space measuring ca. 112 x 96 m that lay to the east of the traditional Athenian Agora and was almost half its size. Despite its modern name "Agora" or "Market," this structure donated to Athens by Caesar and Augustus may have functioned in Roman imperial cult rituals. Published by permission of Ribapix, the RIBA Library Photographs Collection.

Plate II. Nilotic fresco from the House of the Physician, Pompeii. Many of Pompeii's Nilotic scenes, like this detail from a (mid-1st c. CE) wall painting from the House of the Physician, depict dwarfs and/or pygmies as well as hippopotami, crocodiles, ibises, and other birds. The pygmies or other human actors are often shown engaged in sexual activity or with exaggerated genitalia, or engaged in absurd behavior (as here). Such elements, which may strike modern viewers as extraordinary, have been interpreted variously: as referring to Egypt's *truphe* or luxurious abundance and bliss; as exoticizing Egypt and thus removing it from the human sphere; and/or as parodying and belittling Egypt, which seemed to pose a real threat with Cleopatra. Photo Credit: Scala / Art Resource, NY.

Plate III. Roman–Egyptian mummy (1.33 m L) with an inserted panel portrait of an adolescent youth, dated ca. 100–120 CE, from Hawara (southeast of Lake Fayum). Mummy portraits were usually painted in tempera or encaustic (pigmented hot wax) on a thin sheet of wood, often imported limewood (also known as linden wood) or indigenous sycamore fig wood. The wrapping of this mummy suggests a common depiction of Osiris (see Plate V) and gold studs have been added to the diamond-shaped hollows made by the linen. This encaustic portrait and mummy are at the British Museum of Art (EA 13595; Object number 1888,0920.39). © Trustees of the British Museum.

Plate IV. Portrait of a young woman from Antinoopolis, ca. 130 CE. This lovely young woman is depicted as perhaps being in her early 20s, with realistic and unusual elements that suggest her wealth and status. Her right ear is crumpled realistically. She wears fine beaded earrings, a gold-headed stickpin in the braid at the top of her head, and a prominent green gem mounted on a gold oval brooch. The gold leaf added below her face has been related to the traditional Egyptian belief that gold was "the flesh of the gods" and ensured immortality and divinity when applied to an image or the corpse of the dead. Painted in encaustic on cedar wood, the portrait is now in Paris at the Musée du Louvre, Département des Antiquités Grecques, Étrusques et Romaines MND 2047 (P 217). Photo Credit: Réunion des Musées Nationaux / Art Resource, NY.

Plate V. Mummy shroud for a young man in tempera on linen (185 cm H, 130 cm W); presumably from Memphis. The full and curly hair and beard of the deceased suggest a date of about 170–180 CE. He wears a long tunic with dark stripes and (above it) a white mantle. In his left hand he carries a funerary garland. He is accompanied by the Egyptian gods of the underworld, Osiris and the jackle-headed Anubis, who guides him tenderly. Now in Berlin, Staatliche Museen, Äegyptisches Museum und Papyrussammlung 11651. Photo Credit: Erich Lessing / Art Resource, NY.

Plate VI. "Dionysus mosaic" from Sepphoris, Syria Palaestina (formerly Judaea), dated ca. 200 CE. This apparently comes from a *triclinium*, or room for feasting, although the use of the building the mosaic decorated is not identified securely. The large mosaic includes these two panels, which depict Dionysus in a triumphal procession and a drunken Heracles (called Hercules by the Romans and identified by his club hanging in the upper left of the right-hand panel). Explanatory inscriptions are in Greek: "Procession" identifies the Dionysus panel, and "Drunkenness" the Heracles one. The unidentified building this decorated is situated only 40 m from a rabbinic court. Published by permission of Eric and Carol Meyers and the Excavations of Sepphoris, Israel.

CHAPTER 6

CHRISTIANS,

A NEW PEOPLE

Introduction

It may appear odd that this book on peoples of the Roman world includes the Christians, a group whose identity seems so obviously predicated on religion. But an important element of early Christians' self-identity has been the fact that they were defined by others as outsiders, sometimes expressed in ethnic terms. Thus Christians' view of themselves as marginal had some justification. As we shall see, at times both Roman authorities and Roman mobs targeted this monotheistic sect, whose true adherents refused to participate in most of the rituals shaping communal life in Rome, in other cities throughout the empire, and in the army. For centuries Christianity was considered an unlawful religion and Christians seen as being opposed to Romans. The conception even circulated that Christians were a "new race," as the second-century Christian text *Epistle to Diognetus* puts it (1.1). Such separatism was contested, as there were always claims that Christianity transcended race, social status, and gender (see Gal. 3:28), as well as political, geographical, and other limits. The use of ethnicity in competing formulations of Christian identity continued after the 313 Edict of Milan, when the emperor Constantine and his coruler Licinius recognized Christianity as a legitimate religion, and even in the works of individual authors. Eusebius, the church father who knew Constantine, generally presented Christianity as universal and triumphalist, but he also constructed Christians as a new race (*Ecclesiastical History* 1.4.4). This chapter thus allows us to explore the unfixed nature of ethnic and other identities in the Roman world as well as the tension between assimilation and opposition to it.

Sources

The evidence is problematic for an investigation of Christians, and especially a distinct Christian identity, before the Roman state began its first systematic persecution of Christians in 250 CE. Christian sources include the New Testament, which comprises the books of the Gospels, Acts of the Apostles, Paul's letters and other epistles, and Revelation, all dating within a century of Jesus' death. The Christian apologists, including Irenaeus of Lugdunum (modern Lyon, France), Clement of Alexandria, and Tertullian of Carthage, were writing primarily ca. 120–230 CE; their defenses of the "new" faith were often responses to anti-Christian adversaries whom they purport to quote in their texts. Also from this period are anonymous pieces that include some of the early martyr narratives (discussed later). Christian writings a century or so later were influenced by the Edict of Milan as well as by the immediately preceding events of the Diocletian "Great Persecution" (303–312/313). The 313 Edict of Milan, transmitted to us by its contemporaries Lactantius and Eusebius, officially granted Christians as well as others the right to observe whatever religion they preferred. Despite a few later official bans or restrictions on Christianity, the Edict of Milan and Constantine's favor were turning points in the history of Christianity, and perhaps also in Roman history. Henceforth Christianity became protected and advanced by the state, and all subsequent emperors were Christians with the exception of one, Julian (later named "the Apostate," r. 361–363; mentioned in Chapter 5 and depicted in Figure 20).

Christian and non-Christian authors provide mixed evidence for the growing religion. Christian sources from before 313 were usually written by individuals who were not part of Rome's elites; they often sound apologetic and defensive, expressing victimhood and persecution. Those dating to the Constantinian period sometimes reflect Christianity's changed circumstances by vilifying former persecutors and polytheistic rituals and religions. And, as a whole, Christian writers strove to distinguish their new religion from Judaism and polytheism; Christians from practitioners of other rites; and the authors' own beliefs from those of other Christians. Early Christian authors, in short, crafted their words carefully and deliberately, and their many voices and views make it impossible to trace any clear and direct development of Christianity. On the other hand, non-Christian sources for Christians and Christianity are surprisingly few, especially before the later third century, and the quotations or paraphrases of "pagans" that Christian apologists include only to refute them are themselves tendentious. As we shall see later, many non-Christian authors display confusion about the Christians, bolstering the contention that Christians were numerically and socially inconsequential until the mid-third century.

Identifying Early Christians

In contrast to "northern barbarians," Egyptians, and most other groups we have discussed in this book, few visual markers were associated with Christians even by hostile stereotyping. No art or artifacts can definitely be identified as Christian before about 200 CE, and visual ambiguity continued for another century. Early Christians shared Jews' aversion to icons (figured representations of the sacred; see Chapter 5) because of the Second Commandment, which Christians adopted along with the Old Testament. Some Christian signs were made merely by brief actions, or even by the refusal to act. Tertullian, for instance, enjoins believers to make the sign of the cross on their foreheads (rather than, e.g., on their chests, albeit on every possible occasion) and not to wear or decorate doorposts with wreaths during a city's festivals (Tertullian, *On the Garland* 3, 10): it is evident that neither practice would leave any trace. Pliny the Younger associates Christianity with a reluctance to buy meat from sacrificial victims (*Letters* 10.96; see 1 Cor. 8:7–10, Acts 15:29) – again, a symbolic refusal of particular action rather than a more obvious display. Epitaphs and personal belongings like rings did not openly proclaim Christian identity. Until the Edict of Milan, Christians could not have fixed and communally owned meeting halls. So long as Christianity was not officially permitted, clearly identifiable signs of the religion must have been shunned as drawing undue attention to those commissioning or exhibiting them. In sum, it may have been very hard to identify Christians by sight.

Numbers of Christians

Christian statements often suggest that Christianity was a rapidly expanding religion with many adherents; for example, Paul writes, "your [Christian] faith is proclaimed in the whole world" (Rom. 1:8; before 60 CE). But rhetorical analysis of such assertions, and the confusion and general indifference of non-Christian sources about early Christianity, indicate that absolute numbers of Christians were not considerable until the third and early fourth centuries despite significant growth for the sect. Keith Hopkins has plausibly estimated (1998, 195) that in 40 CE only some one thousand people, most in Judaea and Syria, believed in the divinity of Jesus (the number includes practicing Jews). By 100 CE the number of Christians had grown to perhaps seven thousand, or 0.01 percent of the total population of the empire; by 200 CE, to two hundred thousand, or some 0.035 percent of the total population; by 250 CE and the beginning of state-organized persecutions, to 1.1 million, about 2 percent of the population. By about 300 CE, Christians may have numbered 6 million, or 10 percent of the empire's population, a remarkable rise given earlier figures (Fig. 60). Although these numbers can only be rough, including the estimated general population of 60 million at Rome's height in the second century, the proportions are suggestive. For over two centuries after Christianity emerged, it seems, Christians must have had strong motivation to convert others so as to swell their numbers. But by most criteria new converts would have been indistinguishable from their non-Christian kin and neighbors. Christians' relatively low numbers and resulting lack of a noticeable presence seem to have encouraged their own self-definition by various means. One of these was by identifying themselves as a "new race," justifying our including them in this book on peoples of the Roman world.

Christianity's Earliest History

The religion centered on Jesus as the Messiah (or Christ, "the anointed one") developed first in the villages of Judaea, where the charismatic

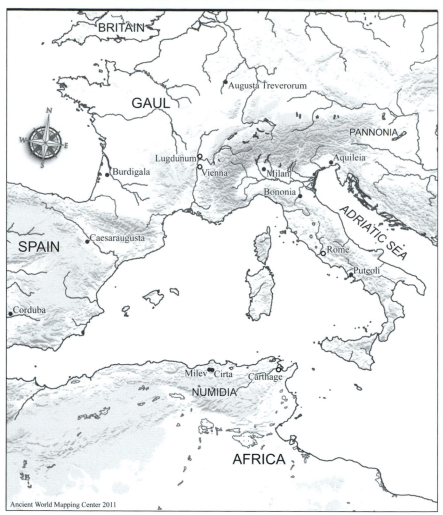

60. Map with early Christian martyrdom sites (before 250 CE) and other locales important to Christians before the rule of Constantine. Martyrdom sites are noted with a circle (○) rather than the dot (●) used for other cities. Note that with the Third Jewish Revolt (132–135 CE) Judaea was renamed Syria Palaestina and Jerusalem was renamed Colonia Aelia Capitolina. Map © 2011, Ancient World Mapping Center (www.unc.edu/awmc). Used by permission.

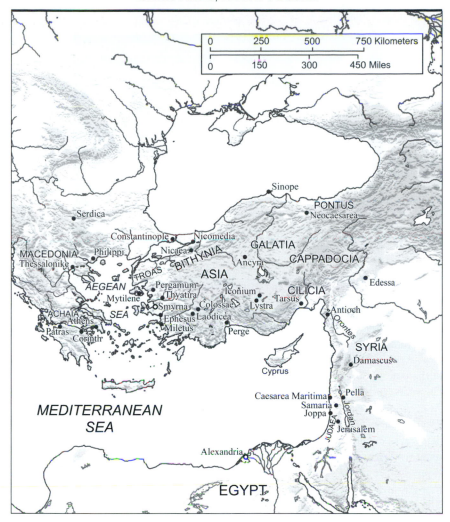

Jesus himself had lived and died; but within a generation it had been transformed into a more distinct and urban phenomenon that attracted shopkeepers, artisans, and others with some leisure, resources, and education. At first individual Christians, and (more influentially) individuals like Paul who proselytized for the new Christian belief, traveled to, settled in, and converted others in cities in Syria and the Greek East and in Rome; by the later second century Christians are also known to have existed in cities in Gaul and elsewhere in the West (see later,

61. Tombstone of the Christian Licinia Amias, one of the oldest identifiable Christian inscriptions (perhaps dating to ca. 200 CE). This was found in the area of the Vatican necropolis in Rome. It combines Greek and Latin, as well as novel Christian symbols and Roman phrases conventional in polytheistic epitaphs. At the top we see a wreath of victory. The now fragmentary inscription reads: "To the Spirits of the Dead. Fish of the Living. For Licinia Amias, who well deserves it; she lived ...." The D M, the dedication to the Spirits of the Dead, is a traditional element in Roman epitaphs. "Fish of the Living," however, is a Christian expression for those who were reborn through baptism. The Christian concept is strengthened by the representation of fish and an anchor, both Christian symbols. The tombstone is now in the Museo Nazionale Romano, Terme di Diocleziano, inv. 67646. Published by permission of the Ministero per i Beni e le Attività Culturali – Soprintendenza Speciale per i Beni Archeologici di Roma.

and Fig. 61). There was no distinct Christian "homeland" or geographic identity, although in the fourth century Jerusalem and the "Holy Land" became celebrated as the cradle of Christianity. Initially, the Roman authorities considered Christianity as simply a sect of Judaism, like the Samaritans, Essenes, and other groups active in Judaea at the time, and its adherents enjoyed whatever legal privileges were then accorded the Jews, including the right to worship their monotheistic religion (see Chapter 5). Pontius Pilate, the Roman governor of Judaea from about 26 to 36 CE, at first refused to hear the complaints against Jesus, agreeing to preside at Jesus' trial only after the Sanhedrin, local Jewish judges, handed Jesus over to him on charges of sedition against Rome. Jesus was crucified around 33, but the Gospels strongly suggest that Pilate neither was convinced that he constituted a threat nor believed his alleged claim to be a king. The ambiguous relationship between Romans and early Christianity was thus manifest even before the religion became a distinct one (see subsequent discussion).

Perhaps around 36 CE occurred the conversion of the Jewish Saul of Tarsus, Cilicia (in south-central modern Turkey), who was thereafter known as (Saint) Paul. Originally hostile to the new movement, which was already spreading outside of Judaea, Paul was converted to Christianity while traveling on the road to Damascus in Syria on his way to persecute Christians. Over the next twenty years his missionary journeys took him to Syrian Antioch, Jerusalem, Cyprus, Asia, Corinth, Ephesus, and Thessalonica, among other cities. Paul had been well educated in the Greek educational system (see Chapter 3) and was thus persuasive and literate. His craft as a tent maker enabled him to find work wherever he traveled. Furthermore, he was a Roman citizen, with legal rights that he invoked when arrested for questioning during a riot in Jerusalem in the late 50s. Around 60 Paul was sent to Rome for trial, for as a Roman citizen he had appealed to "Caesar" (the emperor) and had the right to be heard by Rome's supreme authority. Following a period of house arrest in the capital city for two years (Acts 28:16–30), he was released. But he was arrested again and eventually beheaded in Rome sometime in the later years of Nero's reign.

In the meantime, however, Paul, and others, had begun to convert non-Christians to the new religion, and to differentiate Christianity from Judaism. One Christian distinction was that converts to Christianity did not have to undergo Jewish conversion requirements such as ritual immersion, acceptance of the Torah, and male circumcision (see Acts 15). The followers of Jesus were further differentiated from other Jews and provincials by the new name "Christians," which was first used in Syrian

Antioch, where Paul had stayed for many years (Acts 11:26). Even so, around the middle of the first century those who wanted to call themselves Christians, or who were thus called by others, perhaps numbered less than a thousand, as already observed. They must have been hard to recognize, especially by Roman authorities. Although antagonism between Christians and Jews may have been increasing (see Acts 6:8 – 8:1), conflict among and against Rome's peoples was much more obvious in Britain (see Chapter 2), Judaea and Alexandria (see Chapter 5), and elsewhere.

The Earliest Roman Testimony about Christians

The little evidence we have from early non-Christian sources generally confirms the lack of a clear identity for Christians in the first and early second centuries. Pliny the Younger, Suetonius, and Tacitus, whose relevant works date ca. 110–130, all exhibit confusion about who the Christians were. Suetonius reports that Claudius expelled Jews from Rome because they were "constantly making trouble, with Chrestus as instigator" (Suetonius, *Life of Claudius* 25.4; see Chapter 5). This passage has many problems: it lacks chronological context; it speaks of *Chrestus* (usually understood as *Christus* or Jesus, the anointed one) as though he were still alive; and it apparently conflates Jews and Christians. Claudius' "expulsion" is often dated to 49 CE, and Suetonius' notation suggests that confusion about Christians and Jews lasted into the second century.

Yet earlier attempts had been made to single out Christians, and some of Suetonius' contemporaries display a better understanding of the religion. Christians were scapegoated by Nero (r. 54–68) for the Great Fire of Rome in 64 CE, which seriously damaged most of the city. Writing around 117 CE, Tacitus holds that Nero fixed the blame on those

> whom, hated because of their crimes, the [Roman] crowd called
> "Chrestians" (*Chrestianos*). The originator of that name, Christ

(*Christus*), had been executed by the governor Pontius Pilate during Tiberius' rule. The pernicious sect, repressed for the time being, had broken out again not only in Judaea, the origin of this evil, but even throughout the City.... And so first were seized those who confessed the faith; then on their testimony a huge crowd was convicted, not so much for the charge of the fire as because of hatred for the human race. (*Annals* 15.44)

Here, the Christians are said to be set apart in part by their "hatred for the human race" (*odio humani generis*), a point that resonates with later Christian self-definitions as a new race, or at least as outsiders. (In Suetonius' *Life of Nero* 16.2, the biographer comments that under Nero "Christians, a race of men (*genus hominum*) marked by exceptional and deadly superstition," were punished.) Tacitus speaks of a "huge multitude" being convicted in the aftermath of the fire of 64, but this cannot refer merely to Christians. The rhetorical exaggeration fits other hyperbole the historian uses when he imputes death and devastation to imperial actions. Moreover, at this time Rome probably contained only a few hundred Christians. They met in houses in small groups, and they would have been difficult to locate in the turmoil that followed the conflagration.

If indeed many individuals perished in Nero's reprisals after the fire, some were surely Jews or others swept up in the hysteria. But our information is deficient; we do not even know if the deaths included (Saints) Peter and Paul, although both were executed in Rome during Nero's last years. Tacitus' passage relating to the Christians is part of a larger section of the *Annals* focusing on Nero and the city of Rome (*Annals* 15.38–44). He concludes his account with apparent sympathy for the Christians, "who had been seized for the savagery of one man," denigrating Nero both for staging unspeakable tortures in the "Circus of Gaius and Nero" in the imperial Vatican gardens and for appearing there as a charioteer. This was later the site of Constantine's St. Peter's Basilica. Constantine chose to locate this basilica, one of the first publicly sponsored Christian churches, over what may have been a second-century

(CE) memorial tomb to Peter, whom many believed had been killed during Nero's persecution staged in the neighboring Circus (see Fig. 53). But the fact remains that when Nero scapegoated Christians in 64 CE he was targeting a small and amorphous group in Rome.

The subsequent three Jewish revolts, which spanned from 66 to 135, must have differentiated Christians more clearly from Jews even as they scattered the inhabitants of Judaea and resulted in the deaths of countless Jews in that province and elsewhere. The First Jewish Revolt of 66–70, which resulted in the destruction of the Temple of Jerusalem, forced the Jews to rethink many of their rituals and central tenets and dispersed Judaea's population (see Chapter 5). The Third Jewish Revolt, only two generations later (132–135), may have scattered the religious groups even farther apart. As we saw in Chapter 5, Bar Kokhba was a messianic leader who aimed to rebuild the Temple and restore Judaism. Neither aspiration could have attracted Christians, who must have tried to distance themselves from the growing insurrection. Justin Martyr, a Christian apologist and martyr (d. ca. 165; see later), reports that during the revolt Bar Kokhba singled out Christians for torture unless they denied Jesus Christ and uttered blasphemy (Justin Martyr, *First Apology* 31.6). Whether or not this story is true, it emphasizes the significance of distinctions being drawn between Christians and Jews by the time Justin Martyr wrote.

Pliny's and Trajan's Letters about Christians in Bithynia

In the meantime, however, an important precedent had been established, even if somewhat haphazardly, for official Roman dealings with Christians. This was set in an exchange of letters between the emperor Trajan and Pliny the Younger (*Letters* 10.96–97), after the latter had been appointed in 111–112 CE to oversee the province of Bithynia (Bithynia roughly corresponds to northwestern modern Turkey). Pliny wrote to Trajan for advice about what to do in trials of Christians, into which he had been brought as the emperor's representative. He confesses ignorance about permissible charges and various circumstances, such as the age of the defendants and the degree of their repentance and renunciation of Christianity. In particular, he wonders whether mere identification as Christian (*nomen* [*Christianum*]) or the misdeeds associated with being Christian (*flagitia cohaerentia nomini*) should be punished. He then details for Trajan what he has done so far in the trials, including those begun after an anonymous pamphlet denounced numerous people as Christians: Pliny oversaw repeated interrogations and tested the accused by having them pray to the gods and offer incense and wine before a statue of Trajan, and also by forcing them to curse Christ. He deplores the obstinacy of those who refuse to renounce their beliefs, saying that their intransigence and inflexible stubbornness ought to be punished. He reports that some professing Christianity described their religious practices, which included singing a hymn to Christ as to a god, binding themselves by oath to ethical behavior, and eating ordinary food together. Pliny ends his request for advice by stressing that "many" were endangered, and that this "superstition" had spread to cities, villages, and farms (Pliny, *Letters* 10.96). Again we can see a Roman fear of being overwhelmed by others.

More important, however, is Trajan's measured reply, which subsequently had the force of law. Responding "It is not possible to establish any general rule," Trajan firmly states that Christians should not be sought out; if someone is indicted and convicted of being Christian, he should be punished; but if he proves he is not a Christian by worshipping Roman gods, then he should be pardoned. In any case, anonymous accusations cannot be admitted as valid (Pliny, *Letters* 10.97). Trajan's refusal to accept anonymous accusations is enlightened – as he himself remarks, implicitly contrasting it to Domitian's frightful era (for example, see Chapter 5 on Domitian's test for circumcision) – and he deliberately rejects seeking out Christians. For the next 140 years or so Rome's central government followed this hands-off policy. But as Trajan makes no mention of crimes (*flagitia*) or any kind of behavior at all, his reply implies that punishment is warranted merely by the confirmation of a Christian identity, that is to say, by the acknowledgment of being Christian. His response apparently opened the way to locally initiated persecutions of Christians for more than a century and underpinned the three systematic Christian persecutions of the emperors Decius (250–251), Valerian (257–260), and Diocletian and other tetrarchs (303–312/313).

Christian Martyrdoms

Our evidence for Christian persecutions comes primarily from Christian texts, many called *Acta* (or Acts) of individual or grouped martyrs. These stress the courageous steadfastness of Christians who refused to sacrifice before images of Roman gods and/or the emperor, thus professing or bearing witness to their Christian faith, and who were then accordingly punished. The dehumanizing tortures and deaths of the martyrs, described in these Acts, Eusebius' *Ecclesiastical History*, and other tracts and letters that circulated to different Christian communities, played a major part in the self-definition of Christians, who could see and portray themselves as an oppressed minority. The narratives focus on individual martyrs and their arrest, imprisonment, torture, and death, not on precipitating incidents or underlying socioeconomic circumstances. The martyr Acts, and other early Christian writings like the second-century *Epistle to Diognetus* cited at the beginning of this chapter, are often anonymous and lacking geographical context. At times they are preserved in different versions, and many extant texts date significantly later than the events they discuss. They cannot be considered documentary evidence: their particulars often lack historicity.

The early martyr narratives do, however, illuminate the spread of Christianity, as they are set first in Asia and Rome, then by the latter second century in Gaul and North Africa, and by the third century in Egypt as well (see Fig. 60). In the early fourth century another group of Acts is set in Pannonia, showing Christianity's impact there by that date. The Acts portray men and women, rich and poor, slave and free, and, until the *Constitutio Antoniniana* of 212 CE granted Roman citizenship to free inhabitants in the empire, provincial subjects as well as Roman citizens.

Although the tortures the Christians endured were despicable, the actual numbers of those martyred are not high and the sites of known martyrdoms not ubiquitous in the empire.

One of the earliest martyrs was Ignatius, bishop of Syrian Antioch, who died before 117. He and two others were condemned *ad bestias*, or to the wild-beast fights in the arena, which has become an iconic image of Christian martyrdom. After condemnation but before his death, Ignatius and his companions traveled northwest from Antioch through Asia (via Smyrna [modern Izmir, Turkey] and Troas [modern northwest Turkey]) and Macedonia, across the Adriatic Sea, and finally to Rome. Ignatius' relative freedom of movement, like Pliny the Younger's near-contemporaneous puzzlement about Christians in his province of Bithynia, reveals a general lack of interest in Christians and their beliefs on the part of Roman authorities. Around 155 Polycarp and eleven others were martyred in Smyrna, and around 165 Justin Martyr and six others were martyred in Rome. In 177 untold numbers perished in Lugdunum and Vienna (Vienne, France), with one martyr, Sanctus, having done nothing more than state that he was a Christian (*Christianus sum*, "I am a Christian"; see Pliny's exchange with Trajan, previously cited). In 180 seven men and five women were executed in (the unlocated) Scillium in North Africa after a trial in which one, Speratus, rejected the "empire of this world" and swore allegiance to the "lord who is the emperor of kings and of all nations" (thus expressing a universalist understanding of Christianity). Around 200 the deaths in Carthage of some six martyrs, whose punishments involved being "thrown to the beasts," are famous from the moving narrative known as the *Acts* or *Passion of Perpetua and Felicitas*. Claiming to contain the very words of Perpetua, one of the martyrs, it poignantly displays a woman's point of view; furthermore, Perpetua's Christian slave, Felicitas, who gives birth in prison, is portrayed very sympathetically. In the early 200s, in Alexandria, a mother and daughter, Marcella and Potamiaena, were tortured and killed for being Christian.

When martyrdoms were not simply the result of mob violence – like the horrendous deaths of four Christians killed during widening general riots in Alexandria early in 249 – the *Acta* and other martyr narratives corroborate Roman authorities' generally hands-off approach until the Decian and subsequent state-organized persecutions. We usually do not hear of specific charges for arrests, although high Roman officials often appeared at the trials and executions. The governor of Asia, Lucius Statius Quadratus, was at the wild-beast fights in Smyrna in 155 and repeatedly offered the martyrs the opportunity to recant and be released. The urban prefect Rusticus oversaw the trials involving Justin Martyr in Rome around 165. At the final trials at Lugdunum in 177 the Roman governor was present, and he wrote to the emperor to ascertain the appropriate treatment of Roman citizens who confessed Christianity. (They were to be executed by the sword.) The governor of Africa, Publius Virgellius Saturninus, presided in 180 at Scillium, where the reported circumstances lack the mob hysteria marking the other martyrdoms. The prefect of Egypt presided over the trial of Potamiaena and her mother. In general in the martyr narratives, the various Roman authorities repeatedly urge Christians arraigned before them to disavow their Christian beliefs and save themselves. This perhaps indicates a general promotion of assimilation on the part of Rome.

The Statewide Persecutions of 250–251, 257–260, and 303–312/313

In drawing attention to Christian heroism the early martyrdom tales do not differ significantly from those associated with the statewide, systematic persecutions initiated by the emperors Decius, Valerian, and Diocletian. These later persecutions, which seem ultimately to have involved Roman officials going door-to-door in an attempt to force all Romans to sacrifice to the gods (i.e., to remain within the polytheistic state religion), clearly distinguished who was Christian. They have also been credited with increasing the numbers of Christians from about

2 percent of the empire's total population ca. 250 CE to 10 percent some fifty years later.

The emperor Decius' persecution, begun in 250, seems to have been triggered by the demand that all Romans participate in sacrifices for his own accession. Egyptian papyri record some forty "certificates of sacrifice" that document individuals' participation in rituals including prayers, libation, sacrifice, and eating of the sacrificial offerings. The papryi complement Christian sources that report events in Alexandria, Smyrna, Neocaesarea (in Cappadocia, now central Turkey), Carthage, Spain, and Rome. Many Christians apparently complied with Decius' order in some way, except in Rome itself. In some cases one member of a family is certified as sacrificing for the whole family. Relatively few Christians seem to have been physically harmed before Decius' death halted the persecution in 251. But the persecution left behind lingering questions about what to do with the many Christians who had recanted, or formally denied, their Christianity. For decades Africa and other areas in the west experienced profound struggles among Christian leaders and communities over whether such apostates should be allowed to obtain forgiveness for renouncing their faith and thus be readmitted to communion.

The persecution initiated in 257 by Valerian (r. 253–260) was aimed more at individuals in the upper levels of the Church's hierarchy. All Romans were supposed to acknowledge Roman religious rituals before a Roman official, but Cyprian, the bishop of Carthage who was swept up into the persecution, reports also that, upon refusal, "bishops, presbyters, and deacons [the three highest-ranking local Church administrators] are to be put to death immediately; senators, high-ranking officials, and Roman equestrians are to lose their status and their goods, and if they still continue to be Christians, they are to be executed; matrons are to lose their property and be sent into exile; and all members of the imperial household who have confessed either earlier or now will have their goods confiscated and they themselves be sent in chains to the imperial estates" (Cyprian, *Letters* 80.1.2). Furthermore, church property was confiscated and access to Christian cemeteries restricted. The Christian sources cite Carthage, Alexandria, Rome, and Numidia as the settings for the atrocities they detail. At Valerian's death in 260, however, his son and co-emperor, Gallienus, rescinded the orders and may have even allowed Christians to reclaim their confiscated property. The history of Valerian's persecution discloses the Church's proliferation of its hierarchy, its inclusion of highly placed individuals, its control of property, and the use of cemeteries as holy places. Nonetheless, this tighter organization and greater financial power were met with general state indifference to Christians and Christianity for the next few generations.

In 303 Diocletian initiated the third and longest statewide persecution: it was to last about ten years, until 312/313. At least at its beginning it was operative throughout the Roman empire, which was by now divided officially into over a hundred provinces ultimately supervised by two eastern and western emperors, Galerius and Diocletian. (Diocletian, in the West, was the supreme leader, and his new organization of Rome's provinces remained in force after his retirement in 305.) The third state persecution, often called "The Great Persecution," terribly affected communities, families, and Church property. It first targeted Christian leaders and then spread to all Christians. Many recanted their faith and sacrificed to Roman gods, but there were also many who willingly chose martyrdom. Christian texts such as the New Testament were seized, highlighting the established significance of sacred writings to the religion. Rapidly changing political and military events during these years, however, made for uneven enforcement of the persecution. The eastern part of the empire experienced more turmoil than the western, for the eastern emperor Galerius was notoriously brutal in his actions against the Christians. Ironically, when Galerius finally contracted a gruesome disease, in 311 he issued an Edict of Toleration asking all, even Christians, to pray for his "safety" and that of the state and themselves. His edict even admitted that the policy of persecution had failed. But when he died that same year his successor, Maximinus Daia, resumed the savage persecution. It was officially stopped only by the Edict of Milan in 313.

Constantine the Great

Among the many competing for power after Diocletian's retirement in 305 was Constantine, who in 306 began his military push to become the successor of the western emperor. In 312, at the Milvian Bridge north of Rome, he overcame one rival, Maxentius, reputedly with divine help vouchsafed him by his vision of a cross and the words "In this, conquer." Among the steps he took to defeat his many competitors was allying himself with a claimant to the rule of the East, Licinius. Among their first joint actions in 313 was the aforementioned Edict of Milan, which legitimized Christianity and all other religions, allowing everyone in the Roman state to worship however he or she wished. Around the same time Constantine began openly to support Christian communities and its hierarchy, and to interest himself personally in matters of Christian doctrine (such as the question of whether Christ was equal or subordinate to God). He himself was baptized on his deathbed in 337, having postponed this sacrament to the last possible minute, as did many at the time. He died peacefully in Nicomedia (modern Izmit, Turkey), near the new imperial capital he had established at the city of Byzantium; in his honor it had been renamed Constantinople ("City of Constantine"; see Chapter 3 and Fig. 31).

Before his death in 337 Constantine had reunited the Roman empire politically – although it was to split irreparably into separate eastern and western units by the end of the fourth century – and it is sometimes said that he also wanted to unify it under one religion, Christianity. This purported aim points to the existence, from the start, of many competing understandings of Christ, God, liturgy, and the power of the Church hierarchy, as well as other matters. Such variations, some of which were known as heresies or schisms as early as the second century CE, would continue to divide Christians and even pit them against one another. Although Constantine himself participated in the gathering of Christian bishops in Nicaea in 325 that resulted in the Nicene Creed – now part of many Christian services including the Roman-rite Mass – significant numbers of Christians never accepted the Nicene Creed's statement of the divinity of Jesus. Other Christian controversies arose or resurfaced as well. Nonetheless, the 313 Edict of Milan, Constantine's support of Christianity, and his own baptism as a Christian all changed the identity of Christians in the Roman world.

Some Christians on Christian Identity

Christian texts did not aim to document the legalities of Roman–Christian interaction but to edify Christians and non-Christians about the faith. They illuminate the formation of Christian identity, for they were circulated, responded to, and altered, and they influenced other Christian writings; they cannot, however, be seen to have a consistent or lineally developing set of beliefs. In one of the earliest of the *Acta*, the *Martyrdom of Polycarp* (usually thought to have been written around 160 CE) that describes the horrifying martyrdoms in Smyrna ca. 155, the anonymous author speaks of the "nobility of the God-loving and God-fearing race of Christians." Other Christian writers similarly use what Denise Buell (2005) has called "ethnic reasoning," or "ethnoracial imagery," as they propose a common race for themselves that was different from other races. In part the writers were drawing on long-established notions of ethnicity that emphasized religion as an essential component, as we saw in the fifth-century BCE definition of Greekness by Herodotus (Greeks' shared blood or common descent, shared language, shared way of life, and shared religious practices: *Histories* 8.144.2; see Chapter 1).

Various Christian writings imagined Christians as having a common descent and blood, sometimes the blood shed by Jesus on the cross or the essence of the preexistent Logos ("the Word") responsible for the creation of all humanity (e.g., Clement of Alexandria, *Exhortation to the Greeks* 1.6.4; early third century). The First Epistle of Peter, for example, holds that Christians become "God's people" regardless of individuals' origins in "Pontus, Galatia, Cappadocia, Asia, and Bithynia" (1 Peter 2:10 and 1 Peter 1:1, ca. 100 CE). Such concepts helped form for the

Christians an "ethnic" identity that was fundamentally tied to belief and faith.

In many cases a Christian "ethnicity" was contrasted to those of the Greeks and the Jews so as to distinguish Christians from what they were claimed *not* to be, despite the fact that at least the earliest Christians had been converts from Judaism and polytheism. In various arguments, such as those of the mid-second-century Justin Martyr's *Dialogue with Trypho* (e.g., 123.1, 1.130.3), Christians claimed that their race was actually the true, spiritual Israel, and thus more ancient and worthy of respect than the race of the Jews. As Eusebius puts it, "only among the Christians ... can the manner of religion that was Abraham's actually be found in practice" (Eusebius, *Ecclesiastical History* 1.4.14). At the same time, however, some Christian writings also allowed for the incorporation of all peoples into Christianity, at which point they would become part of this new – but primordial – race. The belief that Christianity is "the Church from the nations" is particularly prominent in the works of Eusebius and widespread now among some Christians.

We cannot adjudicate the validity of such claims, nor should we. But we can see both that some Christians consciously positioned themselves among the peoples of the Roman world and that there was never uniformity or unanimity among those identified as Christian. In this latter view, the Christians are analogous to other "peoples" of Rome and to the Romans themselves. Our literary and material evidence, formulaic and stereotypical though it often is, reveals upon examination myriad differences. It urges us to resist generalizations about Christians and other groups identifiable in the Roman empire. Furthermore, the investigation of Christians in the first three centuries of the Empire reveals to us the tension in the Roman world between assimilation and resistance, the struggle to forge an identity in Rome, and the many ways of asserting individual and group distinctiveness.

SUGGESTED FURTHER READING

Brown, P. 1971. *The World of Late Antiquity from Marcus Aurelius to Muhammad.* London: Thames and Hudson.

Buell, D. K. 2005. *Why This New Race: Ethnic Reasoning in Early Christianity*. New York: Columbia University Press.

Clark, E. A., Richardson, H., et al. (eds.). 1996. *Women and Religion: The Original Sourcebook of Women in Christian Thought*. New rev. and expanded ed. San Francisco, CA: HarperSanFrancisco.

De Ste. Croix, G. E. M. 1954. "Aspects of the 'Great' Persecution." *Harvard Theological Review* 47: 75–113.

Dehandschutter, B. 2007. *Polycarpiana: Studies on Martyrdom and Persecution in Early Christianity. Collected Essays*. Leuven: University Press.

Donfried, K. P., and Richardson, P. (eds.) *Judaism and Christianity in First-Century Rome*. Grand Rapids, MI: Eerdmans.

Ehrman, B. D. (ed.). 1999. *After the New Testament: A Reader in Early Christianity*. New York: Oxford University Press. (Chap. 3.8 contains a translation of the *Passion of Perpetua and Felicitas*.)

Hopkins, K. 1998. "Christian Number and Its Implications." *Journal of Early Christian Studies* 6.2: 185–226.

http://earlychristianwritings.com/index.html. A site for information about early Christian writings, from ca. 50 CE to 250. Links take you to translations and commentary; at times the documents can be found even in the original language. *Epistle to Diognetus* is here in two translations, for example (listed as *Epistle of Mathetes to Diognetus*), as are the works of Justin Martyr and Tertullian.

http://www.tertullian.org/rpearse/eusebius/works.htm. A list of editions and translation of the works of Eusebius, with links.

Jacobs, A. S. 2004. *Remains of the Jews: The Holy Land and Christian Empire in Late Antiquity*. Stanford, CA: Stanford University Press.

Johnson, A. P. 2006. *Ethnicity and Argumentation in Eusebius' Praeparatio evangelica*. Oxford Early Christian Studies. Oxford: Oxford University Press.

Lieu, J. M. 2002. *Neither Jew Nor Greek? Constructing Early Christianity*. Edinburgh: T&T Clark.

Lieu, J. M. 2004. *Christian Identity in the Jewish and Graeco-Roman World*. Oxford: Oxford University Press.

Macmullen, R., and Lane, E. N. 1992. *Paganism and Christianity, 100–425 C.E.: A Sourcebook*. Minneapolis, MN: Fortress Press.

Meeks, W. A. 2003. *The First Urban Christians: The Social World of the Apostle Paul*. New Haven, CT: Yale University Press.

Musurillo, H. 1972. *The Acts of the Christian Martyrs*. Oxford: Clarendon Press.

Noy, D. 2000. *Foreigners at Rome: Citizens and Strangers*. London: Duckworth.

Rousseau, J. J., and Arav, R. 1995. *Jesus and His World: An Archaeological and Cultural Dictionary*. Minneapolis, MN: Augsburg Fortress Press.

Salisbury, J. E. 1997. *Perpetua's Passion: The Death and Memory of a Young Roman Woman*. New York: Routledge.

Sanders, E. P. (ed.). 1980 –. *Jewish and Christian Self-Definition*. 3 vols. Philadelphia: Fortress Press.

Selinger, R. 2002. *The Mid-Third Century Persecutions of Decius and Valerian*. Frankfurt am Main: Peter Lang GmbH.

Whittaker, M. 1984. *Jews and Christians: Graeco-Roman Views*. Cambridge Commentaries on Writings of the Jewish and Christian World 200 BC to AD 200, vol. 6. Cambridge: Cambridge University Press.

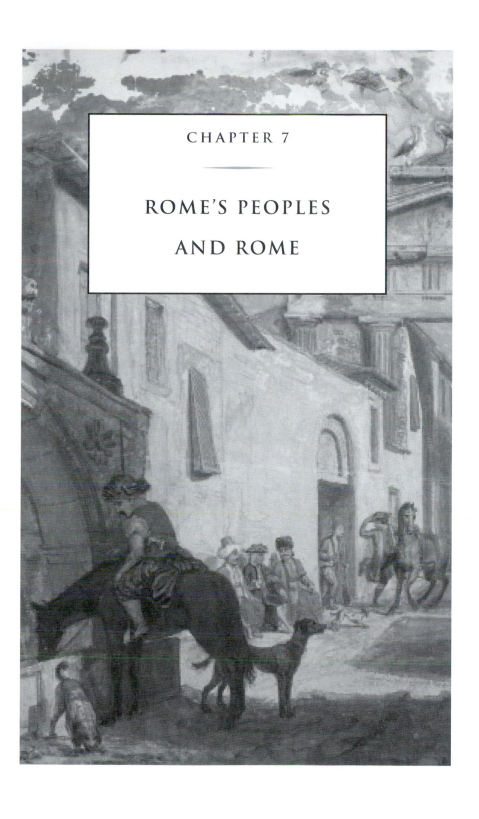

CHAPTER 7

ROME'S PEOPLES
AND ROME

A Typical Roman Family of the
Mid-Third Century CE?

Outside the small city of Sulmo (now Sulmone) in central Italy, Murranus and Decria, apparently husband and wife, erected a large tomb-stone around the middle of the third century CE. Its lengthy inscription laments, in ornate poetic language, the deaths of their children, Primigenius, Severus, Pudens, Castus, Lucilla, and Potestas (whose Latin names loosely translate as "Firstborn," "Solemn," "Modest," "Chaste," "Little Light," and "Power"); it then entrusts the care of the tomb to a grandchild, a boy called Thiasus (Greek for "reveler"). As is common with long Roman epitaphs, the inscription assumes different voices and audiences in its forty-eight lines. Thiasus is enjoined to tell anyone who might inquire that the tomb was installed by his grandfather Murranus, "for misfortunes themselves teach even barbarians to write pitiable things." And in the voice of Murranus the text asks passersby for forgiveness "if any error has escaped me, a barbarian man, Pannonian by birth, undone by many ills and evils." Murranus' diffident words show his awareness of the long-standing stereotype of the northerner as despicably uncultured: by describing himself as a "barbarian ..., Pannonian by birth," he assumes some of the formulaic identity of northerners. On the other hand, he is not identified as a soldier, bodyguard, veteran, or the like in this text, our only information about him and his family, so is not presented as admirably warlike. His inscription emphasizes the unfixed nature of identity in the Roman world. Was Murranus representative of northern peoples, at least in the third century CE? What does Thiasus' Greek name imply, especially in the context of the other, traditionally Roman family names like "Firstborn" (Primigenius)? Is this family typically "Roman"?

Sources and Their Limitations for an Understanding of Cultural Transformation

Turning to images, literature, and texts like the one by Murranus, this book has aimed to bring into relief some of the various peoples who were essential to the Roman world and helped to shape it. In every case the peoples we have examined were not a clearly defined or demarcated group, even if they had come under Roman control through a discrete military action such as Caesar's conquest of the Gauls (58–51 BCE). Even Egypt – which was more or less usurped by Augustus – has been shown as ethnically complex and exerting wide-spreading influence in the form of the Egyptian cults that proliferated far beyond the province. We have also explored depictions of Rome's varied peoples, in their own words and in the words of others. It should now be clear that the words of satirists or other critics cannot reflect any essential realities about any one group or people: such evidence is often inconsistent, self-contradictory, and standardized. Nor can such information represent all Romans or all of any group: we simply have little to no evidence for how the great majority in Rome's world thought, reacted, and acted. Furthermore, images commissioned by the state for the public, or by individuals for their tombstones, may be snapshots in time reflecting only a portion of a community. In the end we cannot truly know any one person's experience as a Roman or as one of Rome's peoples. We cannot tell the difference between assimilation, acculturation, and accommodation, or between resistance and simple lack of contact. On the other hand, the vast and shifting diversity of Rome's population and of Romans' experiences should now be clear, and with what evidence we do have we can venture some conclusions.

Rome's phenomenal geopolitical growth in the Republic and early Empire, together with heightened social and political mobility in the late Republic and Empire, led to continual change that included cultural transformations. The process was never straightforward or uncontested, and it often differed between ruling elite and ruled, Romans and provincials. It also differed among different peoples. The challenges involved in identifying Rome's peoples echo those associated with defining the Romans themselves. But the ongoing, sometimes violent negotiation of Rome and its constituent groups was essential to Rome's own identity as a people who forged their particular history through military and political prowess.

Rome and Northerners and Greeks

Rome's reactions to northerners and Greeks, the earliest groups encountered in this book, may reflect two sides of the Graeco-Roman dichotomy of barbarism versus civilization. With respect to peoples to its north Rome vacillated between outright hostility and apparent satisfaction that these "barbarians" wished to be assimilated because of a desire to obtain Roman civilization (Pliny the Elder's *humanitas*) and citizenship. Almost all our evidence comes from the Romans themselves and frequently in the form of broad stereotype. Romans self-identified with the northerners' admirable fighting qualities, and perhaps also with their supposed lack of guile, even as they prided themselves on superior Roman political cohesion and military discipline.

But in comparing themselves to Greeks Romans often noted their own cultural inadequacy, which would reduce them to "barbarians" according to traditional criteria of language and culture. Beginning in earnest in the mid-Republic, elite and other Romans began to absorb Greek culture and "Greece," fundamentally transforming Roman literature, art and architecture, education, and aesthetics. The Greek language was used for Roman administrative and literary purposes. By the late third century BCE, for example, Fabius Pictor represented Rome at the Panhellenic shrine of Delphi and wrote in Greek the earliest prose history of Rome. Many later Roman authors, including emperors, also wrote in Greek. Greek sculpture, architecture, and other visual arts heavily influenced Roman endeavors in these fields; in turn, by the second century

CE visual arts in the Greek East were influenced by Roman materials, methods, and aesthetics. Criticism of "Greeks" and Greek sophistication reveals sporadic Roman anxiety about such cultural change, however, and Roman pride in their military superiority over the Greeks allowed them to offset feelings of intellectual and artistic inferiority.

The long histories of northerners' and Greeks' interactions with Romans mean that by the second century CE we cannot disentangle "Romans" from these other two groups. There had been too many massive enslavements in the north and in the Greek-speaking East, and too much subsequent manumission; too many northern and "Greek" men forced or induced to serve in Rome's military; too wide a diffusion of Greek literature and aesthetics; and too many individuals from local ruling elites coopted to participate in Roman administration and rule. The mixture seems indissoluble. On a lower scale, we have the unique third-century CE inscription of the "Pannonian barbarian" Murranus and his family from rural central Italy. But similar ethnic and cultural indeterminacy characterizes Antoninus Pius, the mid-second-century CE emperor whose family hailed from Nemausus, as well as Philopappus and Balbilla, from Commagene and Athens a generation earlier, not to mention the paradoxical Favorinus, the Gaul who spoke Greek and who quarreled with the emperor yet was allowed to live.

Rome and Egyptians

Integration into Rome's ruling elite never occurred for two other Roman peoples we have investigated, the Egyptians and the Jews, and the history of the Christians is even more divergent. This makes more difficult the task of gauging assimilation and resistance, acceptance and intolerance. Furthermore, the complexity of these peoples' interactions with Rome is underscored by the facts that Egyptians and Jews used Greek in their dealings with the Roman state and that Greek was the common language for early Christian texts. "Rome" was never uniform, nor were the peoples it encountered.

Egypt, subjugated by Rome only at the end of the Republic, was long kept separate from the rest of the Roman world other than its annual, essential tribute of grain. Access to it was restricted by the emperors, and few Egyptians left the province. But individuals elsewhere in the Roman world were fascinated by Egypt's ancient power and engineering, and Romans willingly appropriated such achievements, to judge from Rome's obelisks, other Egyptian pieces, and the pyramid of Cestius in Rome, for example. Egypt's deities were also a source of continuous interest, and Egyptian cults, especially those of Isis and Serapis, spread widely. Images (however stylized) evoking Egypt appeared in Rome's world, although we cannot be certain of what they symbolized for those who commissioned or viewed them. In turn, the Roman takeover of the Nile valley also meant changes in Egypt, which Roman Egypt's abundant papyri and mummy portraits allow us to see in greater detail than is possible for other provinces. Notably, we find no complete transformation into Romans of Egyptians (if there was any such clearly defined group), but rather hybrid cultural forms in which Greek, Roman, and Egyptian marks of distinction all figured. Similar hybridization of Roman and indigenous elements can be seen on tombstones and in literature of northerners, Greeks, and some other groups.

Rome and Jews

Jewish assimilation and resistance in the Roman world will always be disputed, in part because of the relatively abundant literary evidence that includes the works of Philo and Josephus. Their eloquent Greek words represent Jewish interests for a Roman audience similarly familiar with Greek literature and thought. Josephus is particularly valuable for recording the accommodations Roman authorities made to Jewish religious and cultural traditions, often providing details we would not have otherwise and the likes of which are generally lacking for other groups. His and other evidence indicates fairly wide Jewish Diaspora settlement in cities of the Roman world, not infrequent conversion to Judaism, and, from the third century CE into the later fourth, a usually peaceful modus vivendi for Jews and most others.

On the other hand, the three major Jewish revolts were the fiercest and most sustained known opposition to the Roman provincial system. The First and Third Jewish Revolts, both centered in Judaea, remind us of the importance of geographical origins for some peoples. The Second Jewish Revolt refutes assuming Diaspora Jews' assimilation in Rome's provincial cities and reveals the tenacity of non-Roman identity. Furthermore, the disappearance of Jews from Rome's highest circles by the end of the first century CE sheds harsh light on Rome's acceptance of peoples. Romans acknowledged Jews' resolute dedication to their religion, traditions, and community, a characteristic resembling Rome's own sense of duty and the importance that Romans accorded to custom. But this same tenacity could infuriate them, apparently to the point where they set out to extirpate the Jews at Masada and at the time of the Third Jewish Revolt.

Rome and Christians

The Christians presented distinct dilemmas for the Romans. In contrast to the other peoples we have discussed, they were not subjugated in Rome's apparently inexorable drive to conquer and expand. Rather, the Christians fashioned their own identity from shared religious beliefs and practices. As Pliny the Younger and later Roman officials discovered, for many their Christian identity came foremost, taking precedence over a Roman identity verifiable by participation in imperial cult. Christians' monotheism distinguished them from Jews even when Jews sporadically were benefiting from accommodations with Rome. Furthermore, Christians' beliefs excluded them from participating in the many common rituals that made up the fabric of Roman life, since most of those – civic processions and celebrations, homage to the emperors and imperial family, army ceremonies, and the like – involved religion in some way. Christian identity could not be adjusted to that of the Romans. This led to the uneasy compromise struck in 111/112 CE by Trajan, according to which Christians would not be sought out but could be punished for refusing to renounce their beliefs in front of Roman officials. Romans do not seem to have feared their own possible transformation by Christians (as, for example, they feared being made "soft" by the East). Rather, they seem not to have been able to understand – or stand – what they perceived as Christians' intransigent separatism. In the end, Constantine's open support of Christianity after 312/313 and his own conversion to the faith, which precedents subsequent emperors followed, contributed to far-reaching changes in the Roman empire. But those changes are beyond the scope of this book, as is how this later empire dealt with the peoples and other diversities it inherited.

Romans recognized that their territorial growth inevitably led to cultural transformation, both of themselves and of those they conquered. In general, they did not set out consciously to make other peoples "Roman" or to efface cultural distinctions, although the Third Jewish Revolt is an apparent exception to this generalization, and many of Rome's brutal conquests were tantamount to genocide. The acquisition and organization of lands and peoples were simply what Rome did. Assimilation and "Romanization," or lack thereof, were secondary concerns.

Conclusions

In the second century BCE, during the rule of Augustus, after the First Jewish Revolt, and at various other times, Romans expressed their fears of cultural change by expelling different groups and people, passing laws about citizenship, and individually voicing ethnic and stereotypical prejudices. The state-organized Christian persecutions of the third and early fourth centuries also reflect a desire for conformity and a paramount Roman identity. Although the many poor individuals and families just striving to survive in Rome, the crowded cities of Antioch, Alexandria, Carthage, and elsewhere seem usually to have been indifferent to origins and ethnic identities, we have also seen outbreaks of mob violence against Jews, particularly during the Jewish revolts from 66 to 135 CE, and against Christians in the sporadic local persecutions of the second and early third centuries. As is suggested by Tacitus' description of Nero's arrest of Christians after the Great Fire of Rome in 64 CE, mob violence against Rome's peoples may have been incited by Roman anxiety about separatism, damned as "hatred of the human race." It seems also to have been associated with times of crisis that encouraged people to despair of the gods' approval of Rome.

However, such expressions of fear and outbreaks of intolerance did not halt Rome's expansion and absorption of others within its lands. Rome depended on appropriating as its own whatever it found useful and outstanding in others, including other peoples themselves (Tacitus, *Annals* 11.24). Its struggles with such inclusions contributed to its remarkable history, as we have seen in this book. Rome was shaped by its successes and failures alike, and its world was always one of many peoples.

SUGGESTED FURTHER READING
Michael Kulikowski will be publishing the Murranus inscription in *Classical Quarterly* (forthcoming).

TIMELINE

BCE

1800–1200	Bronze Age
1400–1100	Mycenaean contacts with Italy and Sicily
ca. 1250	Ramses II Pharaoh in Egypt
ca. 1176	Trojan refugee Aeneas founds Lavinium in Italy, and the Roman race
ca. 1000	First undoubted traces of settlement at the site of Rome
900–700	Iron Age in Italy
ca. 800	Phoenicians found Carthage
700s	Writing is introduced into Italy
ca. 775	Greeks begin to colonize in Italy and Sicily
ca. 750	Formation of first city-states
722–333	Parts of area of Judaea are controlled by Assyrians, Babylonians, and Persians
700–400	Etruscan and Greek cities are at their height in Italy; Greek cities flourish in Greek Sicily
500s	Northern Europeans move into Italy and other Mediterranean lands
586	Destruction of Temple of Jerusalem by Babylonians
525	Persian king Cambyses conquers Egypt and Judaea

516/515	Temple of Jerusalem is rebuilt
510/509	Establishment of Roman Republic
499–449	Persian-Greek Wars
ca. 450	Appearance of La Tène culture
430s	Herodotus' *History*
390 or 387/386	Gauls sack Rome
ca. 350–290	Rome conquers central Italy, including Gallic groups
332	Alexander the Great conquers Egypt, establishes Alexandria
327	Rome establishes treaty with Neapolis
304	Ptolemy I Soter is crowned Pharaoh of Egypt
280–275	Pyrrhus of Epirus heads Taras' War against Rome
273	Rome makes treaty of friendship with Ptolemy II of Egypt
264–241	First Punic War, after which Sicily and Sardinia-Corsica become Roman provinces (227)
262–215	Hieron II of Syracuse is allied with Rome
ca. 240–204	Poet Livius Andronicus writing in Latin in Rome
228	First burial of two Gauls and two Greeks in Rome
225	Romans repulse Gauls at Telamon
218–201	Second Punic (Hannibalic) War
217–216	Romans are defeated by Hannibal at Trasimene (217) and Cannae (216)
216	Second burial of two Gauls and two Greeks in Rome
215–205	Rome's First Macedonian War
200	Seleucids of Syria control Judaea
200–196	Second Macedonian War; "Freedom" of the Greeks proclaimed (196)
ca. 200	Fabius Pictor is first historian in Rome; Roman elite engages with Greek literature, philosophy, rhetoric. Plautus is writing plays
ca. 200–ca. 170	Numerous colonies are established in peninsular Italy and the Po valley

197–133	Roman provinces Closer and Farther Spain are established
192–189/188	Rome fights against Antiochus in the Syrian War
187	Via Aemilia is constructed
171–168	Third Macedonian War; end of its monarchy
168/167	Aemilius Paullus' enslavements in western Greece Polybius comes to Rome as a hostage
168/167–142	Revolt of the Maccabees
161	Expulsion of Greek rhetors and philosophers from Rome
155	Greek philosophers Carneades and Diogenes come to Rome as ambassadors for Athens
154?	Expulsion of Greek rhetors and philosophers from Rome
Mid-150s–130s	Roman wars with Celtiberians and other Spanish groups
149–148	After suppression of revolt, Macedon becomes the Roman province Macedonia
149–146	Third Punic War, ending with the destruction of Carthage; territory becomes the province of Africa
146	Destruction of Corinth and victory over the Achaean League
139	Possible expulsion of Jews and Chaldaeans from Rome
133	Capture of Numantia Tribunate and death of Tiberius Gracchus Kingdom of Pergamum is bequeathed to Rome; (129) becomes the province of Asia
122	Domitius Ahenobarbus crushes Allobroges
121	Province of Transalpine Gaul is formed
ca. 117	Province of Narbonese Gaul is formed
114/113	Third burial of two Gauls and two Greeks in Rome

113–101	Confrontation with Cimbri, Teutones, and other Germans
112–105	War with Jugurtha in Numidia
107, 104, 103, 102, 101	Consulships of Marius
105	Serapeum built in Puteoli
ca. 100	Iseum built in Pompeii
91–88/87	Social War
90–89	Extension of Roman citizenship throughout Italy
90–85	War with Mithridates in Asia Minor and Greece; Sulla offers peace terms
86	Sulla in Athens
ca. 86–65	Atticus in Athens
75/74	Kingdom of Bithynia is bequeathed to Rome
73–71	Slave revolt led by Spartacus
69	Cicero's *On Behalf of Fonteius*
66–63	Bithynia/Pontus, Cilicia, Syria (including Judaea) are instituted or reshaped as provinces by Pompey
63–62	Cicero (consul in 63) exposes Catiline's conspiracy
63	Cicero's *Catilinarians*
62	Cicero's *On Behalf of Archias*
59	Consulship of Julius Caesar
	Cicero's *On Behalf of Flaccus*
58–51	Caesar campaigns in Gaul and (55) Germany and (54–53) Britain
	Caesar's *War against Gaul*
56	Cicero's *On the Consular Provinces*, and *On Behalf of Balbus*
55	Roman army enters Egypt to support Ptolemy XII Auletes
	Cicero's *On the Orator*
mid 50s–ca. 44	Diodorus Siculus writes *Library of History*
52	Siege of Alesia
51	Cicero's *On the Republic*

49–45	Civil War between Caesar and Republicans led by Pompey
49	Caesar grants Roman citizenship to Gallic Transpadani
48	Pompey is defeated by Caesar at Pharsalus (August) and is murdered on arrival in Egypt (September)
October 48–mid-47	Caesar in Alexandria establishes Cleopatra VII as ruler of Egypt and fathers a son by her
46	Caesar holds (third) consulship, and is appointed to a ten-year dictatorship
	New "Julian" solar calendar is introduced
	Dedication of Forum of Caesar in Rome
	Cicero's *Brutus*
(April)	Caesar celebrates quadruple triumph
45/44	Cicero's *On the Nature of the Gods*
44	Cleopatra VII visits Caesar in Rome
	Cicero's *Philippics*
(March 15)	Caesar is assassinated
(May)	Octavian arrives in Rome; is adopted posthumously by Caesar
43	Formation of Second Triumvirate
42 (January)	Deification of Julius Caesar
(Fall)	Antony and Octavian defeat Brutus and Cassius at Philippi
	Cisalpine Gaul integrated into Italy
41–40	Antony meets Cleopatra
39–38	Parthian invasions of Syria and Asia Minor are repulsed
37–4 BCE	Herod the Great rules Judaea
32	Italy and the West swear loyalty to Octavian after triumvirate's end. War is declared on Cleopatra
31 (September)	Octavian defeats Antony and Cleopatra at Actium
30	Octavian captures Alexandria; Antony and Cleopatra commit suicide; Egypt taken by Octavian

27	Octavian is renamed Augustus
27–ca. 1 BCE	Extension of Roman control in Spain, the Alps, and central Europe to the Danube River; Raetia, Noricum, and Dalmatia are formed as provinces
25	Galatia becomes a Roman province
late 20s	According to tradition, Vergil reads his *Aeneid* to Augustus
19	Pergamum and Nicomedia establish Temples to Rome and Augustus
9	Endpoint of Livy's history
8	40,000 Germans moved to Roman bank of Rhine
6 BCE–2 CE	Tiberius in Rhodes
2 BCE	Title of *Pater Patriae* is bestowed on Augustus

CE

6–9	Rebellions in Germany, Dalmatia, Pannonia
6	Judaea becomes a Roman province; legion installed in Caesarea Maritima
	Moesia becomes a Roman province
9	Ambush of Varus and his troops in Teutoburg Forest
	Expulsion of Germans and Gauls from Rome
	Pannonia becomes a Roman province
Augustan–early Tiberian period	Strabo writes his *Geography* in Rome
11/13	Narbo's altar for imperial cult is installed
14	Augustus dies and is succeeded by Tiberius
	Promulgation of *Achievements of the Divine Augustus*
14–16/17	Germanicus campaigns in Germany
17	Cappadocia becomes a Roman province
17–19	Germanicus is in the East and Egypt, and dies in Syria

19	Followers of Egyptian and Jewish rites are expelled from Rome
21	Revolt in Gaul
ca. 26–36	Pontius Pilate's governorship of Judaea
ca. 33	Death of Jesus
ca. 36	Conversion of Paul
37	Tiberius dies and is succeeded by Gaius Caligula
37–44	Herod Agrippa rules Judaea
38–41	Anti-Jewish riots in Alexandria. Philo's embassies to Rome
43	Britain becomes a Roman province
46	Thrace becomes a Roman province
47–48	Claudius conducts a census; speech of Lyon Tablet
48–66	Agrippa II and Berenice rule much of Judaea
49?	Claudius expels Jews from Rome
ca. 50s–120s	Composition of the New Testament
54	Claudius dies and is succeeded by Nero
ca. 60	Paul is sent to Rome to appeal to "Caesar" 100,000 trans-Danubians are allowed to settle in Moesia
60–61	Boudica leads a rebellion in Britain
64	Great Fire of Rome; Christians are persecuted as scapegoats
66–67	Nero visits Greece
66–73	First Jewish Revolt, culminating in destruction of the rebuilt Temple of Jerusalem (70) and capture of Masada (73)
67–68	Rising against Nero
68 (June)	Nero commits suicide
68–69	Civil War, which Vespasian finally wins
late 69	Temple of Jupiter Optimus Maximus on Rome's Capitoline Hill is destroyed by fire

69–70	Germano-Gallic revolt
71 (June)	Triumph of Vespasian and Titus celebrating the fall of Jerusalem
70s	Vespasian builds the Temple of Peace in Rome and begins the Colosseum
	Completion of Pliny the Elder's *Natural History*
70s–80s	Revolts in Britain
ca. 70s–120s	Plutarch's literary floruit; Josephus' ca. 70s–110; Juvenal's slightly later
79	Vespasian dies and is succeeded by Titus
80s	Domitian supports Isaeum in Rome
81	Titus dies and is succeeded by Domitian
85–92	Domitian campaigns north of the Danube, especially against the Dacians
88/89	Shrine to Egyptian gods built in Beneventum
96	Domitian is assassinated and is succeeded by Nerva
98	Nerva dies and is succeeded by Trajan
	Completion of Tacitus' *Germania*
100	Pliny the Younger writes *Panegyricus*
ca. 100–110	Tacitus is writing *Histories*
101–102, 105–106	Dacian Wars; Dacia then becomes a Roman province
105–106	Arabia Petraea (Nabataea) becomes a Roman province
ca. 111/112	Pliny the Younger's special governorship of Bithynia-Pontus; Pliny and Trajan exchange letters about the Christians
112	Forum of Trajan dedicated
113	Column of Trajan dedicated
113–117	Trajan's Parthian War
115–117	Second Jewish Revolt
before 117	Ignatius is martyred in Rome
117	Trajan dies and is succeeded by Hadrian
ca. 117	Tacitus is finishing his *Annals*

ca. 120–230	Christian apologists flourish
120s	Hadrian constructs "his" wall across northern England and defines the German-Raetian frontier by erecting a wooden barrier
121–127, 128–131	Hadrian makes extended journeys throughout the empire
after 127	Juvenal, *Satire* 15
130	Hadrian's favorite, Antinous, drowns in the Nile during a tour to view the Colossus of Memnon
132–135	Third Jewish Revolt (Bar Kokhba War)
138	Hadrian dies and is succeeded by Antoninus Pius
ca. 144	Aelius Aristides delivers his oration *To Rome*
2nd c.	"Second Sophistic" flourishes
150s	Anti-Christian violence at Smyrna; martyrdom of Polycarp (155) and others
150s–180s	Apuleius, *The Golden Ass*
161	Antoninus Pius dies and is succeeded by Marcus Aurelius and Lucius Verus
mid 160s–190s	Plague sweeps through the empire
ca. 165	Justin and six others are martyred in Rome
166/67–173, 176–180	First and Second Marcomannic Wars
177	Anti-Christian violence at Lugdunum
180	Marcus Aurelius dies and is succeeded by Commodus Martyrdoms at Scillium, North Africa
192 (Dec. 31)	Commodus is assassinated
193	Civil War; Septimius Severus wins
193	Septimius Severus replaces the Praetorian Guard in Rome with northern troops
End 2nd c.	Rabbi Judah (haNasi) composes Mishnah
ca. 200	Septimius Severus lifts the ban on marriage by soldiers; northern Mesopotamia and Osroene become Roman provinces
203	Martyrdom of Perpetua and others at Carthage

early 200s	Marcella and Potamiaena are martyred in Alexandria
211–218	Caracalla is emperor
212	Caracalla extends Roman citizenship empire-wide (*Constitutio Antoniniana*)
220s	Cassius Dio writes his *Roman History*
ca. 225	Athenaeus of Naucratis' *Learned Banqueters*
226	Sasanid dynasty takes control of Parthia/Persia
235	Maximinus "Thrax," "the Thracian," becomes emperor
249	Rioting in Alexandria
250–251, 257–260	Empire-wide persecution of Christians under Emperor Decius, and then Emperor Valerian
260–274	"Gallic Empire" of Postumus exerts broad control over the West
270	Emperor Aurelian abandons most of the province of Dacia
271	Aurelian fortifies Rome with an encircling wall
273–274	Aurelian regains all areas once controlled by Postumus
284	Diocletian becomes emperor
293	"Tetrarchy" is instituted; Galerius becomes Diocletian's Caesar and Constantius becomes Maximian's Caesar
290s	Provinces are redivided; civil and military positions are separated
303	"Great Persecution" of Christians (in the West to 305; in the East to 311 or 312/313)
305	Diocletian and Maximian relinquish their Tetrarchic positions
306	Constantine is acclaimed Augustus in Britain
312	In the battle at the Milvian Bridge, Constantine conquers Maxentius in Rome and wins the city Constantine disbands the Praetorian Guard

313	Constantine and Licinius unite and issue the Edict of Milan
313–324	Constantine rules the West of the empire, Licinius the East
ca. 315	Completion of Lactantius' *Institutes* and *On the Deaths of the Persecutors*
320	Licinius resumes persecution of Christians
323–324	Constantine defeats Licinius and becomes sole emperor
324	Constantine chooses Byzantium as his capital and renames it Constantinople
	Endpoint of Eusebius, *History of the Church*
324 onward	Constantine promotes Christianity with growing confidence
351–352	Revolt in Syria Palaestina
361–363	Emperor Julian plans to rebuild the Temple of Jerusalem
379–395	Theodosius is emperor, legislates against Jews
410	Sack of Rome by Visigoths led by Alaric

GLOSSARY

Achievements of the Divine Augustus – Autobiography of Augustus, made public after his death in 14 CE.

Acts – Title used for texts describing martyrdoms, especially those that resemble the proceedings of trials ("Acta"). Other names for martyr narratives are "Passion" or "Life."

Aelius Aristides – From the province of Asia, b. 118; leading exponent of the Second Sophistic. His laudatory oration *To Rome* dates ca. 144 CE.

Aeneas – Legendary ancestor of all Romans and survivor of the epic Trojan War traditionally dated to 12th century BCE. *See also* Vergil.

Agrippa II – Last ruler of the Herodian dynasty. After the First Jewish Revolt he lived in Rome before his death at the end of the 1st c. CE. *See also* Berenice.

Alesia – Fortified town in central Gaul (modern Alise-Sainte-Reine, France) where the culminating battle of Caesar's war against Gaul was fought in 52 BCE. *See also* Vercingetorix.

Alexander the Great – Macedonian Greek general who "conquered the world" – the lower Balkans, Asia Minor, Egypt, the Middle East, Persia, and into modern Afghanistan – before his death in 323 BCE.

alienus (pl. *alieni*) – Free individual from outside Roman territory.

Allobroges – Gallic tribe from between the Rhône River and Lake
  Geneva. Neighbors included the Gallic Salluvii, Arverni, and
  Helvetii, and the Greek colony of Massalia (Roman Massilia;
  modern Marseilles, France).

Ambrones – Germanic tribe originating in the North Sea region.
  Moved into Roman territory, with other Germanic tribes, at the
  end of the 2nd c. BCE.

Antinous – The emperor Hadrian's younger male lover, originally from
  Bithynia (now roughly northwestern Turkey), who drowned in the
  Nile in 130 CE.

Anubis – (Black) jackal-headed Egyptian god associated with
  mummification and the afterlife and sometimes associated with
  Cerebus, the three-headed dog and guardian of the Graeco-
  Roman underworld.

apologist – Term often used for early Christians who defended and
  explained their faith in writing, especially those in the period ca.
  120–230 CE.

Appian – Historian and official from Alexandria who witnessed civil
  unrest there during the Second Jewish Revolt of 115–117 CE;
  his *Roman History* is arranged according to the peoples and lands
  Rome conquered.

Archias – Aulus Licinius Archias, poet from Syrian Antioch made
  famous by Cicero's *On Behalf of Archias* (delivered 62 BCE) on
  Archias' Roman citizenship.

Atticus – Titus Pomponius Atticus (110–32 BCE), Cicero's friend and
  confidant who spent many years in Athens.

Augustus – *See* Octavian, and *cognomen*.

Aulus Gellius – Mid-2nd-c. CE author of *Attic Nights*, miscellany book
  on authors, history, grammar, law, customs, and the like.

Bar Kokhba – Name (meaning "Son of a Star") assumed by Ben
  Kosiba, the messianic and nationalistic leader of the Third Jewish
  Revolt (132–135 CE).

BCE – "Before the Common Era," used in this book rather than BC
  ("Before Christ").

Berenice – Sister of Agrippa II and his apparent coruler of parts of
Judaea (with Roman support). Granddaughter of Herod the Great;
lover of Titus. 28 CE—post-70s.

Boudica – Queen of the Iceni tribe in southeastern Britain who
headed a rebellion (60–61 CE) of various tribes in the province.

Brennus – Gallic leader of the Gallic Sack of Rome dated to 390 or
387/386 BCE.

c. (pl. cc.) – Century (pl. centuries).

ca. – Circa, about, roughly.

Caesar – Gaius Julius Caesar, statesman and author, responsible for the
conquest of Gaul in 58–51 (and its description in the seven books
of *War against Gaul*) and often blamed for destroying the Roman
republic before his assassination in 44 BCE.

Caligula – Emperor 37–41 CE; intended to have his image placed in
Jerusalem's Temple.

Canopus – Famously luxurious suburb of Alexandria, Egypt.

Cassius Dio – Roman author and statesman originally from Nicaea,
Bithynia, whose *Roman History* was written in the 220s CE.

Cato the Elder – Statesman and author (234–149 BCE) known for
proverbially austere Roman values.

Catullus – Roman poet, ca. 84–54 BCE, from Cisalpine Gaul.

CE – "Common Era," used in this book rather than AD ("Anno
Domini," Latin for "Year of Our Lord").

Celta (pl. *Celtae*) – One of many imprecise terms for Gauls or Celts,
peoples who shared a common background of language and artistic
traditions now identified as the la Tène culture.

Celtiberian – Culture of the Iberian Peninsula fused from indigenous
Iberians and Celtic immigrants.

Cicero – Orator, author, and statesman (106–43 BCE). Works include
On Behalf of Fonteius, 69 BCE; *Catilinarians*, 63 BCE; *On Behalf
of Archias*, 62 BCE; *On Behalf of Flaccus*, 59 BCE; *On the Consular
Provinces* and *On Behalf of Balbus*, 56 BCE; *On the Orator*, 55 BCE;
On the Republic, 51 BCE; *Brutus*, 46 BCE; *On the Nature of the Gods*,
45/44 BCE; *Philippics*, 44 BCE; and various collections of letters.

Cimbri – *See* Ambrones.

Cisalpine Gaul – The area of the Italian peninsula generally south of
the Alps but north of the Apennines; although some inhabitants
received Roman citizenship in 49 BCE, the area remained a
province until 42 BCE.

Claudius – Emperor 41–54 CE.

Clement of Alexandria – Christian theologian and writer, born in
Greece ca. 150 CE, taught in Alexandria before his death ca. 215.

Cleopatra – Cleopatra VII, the last Ptolemaic ruler and the last
pharaoh of Egypt, late 69–30 BCE. Daughter of Ptolemy
Auletes and sister and wife of Ptolemy XIII and Ptolemy XIV,
she ultimately obtained sole rule of Egypt and extended her
dominion. Her liaison with Caesar in Egypt in 48–47 produced
their son Caesarion (Ptolemy XV Caesar); her relationship with
Mark Antony beginning in 41 resulted in three children. The war
by which Octavian gained sole control of Rome was declared
against Cleopatra (not Antony), and resulted in the deaths in 30
of Cleopatra, Antony, and Caesarion.

cognomen – One of three parts of a proper Roman name as used by male
Roman citizens. By the mid-1st c. BCE most Roman men used
a *praenomen* (personal name given by parents), a *nomen* (inherited
family name), and a *cognomen* (which distinguished a family within
a clan). Some who were adopted also used an *agnomen*, whose basis
was their former name. We now refer to most Romans by *cognomen*
or *agnomen*. Caesar's full name was Gaius Julius Caesar: his parents
named him Gaius and his father was from the Caesar family of the
Julian clan. Octavian, the later Augustus, was originally named Gaius
Octavius Thurinus; when adopted by Caesar (posthumously, in 44
BCE), Gaius Julius Caesar Octavianus; when granted the honorific
name Augustus in 27 BCE, Imperator Caesar Augustus. He is
known as Caesar on coins from 44 to 27 BCE.

Constantine – Emperor 306–337 CE; supported Christianity openly
from ca. 312; established Constantinople (modern Istanbul, Turkey).

Constitutio Antoniniana – Decree passed in 212 CE by the emperor Caracalla that provided Roman citizenship to virtually all free inhabitants of the Roman empire.

d. – Died.

Decius – Emperor 249–251; in 250 began the first statewide Christian persecution.

Denarius – Roman coin made of silver. Standard unit of pay for soldiers and a common coin for circulation.

Diocletian – Emperor 284–305; established the "Tetrarchy" or "rule of four" in 293; reorganized Rome's administration, finances, and provincial system; in 303 began the third (or "Great") Persecution of Christians.

Diodorus Siculus – Historian from Sicily who wrote in Greek one of the first "universal histories," the *Library of History*, while he lived in Rome 50s–20s BCE.

Dionysius of Halicarnassus – From the province of Asia, lived in Rome ca. 30–after 7 BCE, where he wrote *Roman Antiquities*.

Edict of Milan – Edict passed in 313 by Constantine and his then coruler, Licinius; granted Christians and all others the right to worship as they pleased and ordered Christian property to be returned.

entablature – The horizontal upper section of a classical building resting on the columns and comprised of the architrave, frieze, and cornice.

Epistle to Diognetus – Anonymous Christian text from the 2nd c. CE.

Essenes – Jewish religious group from 2nd c. BCE to the 1st c. CE; often associated with the Dead Sea Scrolls.

ethnography – Written investigation of a people or *ethnos*, discussing location, customs, religion, and the like.

ethnos (pl. *ethne*) – People, race, tribe.

Eusebius – 4th-c. bishop of Caesarea (formerly Caesarea Maritima), d. 339; connected with Constantine; prolific author whose works included the first church history, *Ecclesiastical History* (to 324).

Fabius Pictor – Quintus Fabius Pictor, Roman senator and general who wrote (in Greek) the first Roman history ca. 200 BCE.

familia – Group of persons under the legal guardianship of a Roman citizen.

Fayum – Fertile oasis in northern Egypt, sometimes spelled Fayoum or Fayyum.

First Epistle of Peter – A book of the New Testament in the form of a letter addressed to various churches in Asia.

Flavian – *See* Vespasian.

Galata (pl. *Galatae*) – See *Celta*.

Gallia Comata – "Long-haired Gaul," unofficial name of temperate France north of the Roman province of Narbonese Gaul.

Gallia Togata – "Gaul in the Roman Toga," unofficial name of Mediterranean France that included the Roman province Narbonese Gaul and was considered thoroughly "Romanized" by the 50s BCE.

Gallus (pl. *Galli*) – See *Celta*.

gens (pl. *gentes*) – People, race, tribe.

Germanicus – Honorific name often applied to members of the imperial family who had successfully fought against Germans; as a proper name, it designates the emperor Tiberius' nephew and adoptive son (15 BCE–19 CE).

Germanus (pl. *Germani*) – Blanket term used for northerners who were not *Celtae* and who generally lived in or originated from north of the Rhine River.

H – height.

Hadrian – Emperor 117–138 CE; family from Baetica (southern Spain); celebrated for his philhellenism, or love of things Greek.

Hannibalic War – Alternative name for the Second Punic War that Rome fought against Carthage 218–201 BCE, derived from the name of Carthage's general, Hannibal.

Harpocrates – Graeco-Egyptian god promoted by the Ptolemies and assimilated to Horus (see Horus); son of Isis and Serapis. Frequently depicted as a young boy with his right index finger held up to his mouth, a gesture Romans thought enjoined silence. Associated with the rising sun.

Hasmonean – *See* Maccabees.

Helvetii – *See* Allobroges.

Herod – King of Judaea, 37–4 BCE, with Roman support.

Herodian – Roman historian writing in Greek in the mid-3rd c. CE whose *Roman History* provides information on the late 2nd and early 3rd cc. CE, especially the Roman emperors.

Herodotus – "Father of Greek History" and author of *Histories*, written 430s BCE.

Horus – Egyptian deity usually depicted with a falcon's head or sometimes as a falcon; son of Isis and Osiris. Thought to be god of the sky, god of war, and god of protection.

hospis (pl. *hospes*) – Guest, also used to mean foreigner.

imperial cult – Term used for public and private rites and prayers in honor of and for the benefit of emperors and members of their family who had been declared deified by the Roman senate. Often associated with other deities, rituals, and temples (such as those dedicated to Rome and Augustus). Failure to participate in the imperial cult became a touchstone in the Christian persecutions.

Isis – Egyptian goddess of motherhood, magic, and fertility, promoted by the Ptolemies and popular throughout the Mediterranean. Depicted as a woman, Isis was the sister and wife of Serapis (also known as Osiris) and the mother of Harpocrates (also known as Horus).

Josephus – Jewish intellectual and aristocrat (37 CE–ca. 100) who joined the First Jewish Revolt against Rome but then defected to Rome. Granted Roman citizenship by Vespasian. Author of works (in Greek) that include *The Jewish War* and *Jewish Antiquities*.

Julian – Emperor 361–363 CE; sometimes called "Julian the Apostate" for his renunciation of Christianity and embrace of traditional polytheism.

Julio-Claudian – Adjective relating to the period (14–68 CE) when Rome's "Julio-Claudian" emperors came from the Julian and Claudian families connected to Augustus.

Justin Martyr – Christian apologist and martyr who died in Rome ca. 165 CE.

Juvenal – Roman satirist of the early 2nd c. who assumed a xenophobic and old-fashioned Roman persona.

Keltos (pl. *Keltoi*) – See *Celta*.

libertus, liberta (pl. *liberti, libertae*) – Freed Roman slaves who had almost full citizen rights.

Livius Andronicus – Rome's first author (ca. 285–204 BCE), who wrote a Latin version of the *Odyssey* and other works after coming to Rome from Taras (modern Taranto, Italy), probably as a slave.

Livy – Roman historian (ca. 59 BCE – 17 CE) from Cisalpine Gaul, whose 142-volume work covered the history of Rome from its origins to 9 BCE.

Lyon Tablet – Modern name of a bronze inscription from Lugdunum (modern Lyon, France) that records a speech the emperor Claudius made to the Senate in 47/48 CE.

m – Meter.

Maccabees – The Hasmonean or Maccabaeus family. Simon Maccabaeus ("the Hammer") defeated the Seleucid rulers of Judaea in the Maccabean Revolt ca. 168/167 BCE; the family later ruled an independent Jewish state, the Hasmonean Kingdom, until the establishment of Herod the Great's power over most of Judaea in 37 BCE.

manumission – Freeing of a slave by his or her slave owner.

Marcus Aurelius – Emperor 161–180 CE; wrote philosophical *Meditations* (in Greek); involved in the Marcomannic Wars along and south of the Danube River.

Mark Antony – Marcus Antonius, general and protégé of Julius Caesar and key in the civil wars and strife after Caesar's assassination in 44 BCE. Mark Antony was part of the Second Triumvirate, during which he became involved with Cleopatra VII. He and Cleopatra both killed themselves in Alexandria in 30 BCE.

Martial – Roman poet originally from Spain; wrote *On the Spectacles* in 80 CE.

Minucius Felix – Christian apologist and author of the dialogue *Octavius* (probably dating late 2nd/early 3rd cc. CE).

natio (pl. *nationes*) – People, race, tribe.

Nero – Last Julio-Claudian emperor; r. 54–68 CE. He scapegoated, tortured, and killed Christians as responsible for the Great Fire of Rome in 64 CE.

nomen – See *cognomen*.

obverse – One of the two sides of a coin, normally that with the larger-scale image (especially if it is a head). In depictions of the two sides of a coin the obverse conventionally is to the left.

Octavian – Julius Caesar's grand-nephew, adopted in Caesar's will as his son. Ultimate survivor of the civil wars and strife following Caesar's assassination in 44 BCE, and the first *princeps* or Roman emperor. In 27 BCE he was awarded the honorific name Augustus; died in 14 CE. *See also* Mark Antony, and *cognomen*.

Osiris – Egyptian god of the dead and of rebirth, brother and husband of Isis and father of Horus. Often depicted as a green-skinned man dressed as a Pharaoh.

Parthia, Parthians – Monarchy based in the region of modern northeastern Iran, but spreading westward and elsewhere. One of Rome's most organized foes from early 1st c. BCE to 224 CE. Trajan fought the Parthian War in 113–117 CE.

peregrinus (pl. *peregrini*) – Free, non-slave inhabitant of a Roman province.

Philo – Jewish philosopher and writer from Alexandria, Egypt, who in 38–41 CE represented to Caligula the Jewish community in Alexandria. His works include *Against Flaccus* (Prefect of Egypt, 32–38) and *Embassy to Gaius* (both in Greek).

Plautus – Roman playwright of late 3rd–early 2nd cc. BCE.

Pliny the Elder – Author and statesman from northern Italy whose only extant work, *Natural History*, was published ca. 77–79 CE.

Pliny the Younger – Author and statesman from northern Italy, nephew of Pliny the Elder; the last of his ten books of *Letters* is correspondence he exchanged with Trajan when Pliny was appointed to supervise Bithynia-Pontus 111/112. His *Panegyric* is the write-up of a senatorial speech he delivered in 100 CE praising Trajan.

Plutarch – Prolific author of the late 1st–early 2nd cc. CE whose works
(in Greek) include *Parallel Lives* of Greek and Roman statesmen
and generals, and moral essays.

Polybius – Greek statesman and author who came to Rome as a hostage
in 168/167 BCE and remained; his *Histories* (later 2nd c. BCE; in
Greek) analyzed Rome's rise to dominance in the Mediterranean.

Pompey – Roman general responsible in 66–63 BCE for reorganizing
(and in some cases conquering or reconquering) for Rome much
of what is now Turkey and the Middle East. After allying politically
with Julius Caesar in 60 BCE, Pompey later led the "Republican"
opposition against Caesar. Defeated at the Battle of Pharsalus
(modern Farsala, central Greece) in August 48 BCE. Murdered
later that year when seeking refuge in Egypt.

populus (pl. *populi*) – People, race, tribe.

Posidonius of Apamea – Influential ethnographer and philosopher who
traveled through the Roman world; d. ca. 51 BCE.

praenomen – See *cognomen.*

princeps – Term used for emperors from Augustus to Diocletian to
designate their stance as "first among equals" rather than monarchs.

proselytize – Attempt to convert others to one's faith.

provincialis (pl. *provinciales*) – Individual from a Roman province.

Ptolemy Auletes – Ptolemy XII Auletes, King of Egypt 80–58 and
55–51 BCE. Intrigued with the Romans, first to retain Egypt's
autonomy, and then to gain military backing for his restoration in
55. Father of Ptolemy XIV and Cleopatra VII.

Ptolemy, Ptolemies, Ptolemaic – Ptolemy I (Soter) took over Egypt as a
kingdom after the death in 323 BCE of his commander, Alexander
the Great. The dynasty he established is called, collectively, the
Ptolemies. Most kings were named Ptolemy. The adjective
"Ptolemaic" qualifies aspects of their rule of Egypt until 30 BCE.

Quintilian – Rhetorician and author of *Institutes of Oratory* (ca. 95
CE); born in northeastern Spain, he came to Rome. Lived
ca. 35–ca. 100 CE.

r. – Ruled.

recant – Make a formal renunciation of a belief or statement.

reverse – One of two sides of a coin. *See* obverse.

Romanitas, Romanness – Modern words often used to designate what it meant to be Roman.

Romulus – Founder and first king of the city of Rome, traditionally dated to the mid–8th c. BCE; responsible for Rome's "asylum" and the Rape of the Sabine Women.

Sallust – Statesman and author of the mid–1st c. BCE; his *War against Jugurtha* describes Rome's war against the north African leader Jugurtha, and the Roman general Marius' rise to power in late 2nd-c. BCE.

Samaritans – Religious group from the region of Samaria in Judaea that considered its religion distinct from Judaism.

Second Punic War – Rome's war against Carthage, 218–201 BCE. *See also* Hannibalic War.

Second Sophistic – Roman literary movement that boasted a connection to the past greatness of Greek literature and history. Particularly important in the 2nd and early 3rd cc. CE.

Second Temple Period – Period in Jewish history when the rebuilt Temple of Jerusalem functioned, from 516/515 BCE to 70 CE.

Second Triumvirate – Political coalition of Mark Antony, Octavian (the later Augustus), and Lepidus, 43–33 BCE.

Seneca the Younger – Statesman and author, tutor of Nero; d. 65 CE. Wrote *To Helvia, on Consolation* in 42 CE.

Septimius Severus – Emperor 193–211 CE. Originally from North Africa. The "Severan" emperors, related to Septimius Severus by blood or marriage (or allegedly so), ruled Rome until 235 CE.

Serapis (Sarapis in Greek) – Hybrid Egyptian-Greek god promoted by the Ptolemies and associated with Osiris (*see* Osiris). Depicted as a man, Serapis was the brother and husband of Isis and the father of Harpocrates.

Severan – *See* Septimius Severus.

Social War – Fought between Romans and their Italian allies in
91–88/87 BCE; resulted in the eventual enrollment of the Italian
allies as Roman citizens.

Strabo – Geographer and author from Pontus, who wrote his
Geography (in Greek) during the time of Augustus and Tiberius.

Suetonius – Roman grammarian and biographer of the early 2nd c.
CE whose works include *Lives of the Caesars*. Probably from Africa.

Tacitus – Historian and statesman from Cisalpine or Narbonese
Gaul (ca. 55–120? CE). Works include *Germania* (98), *Histories*
(ca. 100–110), and *Annals* (ca. 110–120).

Tertullian – Christian writer and apologist from Carthage who wrote
in both Latin and Greek, although only some fifteen Latin works
are extant. Lived ca. 160–ca. 220 CE.

Tetrarchy – Modern term for the "rule of four" established by
Diocletian in 293 CE. Diocletian served as Augustus of the West,
Galerius as Augustus of the East, and each had a deputy (*Caesar*).
Although this political setup did not long survive after Diocletian's
retirement in 305, other innovations of Diocletian did, such as his
reorganization of the Roman provinces.

Teutoni – *See* Ambrones.

Theodosius I – Emperor 379–395 CE. Responsible for various laws
and policies against polytheistic and Jewish practices and sites
(e.g., sanctioned the destruction of Alexandria's Serapeum and
Callinicum's synagogue). His sons Arcadius and Honorius ruled the
Roman empire's eastern and western halves respectively, marking
the division of the empire into two.

Tiberius – Emperor 14–37 CE.

Tiberius Gracchus – Roman statesman whose murder when he was
serving as tribune in 133 BCE is often used to mark the beginning
of the "Fall" of the Roman Republic.

Titus – Emperor 79–81 CE; son of Vespasian (r. 69–79 CE) and his
lieutenant during the First Jewish Revolt; brother of Domitian
(r. 81–96).

toga – Ceremonial outer garment of white wool that marked a male Roman citizen. Someone dressed in a toga is called "togate."

Trajan – Emperor 98–117 CE; family from Baetica (southern Spain).

Transpadani – Inhabitants of the Italian peninsula north of the Po (Padanus) River but south of the Alps.

trophy – Heap of non-Roman armor rendered in bronze or stone to commemorate a Roman victory.

Valerian – Emperor 253–260 CE; began the second statewide Christian persecution (257–260).

Varro – Roman statesman and prolific antiquarian author whose works at the end of the Republic included *On Agriculture*, *On the Race of the Roman People*, and *On the Latin Language*.

Varus – Publius Quinctilius Varus, Roman general whose devastating ambush in Germany in 9 CE is credited with Rome's establishment of its northern frontier at the Rhine River rather than the Elbe.

Velleius Paterculus – Roman statesman and author of *Roman History*, composed before 31 CE.

Vercingetorix – Gallic leader of the Arverni who united other Gauls to almost defeat Caesar at Alesia in 52 BCE.

Vergil – Poet (70–19 BCE) responsible for Rome's most famous epic poem, the *Aeneid*, as well as other works.

Vespasian – Emperor 69–79 CE, Titus Flavius Vespasianus came to power through a civil war. He commanded the Roman forces (66–69) during the First Jewish Revolt. With his sons Titus (r. 79–81) and Domitian (r. 81–96) he created the Flavian dynasty.

Visigothic Sack of Rome in 410 (CE) – Led by Alaric.

Vitruvius – Roman architect and author (ca. 75–post 15 BCE) who wrote *On Architecture* in the early Augustan period.

zoomorphic – Animal-formed.

INDEX

This index contains alphabetical entries to ancient authors and also to individual works discussed and quoted in the text. The index references sites both by page number and by Figure number of the map on which the site appears; monuments are found in Rome unless otherwise noted. Romans have been referred to by their most familiar name, despite the inconsistency involved; we thus find in order, for example, Aemilius Paulus, Lucius; Caesar, Gaius Julius; Mark Antony; Postumus, Marcus Cassianus. Unfamiliar terms can additionally be found in the Glossary, which also contains entries for authors and works, political figures, and abbreviations.